LINUX DESKTOP HACKS™

Other resources from O'Reilly

Related titles

Linux in a Nutshell	Linux Device Drivers
Linux Server Hacks	Linux Security Cookbook
Running Linux	Linux in a Windows World
Linux Pocket Reference	
Linux Cookbook	Test Driving Linux
Knoppix Hacks	Linux Unwired

Hacks Series Home

hacks.oreilly.com is a community site for developers and power users of all stripes. Readers learn from each other as they share their favorite tips and tools for Mac OS X, Linux, Google, Windows XP, and more.

oreilly.com

oreilly.com is more than a complete catalog of O'Reilly books. You'll also find links to news, events, articles, weblogs, sample chapters, and code examples.

oreillynet.com is the essential portal for developers interested in open and emerging technologies, including new platforms, programming languages, and operating systems.

Conferences

O'Reilly brings diverse innovators together to nurture the ideas that spark revolutionary industries. We specialize in documenting the latest tools and systems, translating the innovator's knowledge into useful skills for those in the trenches. Visit *conferences.oreilly.com* for our upcoming events.

Safari Bookshelf (*safari.oreilly.com*) is the premier online reference library for programmers and IT professionals. Conduct searches across more than 1,000 books. Subscribers can zero in on answers to time-critical questions in a matter of seconds. Read the books on your Bookshelf from cover to cover or simply flip to the page you need. Try it today for a free trial.

LINUX DESKTOP HACKS™

Nicholas Petreley and Jono Bacon

O'REILLY®

Beijing · Cambridge · Farnham · Köln · Paris · Sebastopol · Taipei · Tokyo

Linux Desktop Hacks™

by Nicholas Petreley and Jono Bacon

Copyright © 2005 O'Reilly Media, Inc. All rights reserved.
Printed in the United States of America.

Published by O'Reilly Media, Inc., 1005 Gravenstein Highway North,
Sebastopol, CA 95472.

O'Reilly books may be purchased for educational, business, or sales promotional use. Online editions are also available for most titles (*safari.oreilly.com*). For more information, contact our corporate/institutional sales department: (800) 998-9938 or *corporate@oreilly.com*.

Editor:	David Brickner	**Production Editor:**	Sarah Sherman
Series Editor:	Rael Dornfest	**Cover Designer:**	Emma Colby
Executive Editor:	Dale Dougherty	**Interior Designer:**	David Futato

Printing History:

March 2005:   First Edition.

 This book uses RepKover™, a durable and flexible lay-flat binding.

ISBN: 0-596-00911-9
[C]

Contents

Credits

About the Authors

Nicholas Petreley began his career in computing in 1983 as an Assembly-language programmer for a signal-processing research and development firm called Adaptronics, located in McLean, Virginia, and he hasn't been able to escape the field since. After getting a taste of writing as a weekly columnist for the *Times* in New Jersey, Nick began spending more time with the English language than with Pascal, C, C++, and the dozens of other languages that previously dominated his life. Nick's former lives also include conference advisor for LinuxWorld Expo, creator of the Golden Penguin Bowl quiz show, editorial director of *LinuxWorld*, editor-in-chief of *Network Computing World*, executive editor of the InfoWorld Test Center, award-winning columnist for *InfoWorld*, and regular technical columnist for *ComputerWorld*. You can find his current articles on Newsforge and in other publications under various pseudonyms. He is a columnist for *Tux* magazine, the author of the Official Fedora Companion, a part-time Evans data analyst, a freelance writer, a creator and maintainer of the VAR-oriented web site (*http://www.varlinux.org*), and a professional open source consultant.

Jono Bacon (*http://www.jonobacon.org/*) is an established writer, developer, and musician. Jono has been working as a full-time writer and technology consultant/developer since 2000, for a variety of publishers and companies. They include *Linux Format, Linux Pro, Linux Magazine, Linux User & Developer, Linux Journal, PC Plus, MacFormat, MacTech, Digital Home*, Newsforge, Sitepoint, and ContentPeople. Jono has also worked as a writer/consultant/developer for Trolltech, Apple, theKompany.com, the University of Wolverhampton, Delta Institute, and others. In addition to this work, Jono has been a part of the Linux community since 1998 and has worked for various free software projects including KDE and Kafka, and he founded Linux

UK, the KDE Usability Study, KDE::Enterprise, and the Infopoint Project. He currently works on various free software projects, as well as for OpenAdvantage in Birmingham, UK, as a professional open source consultant.

Contributors

The following people contributed their writing, code, and inspiration to *Linux Desktop Hacks*:

- Thomas Adam [Hack #9] has been using Linux since 1996. He has used a range of distributions but currently runs Debian. He is an active member of an online magazine, the *Linux Gazette*, for which he has written several articles. He also is a member of The Answer Gang.

- Jim Aspinwall [Hack #99] is the coauthor and author of four books about computers and networking. His writing spans not only books but feature articles and how-to columns for a handful of PC magazines and web sites, including *Computer User*, *PC World*, and *CNET.com*. His hack can also be found in his book *PC Hacks* (O'Reilly).

- Adrian Bradshaw [Hack #57] is a network engineer and open source enthusiast.

- David Brickner [Hacks #69 and #87] is an editor at O'Reilly Media, Inc., where he works on Linux and system administration books. He is the author of *Test Driving Linux* (O'Reilly).

- John Cheng [Hack #65] is an enthusiastic teenage Linux user. John has toyed with Linux and FreeBSD for years, and enjoys it.

- Paul Cooper [Hack #31] is the Assistant Director of OpenAdvantage, the first independently funded vendor-neutral Open Source solutions center in the United Kingdom. Paul researches new (and old) OSS technologies in order to help people find the best OSS tools to use in their organizations.

- Alan Donovan [Hack #97] is a researcher in the field of programming languages and program analysis. He holds degrees from the University of Cambridge and MIT, in whose Computer Science and Artificial Intelligence Laboratory he currently works. His hack can also be found in *iPod and iTunes Hacks* (O'Reilly).

- Rob Flickenger [Hacks #75 and #82] has been hacking as long as he can remember. He recently served as sysadmin for the O'Reilly Network, and is currently working on promoting community wireless networking through efforts like NoCat (*http://nocat.net/*) and SeattleWireless (*http://seattlewireless.net/*). His hacks can be found in his O'Reilly books *Linux Server Hacks* and *Wireless Hacks*, respectively.

- Adam Garside [Hack #58] wanted to be a stuffy philosophy professor but discovered Unix in 1993. He currently maintains perimeter infrastructure and gateway services at Central Piedmont Community College using Debian GNU/Linux exclusively. He lives in Charlotte, North Carolina, with his wife Sherri and two crazy cats.

- Emma Jane Hogbin [Hack #96] is a Toronto-based documentation junkie. She teaches standards-compliant web development at Humber College, and gives public lectures on writing documentation through The Linux Documentation Project. She likes her Scotch peaty, her books handbound, and her rabbits angora. To find out more, visit *http://www. emmajane.net.*

- Stuart Langridge [Hack #95] has several interests, including writing code for the Web, Python, Linux, the usability of applications, and driving a Fiat Coupe. You can read his thoughts on these and many, many other things at his web site, *http://kryogenix.org.*

- Jon Masters [Hack #92] hacks on Linux for real-time scientific instrumentation and is the author of a monthly Embedded Linux column in *Linux User & Developer* magazine. He began his first degree in computer science at the age of 13. Jon is a keen musician and also enjoys cycling, countryside walks, and geocaching.

- Adam McMaster [Hack #45] is currently a full-time student, studying A-levels at Brooke Weston CTC in the UK. In his spare time he enjoys learning about operating systems, programming, and web design, as well as other aspects of computing.

- David Murphy [Hacks #49 and #59] is an open source fan, and supporter of Fedora and Mono.

- Kyle Rankin [Hack #2] is a system administrator who enjoys troubleshooting, problem solving, and system recovery. He has been using Linux in many different forms for over six years, and has used live CDs to demo Linux and troubleshoot machines—from DemoLinux to the LinuxCare bootable toolbox to Knoppix. His hack can also be found in his book *Knoppix Hacks* (O'Reilly).

- Jonathan Riddell [Hack #43] is a freelance computer programmer working on PHP-based web sites. As a KDE developer he maintains Umbrello UML Modeller and organizes the exhibition stands for KDE in Britain. He is a former Scottish champion of white-water canoe racing and is currently organizing the World Gathering of Quakers.

- Ron Wellsted [Hack #68] has been in the computer industry for more than 25 years, working on Unix since 1983 and Linux since 1995.

- George Wright **[Hack #74]** is a student living in London, hoping to study computer science at university when he's old enough. In his spare time he's a developer on the KDE Project and occasionally works on embedded Linux systems.

Acknowledgments

Nicholas Petreley

I would like to thank God, above all, for anything that is excellent in my contributions to this book. I offer many thanks to David Brickner for his patience in giving advice and corrections during the editing process. Thanks as well to the entire O'Reilly production crew. Thanks to Kyle Rankin and Jonathan Oxer for their input during the review process. I would also like to thank my readers, contributors, and assistant web masters for their help, encouragement, and inspiration offered at my web site, *VarLinux.org*. Thanks also to the encouragement of my readers in other publications and to the many wonderful people I've met (either for the first time or for the first time face-to-face) at LinuxWorld Expo and other various conferences. Thanks to my heroes Tim O'Reilly, Bob Young, Jon "Maddog" Hall, Linus Torvalds, Alan Cox, Hans Reiser, Con Kolivas, Richard Stallman, and the many more sung and unsung heroes of the Linux and open source worlds. I thank my family for patiently allowing me to sleep through quality time we would have spent together after I stayed up all night so that I could have more consecutive hours of quiet time to focus on the book. I offer many thanks to Bill Gates, Steve Ballmer, and the talented folks in Redmond whose ongoing work in the areas of security, quality assurance, and product licensing continues to contribute greatly to the increasingly rapid adoption of Linux on the desktop. Finally, any errors or anything lacking in excellence among my contributions to this book I credit entirely to myself.

Jono Bacon

I would like to thank all of my family and friends for helping make my contribution to this book possible. Everyone has been incredibly supportive throughout the long tech edits, ramblings on the phone, endless proofreads, and unashamed plugging of the book when it was completed. I would also like to thank the various groups I am involved with and their encouragement in my work. This includes Wolves LUG, LUGRadio, OpenAdvantage, the Infopoint Project, and the many friends I have met at conferences and in my daily work. Finally, I would like to thank the readers of my work in *Linux Format*, *Linux User & Developer*, *Linux Magazine*, the O'Reilly Network, and the other publications I write for.

Preface

The Linux desktop has come a long way. I know. I've been using Linux as my default desktop work environment for so long I feel like I've experienced almost the entire evolution of the Linux desktop firsthand. I'm guessing it was sometime shortly after 1995 when I started using Linux on the desktop for more than 90% of my work. Linux not only outperformed Windows 95 on my Everex 486 DX2-66, but it also spared me the three Rs that plagued every version of Windows: Reboot, Reformat, and Reinstall. I never had to reboot or reinstall anything to solve a Linux problem. That was enough to solidify my determination to use Linux in spite of its aesthetic flaws.

On the down side, I had to tolerate very spotty hardware support, especially for display and sound cards. Once I had a graphical desktop running, the fonts were hideous. To its credit, Linux let me choose from dozens of window managers. Unfortunately, only a few of them ran reliably, and the user interface on most of them made little sense to someone like me, who was used to OS/2 and Windows. On the other hand, I was immediately spoiled by the fact that almost all Linux window managers let you switch between virtual desktops instantaneously (virtual desktops are separate, distinct desktop workspaces). Windows-based attempts at mimicking this feature were pitiful by comparison. Only a small number of productivity applications were available back then, and few of them were GUI-based. But even then, Linux came with more than enough software to meet my needs. Eventually, I learned it was possible to improve the early Linux desktop experience to make it border on pleasant, but I couldn't do it without becoming proficient at editing an endless list of obscure, text-based configuration files.

As Linux matured, it inspired a hack of the window manager FVWM that emulated the Windows 95 desktop. That, and a few other improved desktops, made Linux more usable, but it still didn't offer mass appeal.

Then along came KDE, a free desktop environment based on the Trolltech Qt C++ library of widgets and functions. Even in its most primitive stages, it was obvious that KDE would eventually challenge the best desktop environments on any operating system. The KDE developers didn't disappoint those who saw the potential. The most recent versions of KDE will knock your socks off and make them dance around the room. You can accomplish virtually anything from the KDE desktop in ways more elegant than I had ever anticipated back in 1995. Hopefully, by the time you've picked up some of the tips in this book, you'll be able to use KDE to amaze your Windows-using friends with the flexibility of Linux.

The GNOME project started somewhat later than KDE. Since its inception, GNOME has switched personalities more often than Sybil. But it is finally coming together as a desktop that targets users who are looking for both power and simplicity. Although GNOME is somewhat less flexible than KDE, you can use GNOME to put on a pretty good show for your Windows-using friends, too.

In a more general sense, the Linux desktop has improved dramatically in all other aspects. Linux fonts are now downright beautiful. Arguably at least, as many productivity applications are available for Linux as for Windows and it is surprisingly easy to run Microsoft Office applications directly on Linux without having to buy a copy of Windows. Most important, there is OpenOffice. org, which matches or exceeds the needs of the vast majority of Microsoft Office users. Plus, there's the Ximian Evolution email and scheduler, which is a Microsoft Outlook clone that outperforms Outlook itself. And the Firefox web browser is gaining so much momentum that even top managers at Microsoft use it rather than Internet Explorer, because Firefox is so much more usable and secure.

In short, Linux desktop environments and applications are no longer chasing the Windows desktop for usability and power. When it comes to choice, desktop usability, and features, Linux actually surpasses Windows in many ways. Admittedly, there are a few glitches to fix—features that still require you to edit text files and a few other holes to fill here and there—but we no doubt are entering the age of the Linux desktop.

This book is designed to help you get the most out of the Linux desktop. These hacks will show you how to spiff up your boot experience with graphical startup screens, ways to log in that you might never have imagined, and various ways to let multiple users access the same machine at the same time, each one using the graphical desktop they like best. This book also shows you how to extend the capabilities of your graphical desktop so that it looks like these functions were built-in from the start. There are even many useful tips for those who prefer to do most of their work at the text-mode console. For example, you don't need a graphical desktop to assign the multimedia keys to control your CD player and multimedia experience.

Though this book plunges into depths far more deeply than what I've outlined here, it still uncovers only a fraction of what you can do with the Linux desktop. Linux multimedia capabilities are improving steadily, and multimedia on Linux will virtually explode as problematic patent issues are addressed (such as the decryption algorithms for playing DVDs). Desktop environments such as KDE and GNOME, among many others, are changing and improving so quickly that by the time you read this book, some of the problems I mention in the text that follows likely will have been solved, the URLs to patches probably will have changed to reflect updates to those patches, and so on (fortunately, it is easy to compensate for these changes, as we point out in the affected chapters). If the evolution of the Linux desktop maintains its current pace, it won't be long before you start hunting for the second volume of *Linux Desktop Hacks (101-200)*.

Why Linux Desktop Hacks?

The term *hacking* has a bad reputation in the press. They use it to refer to someone who breaks into systems or wreaks havoc with computers as his weapon. Among people who write code, though, the term *hack* refers to a "quick-and-dirty" solution to a problem or a clever way to get something done. And the term *hacker* is taken very much as a compliment, referring to someone as being *creative*, having the technical chops to get things done. The Hacks series is an attempt to reclaim the word, document the good ways people are hacking, and pass the hacker ethic of creative participation on to the uninitiated. Seeing how others approach systems and problems is often the quickest way to learn about a new technology.

Linux Desktop Hacks is composed of a variety of methods to help you get the most out of your Linux system. Some are hacks in the true sense of varying difficulty. Sometimes you will create a simple text file to add a menu option, while other hacks require you to edit keyboard configuration files to change how your keyboard operates. This book even shows you how to apply a patch to source code and recompile the program to get new features. This book also includes tips on how to exploit the power of existing program features that you aren't likely to discover on your own. For example, *Linux Desktop Hacks* will show you how to use the KDE and GNOME file managers in ways you might never have imagined.

How to Use This Book

You can read this book from cover to cover if you want, but each hack stands on its own, so feel free to browse and jump to the different sections that interest you most. If there's a prerequisite you need to know about, a cross-reference will guide you to the right hack.

Although you do not have to proceed through the beginning chapters sequentially, they are ordered the way in which a user approaches a Linux system: from the boot process to various methods of logging in, using the graphical X11 system, and exploiting the power of KDE and GNOME. Each chapter covers different approaches to enhancing each step in the chronological sequence, so you can construct an entirely personal desktop experience as you choose the alternatives you like best from each chapter. In the end, you will undergo an original experience—one that does not resemble anyone else's experience from reading these same chapters.

Linux Desktop Hacks also covers some basic instructions, such as how to build a Linux kernel so that even ambitious newcomers can learn how to benefit from some of the more difficult hacks.

How This Book Is Organized

The book is divided into several chapters, organized by subject. The first chapters are organized in roughly the same order a user will experience the topics when starting a Linux computer: booting, a console, a login manager, X11, and a desktop environment. Depending on your personal approach to using Linux, you might want to skip a chapter or two. For example, if you never use a text console to do work, you can bypass Chapter 2 without losing momentum on enhancing and personalizing your system. On the other hand, you might miss out on some handy techniques by skipping a chapter that does not appear to appeal to your work style at first glance, so it won't hurt to check out every hack and tip at some time or another.

Starting with Chapter 9, you will learn how to perform some automation and administration tasks that can help you with hacks you learned in other chapters. In addition, some hacks require you to know how to get deep into the innards of Linux. In some cases, the complex information you need to use a hack appears in the chapter itself. Chapter 10, however, is dedicated to helping you learn how to customize and compile the Linux kernel, which will be useful for hacks that appear in previous chapters if you are not already adept at replacing or customizing your Linux kernel.

Whichever way you choose to use this book, you probably will want to familiarize yourself with the contents first, so here's a brief synopsis of each chapter and what you'll find.

Chapter 1, *Booting Linux*

You have to boot Linux before you can use it. So, why not spiff up the process? This chapter shows you how to add a custom graphical background to your boot manager and even how to design your own. It also shows you how to add a boot splash and progress bar to Debian, one of the only popular Linux distributions left that doesn't automatically provide this capability. This chapter also shows you some tricks for creating graphics consoles, and various ways to boot Linux, including how to bypass the boot manager.

Chapter 2, *Console*

Contrary to popular belief, the text console is not dead, especially if you learn from Chapter 1 how to turn your text consoles into graphical wonders. This chapter shows you how to customize your keyboard to use those special Internet or multimedia keys to play CDs, start up programs, or automate virtually anything you can imagine. Combine what you learn here with some hacks from Chapter 7, and you can learn how to use the console or even your text-based email client to view Microsoft Word or PDF file attachments, while maintaining some of the original formatting. As you'll see, text consoles put an amazing amount of power at your fingertips.

Chapter 3, *Login Managers*

Did you know you do not have to close your applications and log out for someone else to log in, start up their favorite graphical desktop, and use the same machine? You can set up Linux to let you switch between simultaneously running desktop sessions started by different users in several ways. This chapter explores both the easy and more challenging ways to accomplish this feat. You can create multiple KDE or GNOME login screens, or be a macho hacker and start multiple sessions from the command line. You can even ditch X11 login screens altogether and run several sessions using Qingy, a fully customizable graphical login manager that runs on a console.

Chapter 4, *Related to X*

If variety is the spice of life, this chapter will thrill your taste buds more than any other. You will learn how to set up custom-animated mouse cursors, how to add depth to your desktop with window drop shadows, and how to make windows partially transparent. You'll also learn how to create reminders or have your applications display on-screen alerts you can't possibly miss. You will learn how to access other desktops from your computer, including Mac OS X desktops, and you'll find out how to use those Internet and multimedia keys on your special keyboard, plus a whole lot more.

Chapter 5, *KDE Desktop*

In this chapter, you'll explore KDE features you never knew existed. For instance, add custom menu options that are smart enough to appear only when you select a file where the options will be useful. Use Konqueror to manipulate files on other desktops almost as if they were local files. Patch KDE to make the Konqueror sidebar easier to use, and make the process of selecting files more attractive. Add drop shadows to your KDE windows. Use *superkaramba* to turn your KDE desktop into a personalized desktop that hardly resembles KDE. This chapter explains all of this, plus how to use DCOP to automate the way KDE applications behave, and much, much more.

Chapter 6, *GNOME Desktop Hacks*

Want to customize GNOME Nautilus menus to give you many more options for what to do with selected directories and files? How about using *gDesklets* to add clocks, weather monitors, hardware monitors, and other features that really spiff up the desktop? This chapter will teach you how to accomplish these tasks. And, if you like a challenge, you will also learn how to run the latest GNOME development code.

Chapter 7, *Terminal Empowerment*

Not everyone uses KDE or GNOME. Many hard-core geeks who prefer lightweight window managers are also likely to prefer lightweight terminal programs. If you're one such user, this chapter contains some tips on how to make your life easier. Set up your terminals to look and behave the same way, no matter which window manager you're using. Add a little transparency without having to use the bloated terminals from KDE or GNOME. And while you're at it, learn how to view Microsoft Word and PDF documents inside terminals or even within the body of messages in email clients such as Mutt.

Chapter 8, *Desktop Programs*

Beyond the desktop environment you run are the applications you choose to run on it. This chapter covers a diverse range of programs that help improve your desktop experience. You will learn how to start OpenOffice.org faster. Several hacks also enable you to take better control of your email and web browser. The last few hacks deal with networking, and teach you how to scan wireless networks, plot your location or next trip with GPS, and connect to a Microsoft VPN.

Chapter 9, *Administration and Automation*

If you're a Debian user, this is a must-read chapter, because it is one of the few places you'll find a way to restore a Debian system after you have accidentally deleted the package database. Learn how to make your system configure and deconfigure network connections simply by connecting or disconnecting the network cable. This chapter also includes a hack that gives CodeWeavers' CrossOver Office and/or Wine users a relatively safe way to view untrusted Microsoft Word documents that arrive in email as attachments. You will also learn some basics, such as how to keep your computer clock synchronized, how to speed up the loading of C++ programs (namely, almost all of KDE and KDE applications), and how to back up or clone information from one machine to another. In addition, this chapter shows you a trick that restarts a background application every time it accidentally (or intentionally) dies, and it does it with a simple script instead of using complicated daemon tools.

Chapter 10, *Kernel*

This chapter discusses Linux, the kernel. Here you will learn how to compile your own kernel and how to upgrade your system from the 2.4 kernel series to 2.6. It also covers one alternative kernel branch that offers improved desktop performance, and ways to tweak your system performance without modifying the kernel.

Chapter 11, *Hardware*

Your computer isn't much use if you can't configure the hardware attached to it. This chapter covers how to set up various pieces of hardware, such as 3D video cards, USB devices, and Bluetooth devices. In addition, it teaches you how to optimize your display refresh rates, print to printers when you don't have a driver, and control the power features of your laptop. This chapter wraps up with information on using the two most popular portable music players, the iPod and the iRiver, under Linux.

Conventions Used in This Book

The following is a list of the typographical conventions used in this book.

Italics

Used to indicate URLs, filenames, filename extensions, and directory/folder names. For example, a path in the filesystem will appear as */Developer/Applications*.

Constant width

Used to show code examples, the contents of files, console output, as well as the names of variables, commands, and other code excerpts.

Constant width bold

Used to highlight portions of code, typically new additions to old code.

Constant width italic

Used in code examples and tables to show sample text to be replaced with your own values.

Color

The second color is used to indicate a cross-reference within the text.

You should pay special attention to notes set apart from the text with the following icons:

> This is a tip, suggestion, or general note. It contains useful supplementary information about the topic at hand.

> This is a warning or note of caution, often indicating that your money or your privacy might be at risk.

The thermometer icons, found next to each hack, indicate the relative complexity of the hack:

 beginner   moderate   expert

Using Code Examples

This book is here to help you get your job done. In general, you can use the code in this book in your programs and documentation. You do not need to contact us for permission unless you're reproducing a significant portion of the code. For example, writing a program that uses several chunks of code from this book does not require permission. Selling or distributing a CD-ROM of examples from O'Reilly books *does* require permission. Answering a question by citing this book and quoting example code does not require permission. Incorporating a significant amount of example code from this book into your product's documentation *does* require permission.

We appreciate, but do not require, attribution. An attribution usually includes the title, author, publisher, and ISBN. For example: "*Linux Desktop Hacks* by Nicholas Petreley and Jono Bacon. Copyright 2005 O'Reilly Media, Inc., 0-596-00911-9."

If you feel your use of code examples falls outside fair use or the permission given here, feel free to contact us at *permissions@oreilly.com*.

How to Contact Us

We have tested and verified the information in this book to the best of our ability, but you might find that features have changed (or even that we have made mistakes!). As a reader of this book, you can help us to improve future editions by sending us your feedback. Please let us know about any errors, inaccuracies, bugs, misleading or confusing statements, and typos that you find anywhere in this book.

Please also let us know what we can do to make this book more useful to you. We take your comments seriously and will try to incorporate reasonable suggestions into future editions. You can write to us at:

O'Reilly Media, Inc.
1005 Gravenstein Highway North
Sebastopol, CA 95472
(800) 998-9938 (in the U.S. or Canada)
(707) 829-0515 (international/local)
(707) 829-0104 (fax)

To ask technical questions or to comment on the book, send email to:

bookquestions@oreilly.com

The web site for *Linux Desktop Hacks* lists examples, errata, and plans for future editions. You can find this page at:

http://www.oreilly.com/catalog/linuxdeskhks

For more information about this book and others, see the O'Reilly web site:

http://www.oreilly.com

Got a Hack?

To explore Hacks books online or to contribute a hack for future titles, visit:

http://hacks.oreilly.com

Safari Enabled

 When you see a Safari® Enabled icon on the cover of your favorite technology book, that means the book is avaiable online through the O'Reilly Network Safari Bookshelf.

Safari offers a solution that's better than e-books. It's a virtual library that lets you easily search thousands of top tech books, cut and paste code samples, download chapters, and find quick answers when you need the most accurate, current information. Try it for free at *http://safari.oreilly.com*.

## CHAPTER 1

Booting Linux
Hacks #1–9

Some of you might be wondering why this book contains a chapter on booting your computer. If you're a new desktop Linux user, you might think the ideal boot experience should involve only two steps: press the computer's power button, and then log in.

Even experienced Linux users might question why this chapter exists. Talk to any longtime Linux aficionado, and he'll boast that one of the biggest advantages Linux has over that "other" popular x86 desktop operating system is that you almost never have to reboot Linux.

Regardless of what type of user you are, chances are good that you power off and boot your Linux desktop system now and then. So, why not make the experience a little more pleasant by sprucing up your bootloader with a fancy background graphic? One word of warning: if you choose to design your own LILO or GRUB bootloader backgrounds, the process is easy and highly addictive. It could become your next hobby.

And while you're at it, why not add a graphical boot-progress screen to Debian, one of the last of the popular distributions that lacks a boot splash screen with a progress bar?

In addition to teaching you how to accomplish these two tasks, this chapter will also help take you out of the Dark Ages of text-based virtual console screens. Whether you boot to a text login screen or a graphical login screen, there's no excuse for leaving the virtual console screens in archaic 80x20 character text mode. It is especially important to enable frame-buffer consoles if you want to take advantage of even fancier hacks in the following chapters.

Give Your Computer the Boot

HACK #1

Take control of your system and boot the operating system you want, when you want it.

The beginning of all Linux journeys originates with the humble boot-loader—the small bit of code that jump-starts the whole boot process. Knowing how to configure your bootloader is almost requisite for using a Linux system. You also need to understand the bootloader if you want to configure your system to boot more than one operating system.

Within the exciting bootloader world are a number of choices for starting your computer. For x86 machines, there are two main contenders: *LILO* and *GRUB*. If you are running Linux on a Mac, LILO and GRUB are not available, and the main bootloader is called yaboot. Another potential situation in which you might need to boot a computer is when you are trying to boot a CD to install an operating system. Sometimes you can encounter a problem booting from a CD if your computer's BIOS does not support booting from CD-ROM or if your CD-ROM drive does not support booting from a CDR. You can resolve this problem with a tool called the Smart Boot Manager.

This hack explores the GRUB, yaboot, and Smart Boot Manager bootloaders.

Configure GRUB

Without a doubt, GRUB is a far more flexible boot manager than LILO. It enables you to add new kernels or boot parameters without having to install each update to the Master Boot Record (MBR). GRUB also allows you to pass parameters to it or to the kernel at boot time. Many Linux distributions now ship with GRUB as the default bootloader. Although GRUB is reliable and flexible enough to recover from most disasters, it is still advisable to back up your boot sector just in case something goes wrong. To do this, run the following command:

```
root@bar:~# dd if=/dev/hda of=/root/hda.mbr bs=512 count=1
```

GRUB is managed by a central configuration file which is either */boot/grub/menu.lst* on Debian and Gentoo systems, or */etc/grub/grub.conf* on Red Hat-based systems. This file contains a number of entries that indicate the name of the kernel, the root partition where the kernel can be found, and an *initrd* if one applies. Here is an example of a typical Linux kernel stanza in the GRUB configuration file:

```
title       Ubuntu, kernel 2.6.8.1-2-386
root        (hd0,0)
kernel      /vmlinuz-2.6.8.1-2-386 root=/dev/hda3 ro quiet splash
initrd      /initrd.img-2.6.8.1-2-386
savedefault
boot
```

It's important to note how GRUB deals with disks and partition numbers. Unlike Linux, GRUB refers to the first disk as hd0 and the first partition as partition 0. In Linux this is designated as */dev/hda1*. Basically, if the letters that designate the hard drive in Linux were numbers, you would subtract 1 from them. Therefore, an *a* (1) becomes 0, a *b* (2) becomes 1, and so on. Also, you would subtract 1 from the partition number itself. For example, a boot partition located on */dev/hdb3* becomes hd1,2 in GRUB parlance. In the previous stanza, you refer to the location of the kernel (root) as hd0,0, but on the kernel line, you refer to the root partition as */dev/hda3*. Because it is a kernel parameter, it uses the normal Linux method of referring to disks and partitions. The final part of the stanza uses savedefault to make the stanza a default option in the GRUB menu, and the command boot actually boots the system.

If you want to add another operating system, simply add it elsewhere in the configuration file. A Windows stanza looks like this:

```
title       Windows 95/98/NT/2000
root        (hd0,0)
makeactive
chainloader +1
```

When you are booting non-Linux operating systems (most likely Windows), you usually will need to use the makeactive and chainloader keywords. The makeactive keyword is used to set this partition as GRUB's main root filesystem device. The chainloader command is used so that the bootloader can call another bootloader (usually the Windows boot manager) instead of loading a Linux kernel.

If your boot manager is hidden, it is probably because your distribution set it to be hidden. Look for the parameter hiddenmenu in your *grub.conf* file, and comment it out if you want to see your boot menu. You might also have a default option, which specifies the stanza in the file you want to be your default boot configuration. As an example, if you want the first stanza to be the default, use this:

```
default     0
```

Configure the Mac Bootloader

Mac versions of Linux use a different bootloader called yaboot. Although not quite as flexible as GRUB, yaboot takes a similar stanza-based approach to specifying kernels. Here is a typical Linux kernel on the first partition (you should adjust the path on the image line when your kernel is located elsewhere):

```
image=/vmlinux-2.6.8.1
        label=NewLinux
        read-only
        append="quiet splash"
        initrd=/initrd.img-2.6.8.1
```

To enable your system to boot Mac OS X as well, simply add the following option to *letclyaboot.conf* and indicate the correct partition that contains Mac OS X (you can determine the right partition by running a partitioning tool such as *cfdisk*):

```
macosx=/dev/hda4
```

When you have edited the file, you need to run the *ybin* program to write the boot sector. If you use the -v option, you can see the output of the command:

```
root@bar:~# ybin -v
```

Boot from a CD-ROM

The vast majority of Linux distributions are available on CD. Their installation program loads automatically when you boot the computer with the CD in the drive. On newer machines, this process is not a problem (though you might need to enter your BIOS setup program and select the CD drive as the first bootable device). On older computers, this can be an issue because some computers do not support a bootable CD drive. Another common complaint with old secondhand computers is that the BIOS might be password-protected but no one knows the password. This means you can't make the CD drive the first boot device.

Many Linux distributions get around this problem by including a floppy-disk boot image that you can use to create boot floppies. These floppies "jump-start" the installation process and give access to the CD despite any hardware shortcomings. The CDs usually include a tool called *rawrite* that can be used to copy the boot images to the floppies. If this works with your distribution, the problem is solved, but unfortunately not all distributions include a floppy boot image.

Another solution is to use a tool called the Smart Boot Manager (*http://btmgr.sourceforge.net*). This useful little utility creates a boot sector on a floppy disk that allows you to boot from the CD and use the CD installation program. To use the Smart Boot Manager, you need to download it from *http://btmgr.sourceforge.net/download.html* and unpack it to your disk. I recommend downloading the latest version that is statically linked. The software includes a program you can use to install the Smart Boot Manager to the floppy disk in /dev/fd0:

```
foo@bar:~$ sbminst -t us -d /dev/fd0
```

This command installs the English theme into the boot sector on device /dev/fd0. A number of different languages are supported across the different themes. These include:

- cz = Czech theme
- de = German theme
- es = Spanish theme
- fr = French theme
- hu = Hungarian theme
- pt = Portuguese theme
- ru = Russian theme
- us = English theme
- zh = Chinese theme

When you boot into the Smart Boot Manager, you can configure the software from within the program with a simple-to-use text-based windowing interface.

Kill and Resurrect the Master Boot Record

How to (carefully) back up and restore the Master Boot Record (MBR).

The MBR is a 512-byte segment at the very beginning (the first sector) of a hard drive. This segment contains two major parts: the *boot code* in the first 446 bytes and the *partition table* (plus a 2-byte signature) in the remaining 66 bytes. When you run *lilo*, *grub-install*, or *fdisk /mbr* in DOS, it writes to these first 446 bytes. When you run *cfdisk* or some other disk-partition program, it writes to the remaining 66 bytes.

> Writing directly to your MBR can be dangerous. One typo or mistake can make your entire system unbootable or even erase your entire partition table. Make sure you have a complete backup of your MBR, if not your full hard drive, on other media (like a floppy or anything other than the hard drive itself) before you try any potentially destructive commands.

The MBR is very important and crucial for booting your system, and in the case of your partition table, crucial for accessing your data; however, many people never back up their MBR. Use Knoppix to easily create backups of your MBR, which you can later restore in case you ever accidentally overwrite your partition table or boot code. It is important to double-check each command you type, as typing 466 instead of 446 can mean the difference between blanking the boot code and partially destroying your partition table.

Save the MBR

First, before you attempt anything potentially destructive, back up the current MBR. Boot into Knoppix, and type the following command into a terminal:

```
knoppix@ttyp0[knoppix]$ sudo dd if=/dev/hda of=/home/knoppix/mbr_backup
bs=512 count=1
```

Change /dev/hda to match the drive you wish to back up. In your home directory, you should now see a 512-byte file called *mbr_backup*. *Dd* is used to create images of entire hard drives, and in this case, a similar command is used; however, it contains two new options: bs and count. The bs (byte size) option tells *dd* to input and output 512 bytes at a time, and the *count* option tells *dd* to do this only once. The result of the command is that the first 512 bytes of the drive (the MBR) are copied into the file. If for some reason you only want to back up the boot sector (although it's wise to always back up the partition table as well), replace 512 with 446. Now that you have backed up the MBR, copy it to a safe location, such as another computer or a CD-ROM.

The full 512-byte copy of the MBR contains the partition table, so it gets out of sync whenever you change partitions on your drive. If you back up the full MBR, be sure to update your backup whenever you make partition changes.

Kill the MBR

Now you should know how to totally destroy the MBR. To do this, simply use the same command you used to back up an MBR, but replace the input file with /dev/zero and the output file with the drive, overwriting each byte of the MBR with zero. If you only want to blank your boot code, type:

```
knoppix@ttyp0[knoppix]$ sudo dd if=/dev/zero of=/dev/hda bs=446 count=1
```

To clear the complete MBR, including the partition table, type:

```
knoppix@ttyp0[knoppix]$ sudo dd if=/dev/zero of=/dev/hda bs=512 count=1
```

While blanking the partition table in effect prevents you from accessing files on the drive, it isn't a replacement for proper wiping of the complete drive, because the files are still potentially retrievable from the drive. Even the partition table itself is recoverable with the right tools.

Resurrect the MBR

If you deleted your boot sector in the last section, you probably want to restore it now. To do this, copy the backup you made earlier to your home directory in Knoppix and run:

```
knoppix@ttyp0[knoppix]$ sudo dd if=/home/knoppix/mbr_backup of=/dev/hda
bs=446 count=1
```

Because of the **bs=446** element, this command only restores the boot code in the MBR. I purposely left out the last 66 bytes of the file so the partition table would not be overwritten (just in case you have repartitioned or changed any partition sizes since your last MBR backup). If you have accidentally corrupted or deleted your partition table, restore the full 512 bytes to the MBR with:

```
knoppix@ttyp0[knoppix]$ sudo dd if=mbr_backup of=/dev/hda bs=512 count=1
```

How Do I fdisk/mbr?

Knoppix also provides a useful tool called *install-mbr* that allows you to manipulate the MBR in many ways. The most useful feature of this tool is that it can install a "default" master boot record on a drive, which is useful if you want to remove *lilo* or *grub* completely from the MBR so Windows can boot by itself, or so you can install Windows to a hard drive that previously used Linux. The results are the same as if you were to type **fdisk /mbr** in DOS. To remove the traces of *lilo* or *grub* from your MBR, run:

```
knoppix@ttyp0[knoppix]$ sudo install-mbr /dev/hda
```

Replace */dev/hda* with your drive.

See Also

- The *install-mbr* manpage by typing **man install-mbr** in a console.

—Kyle Rankin

HACK #3 Bypass the Boot Manager
Save your system from a broken or missing kernel.

Of all the fantastic things you can do with your Linux box, one of the most nerve-wracking activities is changing or upgrading a kernel. This not only involves the archaic process of compiling the kernel itself **[Hack #88]**, but it also requires you to update your bootloader so that you can actually use the new kernel. Updating the bootloader often involves editing a complex configuration file in which one wrong change can lead to a system that won't boot. Perhaps nothing is more worrisome in the Linux world than a computer containing all your important work and files that doesn't boot, because you screwed up the bootloader. Worrisome as it is, there is a useful hack you can use to get around the bootloader to boot a working kernel, fix the broken configuration file, and restart a healthy, working system.

Bypassing the Installer

The key to restoring your sanity when confronted with a broken kernel is to use the installation disk you used to install Linux on your computer in the first place. Every installation disk boots a generic kernel from the CD-ROM to perform the installation routine. Many of the install disks for distributions such as Debian, Ubuntu, Mandrake, Red Hat, and others include a slim-line shell called BusyBox that you can use to sneak behind the installer and fix your system.

When you run the CD-ROM-based installation program, nothing on your hard disk is affected until you get to the partitioning part of the program. Just before this section, jump to another virtual terminal by pressing Ctrl-Alt-F(n) (such as Ctrl-Alt-F2). If you are installing Linux on a Mac, this can be a little trickier, because you need to press the Apple Option Key-F(n)-F(n). These key combinations switch you to a blank screen where you see a root shell. This shell is a substantially cut-down version of a normal shell, but it has the essential commands to navigate directories, mount disks, and use an editor to change files.

Mounting Disks

Before you can fix the bootloader, you need to identify the problem that is preventing your system from booting. In many cases, the problem occurs because the kernel files in /boot do not have the same name/location as specified in the bootloader configuration. This can occur if, for example, you specify in your bootloader configuration that your kernel is called *vmlinux*, but when you installed a new kernel, the original was automatically renamed by the installer to *vmlinux.old*, thus breaking the bootloader configuration because the bootloader no longer contains the correct kernel name. When this occurs, first you need to access /boot and check the names of your kernel and associated files.

To do this, mount /boot. First, create a new directory for the mount point on your hard disk:

```
foo@bar:~# mkdir /bootmnt
```

Now you can mount your hard disk's boot partition using the notation **/dev/discs/disc[disk number]/part[partition number]**. For example, mount the third partition on the first disk with the following:

```
foo@bar:~# mount /dev/discs/disc0/part3 /bootmnt
```

With your boot partition mounted to /bootmnt you can note the names of your kernels and associated files (such as initrd.img files). Now you need to mount the main root partition so that you can modify your bootloader configuration file. First, create the mount point:

```
foo@bar:~# mkdir /rootmnt
```

Now mount it:

```
foo@bar:~# mount /dev/discs/disc0/part4/rootmnt
```

Of course, your root partition might be something other than *part4* as specified in this command. With the partition mounted in /rootmnt, you need to change the root partition to that mount point so that you can specify a different root partition from the one the installer is running. This will enable you to access your root partition and run commands from it. To do this, use the chroot command on /rootmnt:

```
foo@bar:~# chroot /rootmnt
```

When you have run this command, take a look at the directory structure with ls, and you will see that your normal root partition is visible.

At this point in this process, you have access to your normal range of applications, and if you have a network connection, you can use this opportunity to copy important files and directories to another computer, just in case you can't work out how to fix your kernel or bootloader problem. You can find more information on making network backups with scp and rsync in "Make Network Backups" [Hack #83].

To restore your system to its previous working form, you can enter /etc and edit the configuration file for the bootloader using the notes of the filenames that you took from the /boot partition earlier. Then run the command to re-create the bootloader (such as lilo or ybin) and reboot the machine.

Hacking the Hack

If you system is failing to boot the kernel, it could be that your kernel has become corrupted or is incorrectly installed. At this point, you should try to reinstall the kernel from a package if one is available. As root, you can do this with an RPM file using the following code:

```
foo@bar:~# rpm -Uvh kernel.rpm
```

You can reinstall a Debian package using this code:

```
foo@bar:~# dpkg -i kernel.deb
```

Instructions to compile a kernel are in "Compile a Kernel" [Hack #88]. You can compile a new kernel from the chrooted environment you used earlier in this hack.

Set a Bitmap Boot Screen for LILO

#4   You can have a splash screen for just about everything these days, including your bootloader.

Most people use either the time-honored LInux LOader (LILO), or the GRand Unified Bootloader (GRUB). This hack shows you how to download a LILO splash screen and configure it to appear with LILO when you boot your machine. This hack assumes your video card supports VESA frame buffers that will render a 255-color, 640x480 graphics screen in bitmap format (practically every decent graphics card made in the last several years works). It is not necessary to configure your Linux kernel to support frame buffers. When LILO displays the splash screen, the Linux kernel isn't loaded yet, so LILO cannot depend on the kernel for frame-buffer support.

On the other hand, this hack works nicely with all the other frame-buffer hacks, such as "Jazz Up Your Debian System Boot" [Hack #8] and "Scrap X11 for Fancy Login Consoles" [Hack #20], so you might want to combine all these hacks to get the most out of your card's frame-buffer support.

You won't find a cornucopia of preconfigured LILO splash screens on the Internet, but a few do exist. Most of the downloads include a *README* file that includes instructions on the lines you need to add to *lilo.conf* to make the LILO boot splash work. Some of the URLs listed here have the instructions written on their respective web pages. Here are most of the splash screens available on *http://www.kde-look.org*:

Tux Lilo Selection Screen
 http://www.kde-look.org/content/show.php?content=16756

Lilo Waterdrops Theme
 http://www.kde-look.org/content/show.php?content=16739

EnterTheLinux lilo/grub splash screen
 http://www.kde-look.org/content/show.php?content=11098

KeramikBlue Lilo Bootscreen
 http://www.kde-look.org/content/show.php?content=2492

Slackware Lilo splash screen/Slackware Bootsplash Lilo
 http://www.kde-look.org/content/show.php?content=17113
 http://www.kde-look.org/content/show.php?content=15643
 http://www.kde-look.org/content/show.php?content=16739

This hack uses the first splash screen in the list, the Tux Lilo Selection Screen, as an example. Visit the URL and download the file. Then log in as root, extract the file, and copy the bitmap file (*.bmp) to the /boot directory:

```
$ su -
Password:
# tar zxvf 16756-Lilo-Tux.tar.gz
lilo-boot-tux.bmp
README.TXT
# cp lilo-boot-tux.bmp /boot
```

Now view the README.TXT file. In it are the instructions to put the following lines in your lilo.conf file. Start up your favorite editor and add these lines:

```
install=bmp
bitmap=/boot/lilo-boot-tux.bmp
bmp-table=48,15,1,12
bmp-colors=250,,,255,,
bmp-timer=300p,184p,250,,
```

These lines tell LILO to install the ability to display a bitmap and instruct LILO as to which graphical bitmap file to use. The bmp-table, bmp-colors, and bmp-timer lines tell LILO where to place the menu and countdown timer (after which LILO automatically boots the default selection), and which colors to use. "Create Your Own LILO Boot Splash" [Hack #5] provides more details about these lines.

Now run the lilo -v command to effect the change:

```
# lilo -v
```

Reboot your system, and you should see a brand-new graphical LILO startup screen.

> If you are running certain versions of SUSE Linux, you can use a special version of LILO to display animated LILO boot splash screens. You can get more information about this from *http://www.gamers.org/~quinet/lilo/*, along with some sample animated LILO boot graphics.

The next hack provides complete instructions on how to create your own LILO boot splash [Hack #5].

Avoid downloading LILO boot screens that are designed to use the message= command in the *lilo.conf* file. This technique works on only a few distributions of Linux, and it is difficult to find all the utilities necessary to make it work. Because the bitmap approach is at least as effective (if not better), it's probably a waste of time trying to make the message= technique work.

If you can't resist and you do try using the message= technique, note that message= and the bitmap approach are mutually exclusive. You cannot use both simultaneously.

Create Your Own LILO Boot Splash
Create or modify any picture for use as a LILO boot splash background.

You can easily start from scratch and create any kind of LILO boot splash background. Just make sure you consider the following:

- The image resolution must be 640x480.
- The image must be a bitmap.
- The image must comprise 255 colors or less, and it must be indexed.
- You should plan to create or allocate two areas on the screen—one for the LILO menu and one for the LILO timer, which ticks down until it automatically boots.

This example bases the LILO boot screen on a KDE screenshot with a Konsole window open (Figure 1-1). The idea is to place the LILO boot menu within the Konsole window, and the countdown timer where the clock appears on the KDE panel. I set up the KDE screen the way I wanted it to look. If you take a similar approach, do not use a complex and colorful background, because it probably will not translate well into 255 colors. I recommend you use the Gimp to take the screenshot and modify it for use as the LILO boot screen. "Take a Screenshot from the Command Line" [Hack #12] shows you one method of taking screenshots. Here's how to do it with the Gimp:

1. Arrange the KDE screen like the one shown in Figure 1-1.
2. Switch to another virtual desktop, and start the Gimp (starting the Gimp in another virtual desktop ensures that the Gimp won't appear in the screenshot).
3. Select File → Acquire → Screen Shot. This brings up a dialog box.
4. Select the Whole Screen radio button.

5. Give yourself about 5 seconds by entering **5** in the "Grab after [] Seconds Delay" field.

6. Click the OK button.

7. Switch to the virtual desktop you arranged to be the boot screen, and do it in less than 5 seconds! The Gimp should snap a screenshot and present it for your use.

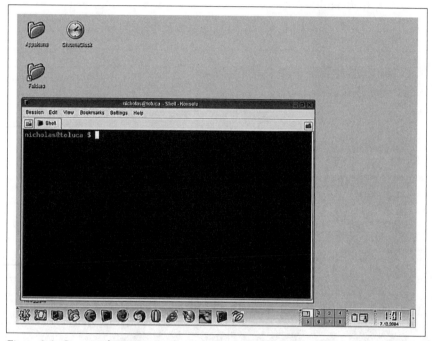

Figure 1-1. Converted KDE screenshot

The next thing you want to do is convert this screen to meet the LILO requirements for a 640x480 bitmap with 255 indexed colors. Here's how to do that:

1. Right-click the image in the Gimp window, and select Image → Scale Image.

2. Type **640** in the New Width field and **480** in the New Height field.

3. Change the Interpolation combo box control to read Cubit (Best).

4. Click the OK button.

5. Right-click the image again, and select Image → Mode → Indexed.

6. Change the number of colors to 255.

7. Check the No Color Dithering radio button.

8. Click the OK button.

This should create a blank area where the clock appears, because that is where the default countdown timer will go. Generally, you would choose a color similar to the panel color, but for this example, you can play it safe by using the color white. Here's how to create that blank area using the Gimp:

1. Select the entire rectangular area where the clock appears.
2. Right-click the image and select Edit → Fill with BG color (which is white by default).

See Figure 1-2 for an example of what the result should look like.

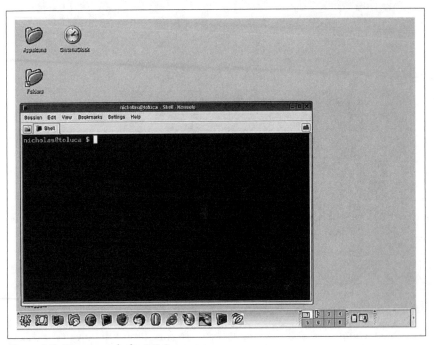

Figure 1-2. Bitmap ready for LILO

Now you need to know the XY coordinates on the picture for those places you plan to place the menu and the timer.

Position your mouse cursor approximately in the upper-left corner of the black inner portion of the Konsole (somewhere beneath the prompt). Look at the lower-left corner of the Gimp window, and you should see the coordinates for your mouse position, which will be the upper-left corner of your boot menu. My selection indicates the coordinates 55, 214. Here is the definition of the LILO menu you need to put in the *lilo.conf* file:

```
bmp-table=<x>,<y>,<columns>,<lines>
```

Let's assume you have up to six entries in your LILO menu. You need only one column to display that many. So, plug in the coordinates, along with these details:

```
bmp-table=55,214,1,6
```

Now you need to know the coordinates for the timer. Position your mouse cursor in the upper-left area of the white rectangle where the clock used to be. This is where the timer will appear. On my screen, the coordinates I chose were 582, 455. The format of the timer definitions looks like this:

```
bmp-timer=<x>,<y>,<fg color>,<bg color>,<shadow color>
```

You know the coordinates already, so you can fill in that much:

```
bmp-timer=582p,455p,<fg color>,<bg color>,<shadow color>
```

Note that the coordinates are followed by the letter p, which tells LILO that the numbers represent pixel coordinates.

Now it's time to pick colors.

Picking Colors

Here's the only really tricky part of creating the boot image specification for *lilo.conf*. You have to specify the colors to use for the menu and the timer. You specify these colors using an indexed palette. There is no standard palette of colors; the Gimp creates one based on the colors in your particular image. When you converted the image to use 255 indexed colors, the Gimp created a palette for the 255 colors, and you must use one or more of those colors for your menu and timer.

Here's how to display the palette for your image: right-click the image and select Dialogs → Indexed Palette.

Here's the trick to defining colors for your menu and timer. Click one of the colored blocks in your palette. You should see the Color Index Number field change to the number of that block. I happened to click a light yellow block, and that was block number 235. Click other colors and you'll see the color index number change accordingly. The color index number is the number you will use to define the colors for your boot menu and timer.

Let's make the color of the timer black on white, with no shadow. On the Index Palette Colormap, find a square that is white and click it. Make a note of the color index number (in my case the number is 254). Click a square that is black and note the color index number. In my case, the black square has a color index number of 0. Now that you have these color index numbers, you can finish the bmp-timer definition, which defines the foreground as black (color index 0) and the background as white (color index 254):

```
bmp-timer=582p,455p,0,254,
```

The last comma has nothing after it, because you are not specifying a shadow color.

Next, define the colors for the boot menu options, which is the menu you use to select which operating system to boot. The format of that line is as follows:

```
bmp-colors=<fg>,<bg>,<sh>,<sel-fg>,<sel-bg>,<sel-sh>
```

The foreground color of the menu selection is defined by the `<fg>` option; `<bg>` is the background and `<sh>` is the shadow for the text, if you want a shadow. The color of the foreground of the selected menu entry is controlled by the `<sel-fg>` option; `<sel-bg>` is the color of the background of the selected entry, and `<sel-sh>` is the color of the text shadow, if you want one.

Assume you want the menu text colors to be white on black, with no shadows. You already have color index numbers for black and white (0 and 254, respectively), and you know to leave the entry blank for no shadow. So, here is what the line should look like at this point:

```
bmp-colors=254,0,,<sel-fg>,<sel-bg>,<sel-sh>
```

Now you need to define the colors for the current highlighted menu selection. Because the menu background is black, I picked something that would create a sharp contrast for the highlighted entry: purple text on a yellow background.

Click a purple block in the indexed palette and note the color index number. The index number in my case is 74. Click a light yellow block and make a note of that color index number. In my case, that number is 242. There is no shadow, so leave the shadow entries blank. Now you can fill in the rest of the information for the `bmp-colors` line:

```
bmp-colors=254,0,,74,242,
```

Logged in as root, save the image as *lilo-kde.bmp* and copy it to the */boot* directory:

```
# cp lilo-kde.bmp /boot
```

Now you need to edit */etc/lilo.conf*. Here is the complete entry you want to put in the *lilo.conf* file for this LILO splash screen. You might have to adjust some of the coordinates and color index numbers depending on how you fashioned your KDE screenshot:

```
install=bmp
bitmap=/boot/swirl.bmp
bmp-table=55p,214p,1,6
bmp-colors=254,0,,74,242,
bmp-timer=582p,455p,0,254,
```

Now run lilo to rebuild the boot record and complete the job:

```
# lilo -v
```

Reboot and you should see the LILO boot menu appear in the Konsole area and the timer appear in the area where the clock was on the panel.

Here's a summary of the steps to follow to create a LILO boot splash image:

1. Download or create your own 640x480 image.
2. Set the image to have an indexed palette of 255 colors or less.
3. Choose two areas of the image: one for the menu, and one for the timer.
4. If necessary, create rectangles suitable for the menu and timer.
5. Find the coordinates where you will put the menu and timer.
6. Choose the colors for the menu entries, selected menu entries, and timer, and find the numbers for those colors by selecting the appropriate squares in the Index Palette Colormap.
7. Save the image as a bitmap file and copy it to /boot.
8. Create the appropriate lines in lilo.conf, based on the information you've collected.
9. Run lilo to rebuild the boot record.
10. Reboot.

HACK #6 Display a GRUB Boot Splash Background

Add a graphical background to your GRUB bootloader.

By default, the GRUB bootloader looks rather bland. It's a menu in a box with some instructions below the menu. It is possible, however, to customize GRUB to display a graphical background. This hack blends nicely with other custom screen hacks such as "Jazz Up Your Debian System Boot" [Hack #8] and "Scrap X11 for Fancy Login Consoles" [Hack #20], because each lets you customize the look of your screen at the different stages of booting up Linux, and starting up terminals or window managers.

It's hard to find many premade backgrounds for GRUB. You can view thumbnails of some available images at *http://ruslug.rutgers.edu/~mcgrof/ grub-images/images/*, and download those images from *http://ruslug.rutgers. edu/~mcgrof/grub-images/images/working-splashimages/*. Place the image in the /boot/grub directory.

For example, let's assume you downloaded the file *frag.xpm.gz*. Log in as root, and copy that file to the /boot/grub directory:

```
# cp frag.xpm.gz /boot/grub
```

Now use your favorite editor to add or change the following line in your */boot/grub/grub.conf* file:

```
splashimage=(hd0,0)/boot/grub/frag.xpm.gz
```

The preceding line assumes that your */boot* directory is located on the first partition on the first disk on your system. Change (hd0,0) to point to the disk and partition where your */boot* directory resides, if it is different from the example.

Reboot and *voilà*: you now have a new background splash screen for GRUB. "Create a GRUB Boot Splash Background" **[Hack #7]** provides full details on how to make your own personal backgrounds.

Create a GRUB Boot Splash Background
HACK #7
Create your own personalized boot splash backgrounds for GRUB.

The default GRUB bootloader screen is rather bland, but you can spice it up a little by creating your own custom graphical background screen for the bootloader. GRUB imposes a number of limitations on the image size and number of colors. It also doesn't let you move the menu. The menu appears in a rectangle near the top of the screen, with some text instructions below the menu. This makes it relatively easy to create a graphical background screen for the GRUB bootloader, because you can focus primarily on making the bottom one-third of the screen interesting. That is not to say you cannot use other areas of the screen, but you should be careful. For example, don't make it difficult to read the GRUB instructions by placing complex graphics behind the text.

Here are the rather strict requirements for the image:

- It must be sized at 640x480.
- It must be a *.xpm* format image file (gzip compression is optional).
- It must contain no more than 14 colors.

Most people will cringe at the 14-color limit, but it is rather amazing what you can do with just 14 colors. Cartoon images are quite suitable for this narrow range of colors, and the narrow range of colors to represent the official Linux penguin (Tux) works fine.

Find or create any image you want to try as a background for GRUB. If you create an image yourself, it's best to create a 640x480 image and use as few colors as possible so that you don't lose the fidelity of the image when you later reduce it to 14 colors. Don't worry about using your graphics editor to limit yourself to 14 colors, however. It is possible to use the Gimp to reduce your image to use 14 colors, which can be a good way of fine-tuning the results you want.

Here is what you need:

- A graphics editor, such as the Gimp, if you want to create or modify an image.
- You must install ImageMagick if it is not already installed. Nearly all Linux distributions provide this on the install CD, and you can use your preferred package manager to install it.

Suppose you have found or created the image *myimage.png*. If you have ImageMagick installed, all you need to do to prepare the image is log in as root and issue these commands:

```
# convert myimage.png -colors 14 -resize 640x480 myimage.xpm
```

The convert command recognizes the extension *png* and knows what format it must convert the image from. It also recognizes the extension *xpm* and knows what format to convert the image to. The -colors 14 switch reduces the number of colors in the image to 14. If the image isn't already sized at 640x480, the switch -resize 640x480 will do that for you.

Next, compress the image (this step is optional, but it saves disk space, which is useful if you plan to install GRUB on a floppy disk and use the floppy as your bootloader). Then copy the image to the */boot/grub* directory (if you have to mount the */boot* directory after starting up Linux, make sure you have it mounted before you start copying files into the */boot/grub* subdirectory):

```
# gzip myimage.xpm
# cp myimage.xpm.gz /boot/grub
```

Now use your favorite editor to add this line to your *grub.conf* file:

```
splashimage=(hd0,0)/boot/grub/myimage.xpm.gz
```

Reboot and you should see your image as the background for GRUB.

 ## HACK #8 Jazz Up Your Debian System Boot

Boot Debian with an optional graphics screen and progress bar, and spiff up your text consoles by running them in graphics mode.

Here's how to add a graphical boot splash to your Debian distribution, the only popular Linux distribution that lacks a built-in boot splash. Windows and Mac OS X have a graphical boot process, as do all the most popular versions of Linux, including Fedora Core (Red Hat), SUSE, and Mandrake. Debian lacks one. (OK, to be perfectly fair, so does Slackware, but currently there's no simple solution for bringing a graphical boot screen to Slackware.) Here's how to bring your Debian system up-to-date with the rest.

You must use a 2.6 version of the Linux kernel for the boot splash to work. If you are using a 2.4 or earlier version of the Linux kernel and are not willing to upgrade to a 2.6 version, you cannot use this hack. This hack also assumes you know how to configure, build, and install a new Linux kernel, and that you already have chosen a version of the 2.6 Linux kernel source code and have that source code on your hard drive. "Compile a Kernel" [Hack #88] provides instructions on how to build and install a Linux kernel if you have never done so. Once you know how to build and install a Linux kernel, you will need to build your kernel with support for frame-buffer graphics, frame-buffer graphics-based consoles, and graphical boot splash screens to make this hack work.

The boot splash portion of this hack gives you a choice of booting in *silent mode* or *verbose mode*. Silent mode displays a graphical background (such as a picture of Tux, the official Linux penguin), and a progress bar to give you a rough idea of where you are during the boot process. You can press F2 at any time to switch to verbose mode, where you see exactly what is happening at boot time. When the boot process is finished, all your virtual consoles work in frame-buffer graphics mode.

Whether you boot to a console or to a graphical login manager, you always have a number of virtual text consoles available to you. You can switch between them by pressing Ctrl-Alt-F1 to get to the first virtual console, Ctrl-Alt-F2 to get to the second, and so on. The difference between a frame-buffer console and a normal console is that the frame-buffer console works in graphics mode, which allows you to display more text on the screen (using smaller fonts), yet keep the text very sharp and readable. The consoles are still primarily for text-based use, but because they are running in graphics mode, you can also have a graphical background behind the text.

At the time of this writing, two substantially different types of patch sets to the Linux kernel are available for boot splash support. The patch set you need for this particular hack is the one that works now, but it is slowly being phased out in favor of an approach that requires far fewer patches to the kernel. This latter approach isn't quite ready for Debian yet. Keep your eye on the web site *http://alioth.debian.org/*. I have been working with other Debian developers to create a more modern boot splash package, and it should eventually show up on that site.

For now, however, you need to work with what's out there. Even so, it's difficult if not impossible to find kernels prepatched or precompiled with the kind of frame-buffer boot splash support you need for this older approach to boot splash. So, you have to patch and compile your own Linux kernel to make this work. You can download a patch from *http://www.bootsplash.de/files*.

Log in as root and change to the directory */usr/src*:

```
$ su -
Password:
# cd /usr/src
```

Choose the patch that matches the 2.6 kernel you are using, and download that patch to the directory */usr/src*. For this example, let's assume you are using the Linux kernel 2.6.8.1, so download the file *bootsplash-3.1.4-sp3-2. 6.8.1.diff*.

It's always good practice to do a dry run with the patch process just to make sure the patch will apply cleanly:

```
# cd /usr/src/linux-2.6.8.1
# cat ../bootsplash-3.1.4-sp3-2.6.8.1.diff | patch -p1 --dry-run
patching file drivers/char/keyboard.c
patching file drivers/char/n_tty.c
patching file drivers/char/vt.c
patching file drivers/video/Kconfig
patching file drivers/video/Makefile
patching file drivers/video/bootsplash/Kconfig
patching file drivers/video/bootsplash/Makefile
patching file drivers/video/bootsplash/bootsplash.c
patching file drivers/video/bootsplash/bootsplash.h
patching file drivers/video/bootsplash/decode-jpg.c
patching file drivers/video/bootsplash/decode-jpg.h
patching file drivers/video/bootsplash/render.c
patching file drivers/video/console/fbcon.c
patching file drivers/video/console/fbcon.h
patching file include/linux/console_struct.h
patching file include/linux/fb.h
patching file kernel/panic.c
```

It looks like there are no errors. Do it again for real by running the patch command, without the –dry-run option:

```
# cat ../bootsplash-3.1.4-sp3-2.6.8.1.diff | patch -p1
patching file drivers/char/keyboard.c
patching file drivers/char/n_tty.c
patching file drivers/char/vt.c
patching file drivers/video/Kconfig
patching file drivers/video/Makefile
patching file drivers/video/bootsplash/Kconfig
patching file drivers/video/bootsplash/Makefile
etc...
```

Now it's time to configure the kernel. Because this hack assumes you have already configured and compiled this kernel without the boot splash feature, all you need to do is configure the boot splash feature and the other kernel features on which boot splash depends.

make menuconfig

When you use **make menuconfig** to configure your kernel, you have to follow the menu options. Here are the menu steps you should follow to set up your kernel to support boot splash and the frame buffer:

1. Select Device Drivers → Graphics support → Support for frame buffer devices.
2. Select the "VESA VGA graphics support" option and press Y.
3. Select "Video mode selection support" and press Y (you should see the selection show [*]).
4. Select "Console display driver support" and press Enter.
5. Select "Video mode selection support" and press Y, after which you should see [*].
6. Select "Framebuffer Console support" and press Y, after which you should see <*>.
7. Exit from this menu. Now select Bootsplash Configuration, and when you see the only selection, "Bootup splash screen," press Y (you should see the selection show [*]).

 You might see a frame-buffer driver specifically written for your video card and be tempted to use it instead of the VESA VGA driver. This can lead to serious problems if you also use an accelerated graphics driver for your video card. For example, *never* select "nVidia riva" frame-buffer support if you plan to use the third-party NVIDIA accelerated graphics drivers. These two drivers do not play well together, and you're sure to have video crashes.

If your system uses an initial RAM disk (*initrd*), now create that initial RAM disk as you normally would. Make a note of the name of the *initrd* file you create. You'll need it later. It's easiest to remember it if you put the kernel version in the name, such as *initrd.img-2.6.8.1*. For example, create the *initrd* file with a command such as this (assuming your root partition is */dev/hda1*):

```
# mkinitrd -o initrd.img-2.6.8.1 -r /dev/hda1 2.6.8.1
```

Install Boot Splash and the Boot Splash init Scripts

Now that your kernel has support for frame buffers, frame-buffer consoles, and boot splash, you must install the boot splash utilities and boot splash startup scripts.

Use your favorite editor to modify your */etc/apt/sources.list* file to include the following line:

```
deb http://www.bootsplash.de/files/debian unstable main
```

Then update the package database and install the necessary files:

```
# apt-get update
# apt-get install sysv-rc-bootsplash
# apt-get install bootsplash bootsplash-theme-newlinux
```

 If you are running a Debian-based distribution instead of true-blue Debian, you will probably have problems installing these packages. You must convert your Debian-based distribution into a true Debian system for these instructions to work. This process isn't difficult, but it is different for each Debian-based product, and an explanation of the necessary steps is beyond the scope of this book.

When Debian installs the *bootsplash* package, the installation dialog presents a list of existing *initrd* images it finds, and it asks you to make a choice about your *initrd* file. If you created an *initrd* file called *initrd.img-2.6.8.1*, as in the previous example, select that file from the list. In this case, the installation program will append the boot splash information to your existing *initrd* file.

If you do not have or need an *initrd* file for this kernel, select none from the list. In this latter case, the configuration program creates an *initrd* file for you called *initrd.splash*.

Set Up Your Bootloader

Most people use either LILO or GRUB as their bootloaders, so let's take a look at both. But first, you must decide what screen resolution and color depth you want for your frame-buffer consoles. The bootloader uses a command something like the following:

```
vga=791
```

The decimal number 791 sets the console to 1024x768 with 64,000 colors. This is usually the safest number to use (not all video cards support all combinations of resolutions and color depths). You can experiment with others. Table 1-1 shows you which numbers represent the various resolutions and color depths.

Table 1-1. *Frame-buffer decimal codes*

Color depth	640x480	800x600	1024x768	1280x1024
8-bit	769	771	773	775
15-bit	784	787	790	793
16-bit	785	788	791	794
24-bit	786	789	792	795

The LILO bootloader is controlled by the settings in the */etc/lilo.conf* file. These settings determine which operating system or kernel version your machine boots with, and which configuration options are passed to Linux at boot time.

Here is a sample entry in the */etc/lilo.conf* file that supports the boot splash and frame-buffer console. Notice the line that sets the vga mode to the decimal number 791. This number specifically refers to the frame-buffer console resolution 1024x768 at 16-bit (64,000 colors) color depth (see Table 1-1). The line append="splash=silent" tells the boot splash sequence not to show all the steps Linux takes during boot time. Instead, you will see a progress bar. If you would rather see all the boot information, change that line to append="splash=verbose". If you choose "splash=silent", you can still press the F2 key during the boot process to switch to verbose mode. However, once you press F2 to switch to verbose mode, you cannot switch back to silent mode.

If you have an *initrd* image, such as *initrd.img-2.6.8.1*, set up your LILO entry like this (substitute your kernel version where appropriate):

```
image=/boot/vmlinuz-2.6.8.1
  label=Linux
  root=/dev/hda1
  initrd=/boot/initrd.img-2.6.8.1
  append="splash=silent"
  vga=791
```

If you do not have an *initrd* image and you selected none during boot splash configuration, set up your LILO entry more like this (substitute your kernel version where appropriate):

```
image=/boot/vmlinuz-2.6.8.1
  label=Linux
  root=/dev/hda1
  initrd=/boot/initrd.splash
  append="splash=silent"
  vga=791
```

Whenever you modify your */etc/lilo.conf* file, you must run the command lilo for the changes to take effect.

Always include a known working boot configuration in your *lilo.conf* file in case the new one does not work. That way you can reboot and choose the working selection to make changes to fix any problems you find.

If you use GRUB as your bootloader, you should have a directory called */boot/ grub* on your system. This directory contains the files GRUB needs to work, such as the GRUB configuration file. The *grub.conf* file is the one that determines which operating systems or Linux versions you can choose, and this is the file you will need to modify to enable the boot splash.

Here is a sample entry in the *grub.conf* file, assuming you have an *initrd* file and you chose it during boot splash configuration:

```
title Debian Splash
  root (hd0,0)
  kernel /boot/vmlinuz-2.6.8-1 ro root=/dev/hda1 vga=791 splash="silent"
  initrd /boot/initrd.img-2.6.8-1
```

Here is a sample entry in the *grub.conf* file, assuming you chose none during boot splash configuration:

```
title Debian Splash
  root (hd0,0)
  kernel /boot/vmlinuz-2.6.8-1 ro root=/dev/hda1 vga=791 splash="silent"
  initrd /boot/initrd.splash
```

Unlike with LILO, changes in *grub.conf* automatically take effect.

Always include a known working boot configuration in your *grub.conf* file in case the new one does not work. That way you can reboot and choose the working selection to make changes to fix any problems. GRUB also gives you the opportunity to boot to a working kernel even if there is no definition for it in the *grub.conf* file. Read the *info* file on GRUB for instructions for performing special operations such as this.

Reboot

Once you have your Linux kernel compiled to support frame-buffer consoles and you have set up your bootloader properly, it is time to reboot. If everything goes according to plan, you should see Tux, the Linux penguin, and a progress bar that fills as the boot sequence proceeds. When your system has finished booting, it will take you either to the first text console or the graphical login manager, depending on how you have your system configured. When you shut down the machine, you should also see the splash screen and the progress bar. In either case, you can press F2 to switch from silent mode to verbose mode. You cannot switch back, however. Once you are in verbose mode, you stay in verbose mode for the duration of that boot or shutdown sequence.

Graphical Consoles

If you normally boot into a text console, you should notice that you now have a graphical background picture of Tux, the official Linux penguin. If you boot to a graphical login manager, press Ctrl-Alt-F1 to get to the first console to see this new feature.

You can control how many consoles display this background by editing the file */etc/default/bootsplash*. Edit the following line to include whichever consoles you want to display the background:

```
BOOTSPLASH_TTYS="1 2 3 4 5"
```

Even if you do not include the number 0 in the list, console 0 (the first console) will always have the background image.

Graphics on the Console

HACK
#9

Make your console a graphics layer to support a higher resolution and color at the command line.

Some of you might be familiar with a picture of Tux the penguin in the upper-left corner of the screen when your system is booting. Ever since kernel 2.2, this popular feature has graced many a Linux boot sequence. To the untrained eye, it simply looks like a penguin, but to the trained technical eye, it is a cunning use of the Linux frame buffer.

A frame buffer is an abstraction for graphics hardware. This abstraction provides a common set of instructions that programs can use to access the graphics hardware on the computer. Most people see the frame buffer as a grinning Tux when the system boots. However, there's more to the frame buffer than a cartoon penguin. Typically, frame buffers are used to render the console graphically so that a resolution can be set on it. Frame buffers are useful in a number of situations, some of which include the following:

Providing a higher resolution
    This allows for the display area to be much larger than before.

Greater color depth
    When you use frame buffers, you can use more colors.

Bypassing X Windows

In some instances, certain Linux programs such as Mplayer can use the frame buffer immediately, thus reducing the overhead of having to run an X Windows desktop such as KDE or GNOME. This is suitable for use on resource-limited embedded systems.

Setting Up the Kernel

Support for the frame buffer comes from the kernel itself. Most stock kernels are supplied with frame-buffer support built into them, so this shouldn't be a problem for most people. To check if your kernel has support already, you can query it:

```
foo@bar:~$ grep -i config_fb /boot/config-$(uname -r)
CONFIG_FB=y
```

If you have frame buffers set, the line `CONFIG_FB=y` will be displayed (in which case you can move on to the next section "Configuring the Bootloader"). If `# CONFIG_FB is not set` is displayed instead, you will need to compile support for the frame buffer into your kernel.

Configuring the Kernel

Details on compiling a kernel are discussed in "Compile a Kernel" **[Hack #88]**, and in this hack, I will simply discuss which options need to be included. The first thing to do is to make sure development features have been enabled within the "Code maturity level" options. Then, to enable frame buffers, go to the "Console drivers" page and enable "VGA text console" and "Video mode selection" support.

There is a subsection under Console called "Frame-buffer support." Underneath that, you need to enable "Support for frame buffer devices," "VESA VGA graphics console," and "VGA 16-color graphics console."

In addition, the subsection "Advanced low level driver options" appears under "Frame-buffer support." Under this menu, you can enable specific levels of pixel support.

Now you can go ahead and compile the kernel.

You might see a frame-buffer driver specifically written for your video card and be tempted to use it instead of the VESA VGA driver. This can lead to serious problems if you also use an accelerated graphics driver for your video card. For example, *never* pick "nVidia riva" frame-buffer support if you plan to use the third-party NVIDIA accelerated graphics drivers. These two drivers do not play well together, and you're sure to have video crashes.

Configuring the Bootloader

When the bootloader loads the kernel, it will pass to it the parameters which you specify and these parameters affect how you use the frame buffer. Just like you would normally tell it which partition is your root partition, you can do the same thing by telling the kernel the values you want to use for the frame buffer.

When using the frame buffer, people commonly require a higher resolution for the command-line console. To set this option, you will need to pass to the kernel the right video mode to use to enable the frame buffer. Refer to Table 1-1 to determine the code to use for your desired video mode.

When you have determined the correct video mode to use, you can pass the kernel the vga parameter to set the mode.

Configure LILO. To configure LILO to use a value from the table (as an example, 1024x768 with 16-bit color), edit */etc/lilo.conf* and find the following line:

```
vga=normal
```

Change this to the mode you want, which in this example is 0x317:

```
vga=0x317
```

Finally, save the file, and as root run /sbin/lilo -v.

Configure GRUB. You configure GRUB in much the same way you configure LILO. The configuration file varies from distribution to distribution, and this is discussed in "Give Your Computer the Boot" [Hack #1]. Edit your grub configuration file and add the vga parameter on the kernel line:

```
title foo
        root (hd0,0)
        kernel /vmlinuz ro root=/dev/hda2 vga=0x317
```

—*Thomas Adam*

## CHAPTER 2

Console
Hacks #10–15

Some people actually prefer to use Linux as a desktop strictly in text mode, without running X Windows at all. If you're among those users, this chapter is definitely for you.

Graphical desktop users have no reason to scoff at this approach. Plenty of text-mode versions of productivity applications are equivalent to the applications most people use on a graphical desktop. For example, the text-mode email client called Mutt is actually more powerful and flexible in handling email than any graphical email program that I've tried. It might not have as many features as a combination email/organizer such as Evolution has, but graphical email programs often force you through several menus and submenus to accomplish a task that takes only one keystroke in Mutt.

If you're under the mistaken impression that you need to run a graphical desktop to use those special multimedia and Internet keys on your keyboard, this chapter will set you straight. You can redefine your keyboard so that your multimedia keys control your CD player, the Internet keys open your email program or web browser, and so on. If you use your imagination, you can automate just about any action.

This chapter focuses primarily on what you do at the virtual console. You can use some of the hacks in the chapter (such as how to colorize files in your pager) in graphics terminals on X Windows desktops. But you must avoid using the first two hacks with terminal emulators in X Windows; "Redefine Keyboard Actions" [Hack #10] and "Energize Your Console with Macro Music Magic" [Hack #11] are designed specifically for the text console. Because X generally redefines the keys the way it wants them, these console definitions will be overwritten, which means you lose the customizations. But at least it won't hurt anything you do in X.

Redefine Keyboard Actions

#10   Fine-tune the way your keyboard behaves when using plain virtual consoles.

This hack describes one of many ways you can customize the default behavior of keys and key combinations for your keyboard. If you just want to make your special function keys on your fancy Internet and multimedia keyboard work, take a look at "Heat Up Your Keyboard with Hotkeys" **[Hack #28]** and "Get Hotter Hotkeys with LinEAK" **[Hack #29]**. But if you want to fine-tune how keystrokes affect virtual text consoles, this is the place for you.

Virtual Consoles

You might recall that people used to attach several text-based terminals to minicomputers and mainframes so that many people could access the computer at once. Each person could log in to the computer and work on his separate text console, because he had his own text-based terminal connected to the main computer.

Linux simulates that kind of behavior with a single terminal and several virtual consoles. Even if your Linux-based computer starts up automatically with a graphical login screen, you can get to the first virtual text console by pressing the key combination Ctrl-Alt-F1. If you want, you can log in and work, using text-based programs. If you press Alt-F2 from here (or Ctrl-Alt-F2), Linux takes you to another virtual console with another login prompt. This simulates another separate terminal hooked up to the computer. Alt-F3 takes you to yet another virtual console and login prompt.

You actually need to use Ctrl-Alt-F*n* only when switching from an X console, such as virtual console 7. Otherwise, you can get away with just Alt-F*n*.

Using the "Other" Alt Key

You might have noticed by now that you can switch from one text console to another only by using the Alt key on the left side of the keyboard. It won't work if you use the Alt key on the right side of the keyboard with F1, F2, or any other function key. This is not an accident. Linux is configured such that the Alt key on the right side of the keyboard plus the F1 key will take you to virtual console 13. The problem is that very few people use as many as 13 virtual consoles, and most Linux distributions don't even enable more than 10 or 11 virtual consoles by default.

Because you don't need to use the Alt key on the right side to switch to non-active virtual consoles, you might as well use that Alt key in the same way the left Alt key works—to take you to virtual console 1, 2, 3, and so on. If you learn how to alter the way the keyboard is configured so that you can use the right Alt key to switch between virtual consoles, you will begin to understand how to make other useful changes in how your keyboard functions.

Here's how to make the change. Dump the current default key settings to a file with the following command (you can log in as root, but a properly configured *sudo* should give you the right to dump the file to the */etc* directory):

```
$ sudo dumpkeys --keys-only > /etc/mykeys
```

Now open the file (as root, preferably with *sudo*) with your favorite editor and locate the following section:

```
keycode  59 = F1              F13            Console_13       F25
    alt     keycode  59 = Console_1
    control    alt    keycode  59 = Console_1
keycode  60 = F2              F14            Console_14       F26
    alt     keycode  60 = Console_2
    control    alt    keycode  60 = Console_2
keycode  61 = F3              F15            Console_15       F27
    alt     keycode  61 = Console_3
    control    alt    keycode  61 = Console_3
keycode  62 = F4              F16            Console_16       F28
    alt     keycode  62 = Console_4
    control    alt    keycode  62 = Console_4
keycode  63 = F5              F17            Console_17       F29
    alt     keycode  63 = Console_5
    control    alt    keycode  63 = Console_5
keycode  64 = F6              F18            Console_18       F30
    alt     keycode  64 = Console_6
    control    alt    keycode  64 = Console_6
keycode  65 = F7              F19            Console_19       F31
    alt     keycode  65 = Console_7
    control    alt    keycode  65 = Console_7
keycode  66 = F8              F20            Console_20       F32
    alt     keycode  66 = Console_8
    control    alt    keycode  66 = Console_8
keycode  67 = F9              F21            Console_21       F33
    alt     keycode  67 = Console_9
    control    alt    keycode  67 = Console_9
keycode  68 = F10             F22            Console_22       F34
    alt     keycode  68 = Console_10
    control    alt    keycode  68 = Console_10
```

The first line in the section that is relevant to the changes we want to make starts with the keycode definition, which is keycode 59 =. A number of columns follow the equals sign, and each column represents what is produced when you combine a modifier (such as Shift, Ctrl, etc.) with that keycode 59. F1 appears in the first column; so, when you press F1 alone (to produce keycode 59), you get F1 with no modifiers (such as Shift, Ctrl, etc.). The second column tells you what you get when you press Shift-F1, and that result is the key F13. The third column tells you what you get when you press Altgr (the Alt key on the right side of the keyboard)-F1, and that takes you to Console_13.

> See the sidebar "How to Interpret Keycode Files" for a more detailed explanation as to why the command switch --keys-only produces this particular type of abbreviated set of definitions for your keyboard configuration.

You want to change this key combination to take you to Console_1 rather than Console_13. All you have to do is change the definition from Console_13 to Console_1. Change Console_14 to Console_2, and so on. Edit each starting line for every keycode definition so that the previous section looks like the following:

```
keycode  59 = F1              F13             Console_1      F25
   alt     keycode  59 = Console_1
   control   alt    keycode  59 = Console_1
keycode  60 = F2              F14             Console_2      F26
   alt     keycode  60 = Console_2
   control   alt    keycode  60 = Console_2
keycode  61 = F3              F15             Console_3      F27
   alt     keycode  61 = Console_3
   control   alt    keycode  61 = Console_3
keycode  62 = F4              F16             Console_4      F28
   alt     keycode  62 = Console_4
   control   alt    keycode  62 = Console_4
keycode  63 = F5              F17             Console_5      F29
   alt     keycode  63 = Console_5
   control   alt    keycode  63 = Console_5
keycode  64 = F6              F18             Console_6      F30
   alt     keycode  64 = Console_6
   control   alt    keycode  64 = Console_6
keycode  65 = F7              F19             Console_7      F31
   alt     keycode  65 = Console_7
   control   alt    keycode  65 = Console_7
keycode  66 = F8              F20             Console_8      F32
   alt     keycode  66 = Console_8
   control   alt    keycode  66 = Console_8
keycode  67 = F9              F21             Console_9      F33
   alt     keycode  67 = Console_9
   control   alt    keycode  67 = Console_9
keycode  68 = F10             F22             Console_10     F34
   alt     keycode  68 = Console_10
   control   alt    keycode  68 = Console_10
```

Save your modifications to the file */etc/mykeys*.

You're not quite done. You still have to load this new set of definitions into the system before the modifications will work. You do that with the following command:

```
$ sudo loadkeys /etc/mykeys
```

Now you can use either the left or right Alt key (plus a function key such as F1) to switch between the most frequently used virtual consoles. The downside, if there is one, is that you can no longer get to Console_13 or higher by pressing Altgr-F1, Altgr-F2, etc. In most cases, however, Linux does not activate consoles above Console_11, so you'll never miss the lost capability.

If you want to have your computer automatically reload the new key definitions at startup, see the sidebar "Keep Your Custom Keys Intact."

Deep-Six the Caps Lock Key

This section describes another thing you can accomplish by changing the keycode definitions.

I hate the Caps Lock key. I am always inadvertently hitting the key, after which I type a full command at the console in caps before I realize what I've done. Naturally, the command does not work, because Linux/Unix is case-sensitive.

Although you can redefine the key in your */etc/mykeys* file with your favorite editor (which would be a good idea if you also implement the previous hack), here are two tricks you can use without having to edit any files. This first trick simply disables the Caps Lock key for consoles so that it has no function:

```
$ sudo echo "keycode 58 = VoidSymbol" | loadkeys
```

Some people like to convert the Caps Lock key into a Ctrl key. Here is the simple command to do that:

```
$ sudo echo "keycode 58 = Control" | loadkeys
```

Again, if you want to have your computer make this change automatically, see the sidebar "Keep Your Custom Keys Intact" for instructions.

How to Interpret Keycode Files

The --keys-only switch makes the keycode definition file a bit shorter and easier to read, because it omits a lot of information you don't need to customize it for our purposes.

When you dump the list of keycodes and their various permutations (which is what happens when you combine them with some other key or key combination, such as Alt, Alt-Ctrl, etc.) with the dumpkeys --full-table command, it prints out 16 columns in an order determined by the numeric value of the first five modifying keys: 0, 1, 2, 4, and 8. Here is a list of the numeric values of all the key modifiers, including the ones that aren't used:

- None = 0
- Shift = 1
- Altgr = 2
- Ctrl = 4
- Alt = 8
- ShiftL = 16
- ShiftR = 32
- CtrlL = 64
- CtrlR = 128

Notice that you can add any combination of modifying keys and still get a unique column number. Ctrl-Shift is 4+1. Although it is possible to use ShiftL, ShiftR, CtrlL, and CtrlR (the left and right Shift and Ctrl keys), these keys aren't assigned by default. That's why you get only 16 key combinations, each represented in a column of a row of combinations for each keycode. If you print out a complete list of keycodes and their functions, you should get 16 columns. Each column would represent, in order:

- The key with no other key pressed (0)
- The key with the Shift key pressed (1)
- The key with the Altgr key pressed (2)
- The key with the Altgr-Shift keys pressed (2+1 = 3)
- The key with the Ctrl key pressed (4)
- The key with the Shift-Ctrl keys pressed (1+4 = 5)
- The key with the Altgr-Ctrl keys pressed (2+4 = 6)
- The key with the Ctrl-Altgr-Shift keys pressed (4+2+1 = 7)
- The key with the Alt key pressed (8)
- The key with the Shift-Alt keys pressed (1+8 = 9)

—continued—

- The key with the Alt-Altgr keys pressed (8+2 = 10)
- The key with the Alt-Altgr-Shift keys pressed (8+2+1 = 11)
- The key with the Alt-Ctrl keys pressed (8+4 = 12)The key with the Alt-Ctrl-Shift keys pressed (8+4+1 = 13)
- The key with the Alt-Ctrl-Altgr keys pressed (8+4+2 = 14)
- The key with the Alt-Ctrl-Altgr-Shift keys pressed (8+4+2+1 = 15)

You don't see all 16 columns when you use the `--keys-only` switch. You see a subset of columns defined by the first line of the output of the command. The first line of the output of the `dumpkeys --keys-only` command is `keymaps 0-2,4-6,8-9,12`. This means the `dumpkeys --keys-only` command displays only the following nine columns: modifiers 0, 1, 2, 4, 5, 6, 8, 9, and 12.

Indeed, the `--keys-only` command might not even print all nine columns, because it does not print columns that are not assigned an action. If nothing happens when you press certain key combinations (such as Shift-Ctrl), the command does not print that column. (The official definition of an inactive key is `VoidSymbol`).

For example, look at the definition line for keycode 59 in the output of our example file:

```
keycode  59 = F1  F13 Console_13  F25
    alt     keycode  59 = Console_1
    control     alt     keycode  59 = Console_1
```

The first column shows F1, which is the key without any modifiers. The second column is F13, which is Shift-F1. The third column is Console_13, which is Altgr-F1. Because the columns are defined as 0-2,4-6, etc., the output skips modifier 3, and the next column we can expect to see is the key with modifier 4, or Ctrl-F1. This produces F25. The next column we should see is modifier 5, which is Shift-Ctrl-F1. But no action is defined for this combination. The fact that nothing happens when you press Shift-Ctrl-F1 would normally be represented by the definition `VoidSymbol` in that column, but the `--keys-only` switch avoids printing out `VoidSymbol`.

As a result, notice that the keycode table format changes for the rest of the keycode combination definitions. The rest of the possible actions for F1 are spelled out in separate lines. That's why the output skips to a new line that says `Alt keycode 59 = Console_1` (this would normally appear in column 8), followed by another line that says `Control-Alt-keycode 59 = Console_1` (normally column 12).

If you want to see a file that has a column definition for every possible key modification combination from 0-15, including all the `VoidSymbols`, issue the command `dumpkeys --full-table`.

HACK #11 Energize Your Console with Macro Music Magic

Redefine keys to issue commands at the command line.

You can exploit the power of the preceding keyboard customization technique to a much greater degree than just redefining the action of a key. You can actually define keys to send strings of characters, which, at the console, means issuing commands.

In this example, you're going to redefine keys to control your CD-ROM as a CD player. Even if you have a plain keyboard, you can simply use unusual key combinations such as Ctrl-Alt-Right Arrow to perform the kind of magic you're about to explore. If you can determine the keycodes generated by any special keys you have on your Internet or multimedia keyboard, you can use those keys instead.

Defining the Magic

First, you want to create a file called /etc/mykeys, or add to your existing /etc/mykeys file if you are combining this hack with "Redefine Keyboard Actions" [Hack #10]. You will place in /etc/mykeys string definitions that represent commands. The cdtool program is really handy for controlling a CD player at the command line without a bothersome user interface. You can use another tool if you prefer, but you'll have to substitute your tool's commands for the ones defined by cdtool.

Assume you are using cdtool to define commands to play a CD, stop playing it, advance to the next track, move to the previous track, etc. First, define labels for the command strings. Here is what you add to /etc/mykeys:

```
string F100 = "cdplay\n"
string F101 = "cdstop\n"
string F102 = "cdplay +\n"
string F103 = "cdplay -\n"
string F104 = "eject\n"
```

Notice that each command string includes a trailing \n. This is the equivalent of pressing the Enter key. If you don't add the \n at the end of each string, the computer "types" the command, but doesn't execute the command until someone presses Enter.

Normal Keyboards

If you have a normal keyboard with no added multimedia keys, decide on a set of keys you want to modify. In this example, you will assign the following keys these actions:

Keyboard command	Action taken
Ctrl-Alt-Insert	Play the CD.
Ctrl-Alt-Right	Play the next track.
Ctrl-Alt-Left	Play the previous track.
Ctrl-Alt-Down	Stop the CD.
Ctrl-Alt-Up	Eject the CD.

Because you want Ctrl-Alt-Insert to begin playing an audio CD in your CD drive, look for the definition for the Insert key in */etc/mykeys*. That keycode is 110. Add a line below the keycode definition that makes the combination control+alt+keycode 110 execute the string represented by F100, which is cdplay\n.

Assume you want Ctrl-Right Arrow to play the next track on a CD. Find the definition in */etc/mykeys* for the Right Arrow key, which is keycode 106. It already has one definition (increase to the next console). Add another definition below that so that Ctrl-Alt-Right plays the next track on a CD (string F102).

When you are finished assigning all the F100-F104 actions to the keys, the relevant section of your */etc/mykeys* file should look like this:

```
keycode 103 = Up
        alt      keycode 103 = KeyboardSignal
        control alt    keycode 103 = F104
keycode 104 = Prior
        shift    keycode 104 = Scroll_Backward
keycode 105 = Left
        alt      keycode 105 = Decr_Console
        control alt    keycode 105 = F103
keycode 106 = Right
        alt      keycode 106 = Incr_Console
        control alt    keycode 106 = F102
keycode 107 = Select
keycode 108 = Down
        control alt    keycode 108 = F101
keycode 109 = Next
        shift    keycode 109 = Scroll_Forward
keycode 110 = Insert
        control alt    keycode 110 = F100
```

Special Keyboards

I have a Logitech Elite keyboard. It has multimedia keys for starting and stopping a CD player, moving forward and backward through the CD tracks, and so on. If you have a similar keyboard you can find out what keycodes these keys generate by using the showkey command. Then, execute showkey, and then press the keys for which you want the keycodes. Here is a sample showkey session:

```
$ showkey
press any key (program terminates 10s after last keypress)...
keycode  28 release
keycode 165 press
keycode 165 release
keycode 163 press
keycode 163 release
keycode 164 press
keycode 164 release
keycode 166 press
keycode 166 release
keycode 171 press
keycode 171 release
```

When you execute the showkey command it tells you that you have 10 seconds in which to enter a keypress. If you don't send one within that time the program will terminate. Ignore the first keycode 28 release in this list, as it represents the fact that I released the Enter key after executing showkey.

Given the order in which I pressed my special keys and the output of showkeys, I was able to create the following table:

Special keyboard key	Keycode
Previous track	Keycode 165
Next track	Keycode 163
Play	Keycode 164
Stop	Keycode 166
Eject	Keycode 171

You should already have defined the strings for the special keys F100-F104, but I'll repeat them here so that you can see the associations more clearly. Assuming you have a Logitech Elite keyboard with the same keycodes, the following section is what you should add to or modify in your */etc/mykeys* file:

```
string F100 = "cdplay\n"
string F101 = "cdstop\n"
string F102 = "cdplay +\n"
string F103 = "cdplay -\n"
string F104 = "eject\n"

keycode 163 = F102
keycode 164 = F100
keycode 165 = F103
keycode 166 = F101
keycode 167 =
```

```
keycode 168 =
keycode 169 =
keycode 170 =
keycode 171 = F104
```

The last thing you need to do is save your work, and then load the new key definitions with this command:

```
# sudo loadkeys /etc/mykeys
```

Now, even if you don't have a multimedia keyboard, you can use your keyboard at a virtual text console to play and manipulate audio CDs. If you want to have your computer automatically reload the new key definitions at startup, see the sidebar "Keep Your Custom Keys Intact."

Keep Your Custom Keys Intact

The only problem with defining a special /etc/mykeys file and loading it manually is that you will lose this customization the next time you boot your Linux system. You can find and replace the default configuration file for your system, but that's not a very good way to make these changes permanent. You'll probably overwrite the modified system key bindings with a new version the next time you upgrade the package that contains the configuration file. It is best to save your custom settings in a file somewhere, such as /etc/mykeys, and load them automatically within a startup script after all the necessary startup scripts have finished. Virtually every Linux distribution I've used gives you a method to add these sorts of extra commands. Here are some samples to show you where you would add the command to load the special key configurations.

You might notice that you don't need to use *sudo* to redefine the Caps Lock key when you make the modification in this file. This file is automatically executed as root, so *sudo* is not necessary.

You need to place the following code into each file. In most instances it needs to be placed at the end of the file, so it doesn't hurt to put it at the end for all files:

```
loadkeys /etc/mykeys
echo "keycode 58 = VoidSymbol" | loadkeys
```

Here are the files you need to edit for various distributions:

Fedora Core 3: /etc/rc.local

Debian: /etc/rc.boot

SUSE 9.1: /etc/init.d/boot.local

Mandrake 10.1: /etc/rc.local

Gentoo ~x86: /etc/conf.d/local.start

Undoing Your Custom Keys and Macros

If you want to set the behavior of your keyboard back to the defaults, all it takes is one simple command:

```
$ sudo loadkeys --default
```

XFree86 and Xorg tend to override settings you make for console use, so you don't usually have to undo them before you start up a graphical desktop.

> On rare occasions, something you define with loadkeys can sneak into your graphical desktop keyboard definitions and cause unexpected behavior. If you run into that problem, set your keyboard configuration back to the defaults before starting your graphical desktop.

Take a Screenshot from the Command Line

HACK #12

Who needs a graphical tool to grab a screenshot? The command line has everything you need.

For many writers and programmers, screenshots are useful for showcasing how an interface or program looks. Although grabbing a screenshot is often as simple as running a small utility or clicking an option, some grabbers are not as flexible as you need them to be. For example, sometimes you might need a screenshot without the screenshot tool displayed in the taskbar, or you might need to take a screenshot in an environment, where you cannot run a graphical screenshot utility. This is a common problem for those who need to take screenshots of installation programs or software on embedded devices.

Take a Screenshot from an X Terminal

Although a graphical screenshot-grabbing tool is the obvious choice for making a screenshot, most of these utilities leave a trace of themselves in the screenshot by having an entry on the taskbar or being visible on the desktop. You can solve this problem by using a collection of command-line tools to take the screenshot from an X terminal or even from within the Run option in the KDE/GNOME main menu:

```
foo@bar:~$ sleep 2; import -window root screen.png
```

This command is actually composed of two separate utilities. The sleep command delays the process for two seconds before the screenshot is taken. This gives you time to minimize windows, expand menus, or make other necessary adjustments before the screenshot is taken. By changing the sleep value you can control the delay before the screenshot is taken. The second command uses the *import* utility that is part of the ImageMagick suite of tools (use your package manager to install ImageMagick if it isn't already on your system) to take a screenshot of the root window (the root window is the entire screen) and name the image *screen.png*. If you want to grab a particular part of the screen, you also can use the –crop option to grab that specific area (such as import -crop 500x400). And if you run *import* without –window your cursor will change to a crosshair, which you can drag over the area you want to capture. For many print and digital media houses, *PNG* is a recommended screenshot format, but ImageMagick supports a range of different formats, so you can use what you need. Read the import manpage for more information.

Take a Screenshot from a Command-Line Terminal

If you need to take a screenshot from a command-line console while X is running elsewhere on the system, adjust the command line and add a few additional features to it. This method is commonly used when you need a screenshot of an installation routine or a program running on an embedded device. To do this, first access the shell that runs behind the installer by pressing Ctrl-Alt-F2; this provides you with a simple shell in which you can run the commands to grab the shot. If you are planning on using this hack while installing a Linux distribution, you might need to copy the chvt, sleep, and import commands onto a floppy disk so that you can mount it and access the programs. You can mount the floppy disk with:

```
foo@bar:~$ mount /dev/fd0 /mnt/floppy
```

Before you can run the command to grab the shot, you need to find out the display number of the running X server. Every X server has a unique display number that is mapped to the particular user who is using X. This number can be used to distinguish between different X displays. You can find this number by checking the $DISPLAY environmental:

```
foo@bar:~$ echo $DISPLAY
```

Now you can run the command. For example, if your display number returns :0.0, the main command to grab the screenshot is:

```
foo@bar:$ chvt 7; sleep 2; import -window root screen.png
-display :0.0 ; chvt 2
```

This command runs through the process of switching to the X terminal, grabbing the screenshot, and switching back to your current command-line terminal. The first command (chvt 7) switches to the X terminal (usually the 7th terminal), and then the second command (sleep 2) pauses the process for two seconds. This pause allows for the machine to switch to the 7th terminal before the screenshot is taken. Then the import command is used to grab the root window on display :0.0 and save the shot as *screen.png*. Finally, the terminal is switched back to terminal 2 (chvt 2). If you run this from a terminal other than 2, you need to change the number on the last command to the relevant terminal number. If you need to store the image to the floppy disk when you run this command, you need to prepend the filename with the mount point of the floppy disk—e.g., */mnt/floppy/screen.png*.

HACK #13 Put Your Command Prompt on a Diet

Change your bash prompt to show extra information without cluttering the area around your command prompt.

This hack saves command-line prompt space without sacrificing the informational value that prompt hacks often add to command-line prompts. Sure, it's great to see the date, time, uptime, and phase of the moon in your bash prompt, but most schemes for providing this extra information create a crowded mess and push more important text off the terminal screen. This hack uses the tput command to place some of that extra information in the upper-right corner of the terminal or console, leaving your prompt neat, clean, and short. Thanks to Giles Orr whose web site on bash prompts (*http://www.tldp.org/HOWTO/Bash-Prompt-HOWTO/*) inspired this example hack.

I'll keep this particular hack simple. You are going to put the current working directory somewhere on the terminal but not at the prompt itself. This hack creates a directory path that always appears in the upper-right corner. Of course, as explained later, you can modify this location.

The tput command is ideal for this type of trick, because tput manipulates the location and color of cursors. Figure 2-1 shows what it might look like when it is configured as the default prompt.

This might seem somewhat superfluous when using an X terminal, because it's easy to put the current working directory in the titlebar. However, not every terminal works that way, and there is no titlebar on a virtual console, so it still comes in really handy, especially when you are working without a graphical window manager or desktop.

Here is the script, with comments on how it works:

```
#!/bin/bash
```

```
function prompt_command {
# save the current position
tput sc
# backwash is where to position the cursor
# to write the whole current working directory
# we back up 2 more for the brackets
let backwash=$(tput cols)-$(echo $(pwd) | wc -m)-2
```

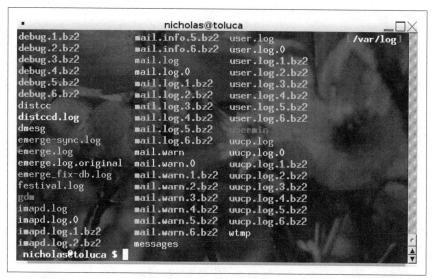

Figure 2-1. The current working directory in the upper-right corner

```
# position the cursor at Y=0, X=calculated length
tput cup 0 ${backwash}
# set foreground color, bold
tput setaf 4 ; tput bold
# wrap the full path in brackets
echo -n "["
# set the color of the current path
tput setaf 6
# show the path
echo -n "$(pwd)"
# set the color of the closing bracket"
tput setaf 4 ; tput bold
# show the closing bracket
echo -n "]"
# return cursor to the saved position
tput rc
}

PROMPT_COMMAND=prompt_command

GREEN="\[$(tput setaf 2 ; tput bold)\]"
WHITE="\[$(tput setaf 7 ; tput bold)\]"
NO_COLOUR="\[$(tput sgr0)\]"

case $TERM in
    xterm*|rxvt*)
        TITLEBAR='\[\033]0;\u@\h \007\]'
        ;;
    *)
        TITLEBAR=""
```

```
                ;;
    esac

    PS1="${TITLEBAR}\
    $GREEN\u@\h \
    $WHITE\$$NO_COLOUR "
    PS2='> '
    PS4='+ '
```

Here's how it works. First, the tput sc command saves the current position of the cursor.

Now let's pick apart the following, somewhat awkward-looking command from the preceding code:

```
    let backwash=$(tput cols)-$(echo $(pwd) | wc -m)-2
```

The goal here is to find out where to move the cursor on the X axis to start printing out the current working directory surrounded by brackets. The column you want is the width of the terminal minus the width of the current directory, minus two more columns (for the brackets).

The tput cols command returns the number of columns in the current terminal or console. The pwd command prints the current working directory, which is echoed and piped through the wc -m command, which returns the number of characters in the current working directory. Then the command subtracts that length plus two more for the brackets. All together, the whole command returns the X axis location of the cursor where the script should start printing the current directory in brackets.

The tput cup <row> <column> command moves the cursor to the specified row and column. In this case, we always want row 0 (the top row), and we calculated the starting location for the column in the previous command.

Now the script sets up some tput variables to determine how the next bit of text placed on the screen will look. The tput setaf 4 command defines the color as dark blue, and tput bold makes it bold. Then the script echoes the open bracket to the screen. The script resets the color and prints the current path, and then resets the color and prints the close bracket.

Then it returns the cursor back to its saved position with tput rc. Finally, it sets the prompt, using variable definitions for tput sequences to set colors.

You probably won't find setaf in the manpage for tput. Indeed, Table 2-1 provides some of the rarely documented features of tput.

> The fact that these features are rarely documented implies it is possible they might not work on some systems (such as some terminals or Linux running on machines other than x86es).

Table 2-1. tput commands

Command for tput	Result of the command
tput setab [1-7]	Set a background color using ANSI escape sequence.
tput setb [1-7]	Set a background color.
tput setaf [1-7]	Set a foreground color using ANSI escape sequence.
tput setf [1-7]	Set a foreground color.
tput bold	Set bold mode.
tput dim	Set half-bright mode.
tput smul	Begin underline mode.
tput rmul	Exit underline mode.
tput rev	Turn on reverse mode.

Table 2-2 shows the ANSI escape sequence commands for foregrounds and backgrounds you can use in place of the colors I've chosen.

Table 2-2. Color commands for tput

Command for tput	Color
tput setaf 0	Black
tput setab 0	BlackBG
tput bold ; tput setaf 0	DarkGrey
tput setaf 1	Red
tput setab 1	RedBG
tput bold ; tput setaf 1	LightRed
tput setaf 2	Green
tput setab 2	GreenBG
tput bold ; tput setaf 2	LightGreen
tput setaf 3	Brown
tput setab 3	BrownBG
tput bold ; tput setaf 3	Yellow
tput setaf 4	Blue
tput setab 4	BlueBG
tput bold ; tput setaf 4	BrightBlue
tput setaf 5	Purple
tput setab 5	PurpleBG
tput bold ; tput setaf 5	Pink
tput setaf 6	Cyan
tput setab 6	CyanBG

Table 2-2. Color commands for tput (continued)

Command for tput	Color
tput bold ; tput setaf 6	BrightCyan
tput setaf 7	LightGrey
tput setab 7	LightGreyBG
tput bold ; tput setaf 7	White

HACK #14 Simplify Changing Directories

This hack makes it ridiculously easy to jump right to your favorite directories from the command line.

Every Linux user probably knows there's an environment variable called PATH. When you type a command, your system looks through all the directories defined in the PATH environment variable until it finds the command. If it doesn't find the command by the time it has exhausted all the directories listed in the path, it tells you it can't find the file.

There's a similar environment variable that is a bit more obscure called CDPATH. You can define CDPATH to include a number of directories to search when you type the following command:

```
$ cd somewhere
```

Here's how it works. Assume for a moment that you're an obsessively organized writer who likes to create directory trees that organize files by types, groups, categories, etc. Let's say you organized your documents such that you have the following directories:

/docs/pub/books/oreilly/linuxhacks/chapter1
/docs/pub/books/oreilly/linuxhacks/chapter2
/docs/pub/books/oreilly/linuxhacks/chapter3

Here's what you want to do. You want to be able to jump right to the *chapter2* directory without having to type the entire path. Here's how to set the CDPATH environment variable so that you can do that:

```
$ export CDPATH=:..:/docs/pub/books/oreilly/linuxhacks
```

Notice that this command does *not* include any of the chapter directories in the CDPATH. That's because you want the CDPATH to define the directory immediately above the directory you want to find. Remember, the system searches the directories listed in the path for the *contents* you specify on the command line. The argument *chapter2* is what you're looking for. *chapter2* exists in the directory */docs/pub/oreilly/linuxhacks*, so that is the directory you want to include in your search CDPATH.

Assuming you have defined `CDPATH` as shown in the previous example, now you should be able to type this command, (almost) no matter what your current directory might be:

```
$ cd chapter2
```

The command should take you immediately to the directory */docs/pub/books/oreilly/linuxhacks/chapter2*.

The Catch

Remember I said you're obsessive about organization? Suppose you also created the following directories according to the same pattern mentioned earlier:

/docs/pub/books/oreilly/bsdhacks/chapter1
/docs/pub/books/oreilly/bsdhacks/chapter2
/docs/pub/books/oreilly/bsdhacks/chapter3

Naturally, you have to add a new path to your `CDPATH` environment variable:

```
$ export CDPATH=.:/docs/pub/books/oreilly/linuxhacks:/docs/pub/books/
oreilly/bsdhacks
```

As with the `PATH` environment variable, you separate different search paths with a colon. The system searches through each path from left to right. Now issue this command:

```
$ cd chapter2
```

Where do you think it takes you? It puts you in the same place as before, */docs/pub/books/oreilly/linuxhacks/chapter2*. That is *not* what you expected or desired. But it happened because the `cd` command searches the `CDPATH` environment variable paths from left to right. It searched the *linuxhacks* location first and found *chapter2*. So, that's where it assumed you wanted to go.

The Solution

One solution is to avoid being obsessive about standardizing the way you structure directories. The other, arguably more realistic solution to this problem is to be extremely careful about how you construct your `CDPATH` environment variable and how you use it. One way to avoid the problem described earlier is to define the `CDPATH` in this way:

```
$ export CDPATH=.:/docs/pub/books/oreilly
```

You have to do a little extra typing to get where you want to go, but you still save some effort. If you want to get to *chapter2* of *bsdhacks*, you simply type the following:

```
$ cd bsdhacks/chapter2
```

One More cd Trick

This is perhaps the simplest of all tricks for cd, yet surprisingly few people know of it. Suppose you are working in the directory */docs/pub/books/oreilly/ linuxhacks/chapter2* and then you change to the directory */usr/X11R6/lib/ X11/fonts/TrueType*. You can jump back to the previous directory simply by typing the following:

```
$ cd -
```

This simple command returns you to the last directory you were using before you changed to the current one.

Colorize Files in Your Pager

Keep your splash of color when terminal commands tend to turn things into black and white.

As a Linux user you might have noticed that filenames appear in different colors when you type ls or dir. Yet when you pipe the colored file listing through a pager such as *less*, the pager ignores the colors and turns the output into black and white. You might notice this when you execute a commonly used command, such as ls -al | less.

Most Linux distributions are configured to display the files in various colors to make it easy to identify symbolic links, executable files, compressed files, and so on. If yours is not configured in such a way, there's an easy way to correct this. Type the following command:

```
$ alias ls='ls --color=auto'
```

This tells your system that every time you type the ls command, it will actually type ls --color=auto for you. Now type the command:

```
$ ls
```

You should see your files appear in different colors, according to their type. If you didn't see colored filenames, you might have a distribution that requires a slightly different switch. Try this instead:

```
$ alias ls='ls --color=tty'
```

Now type the command to test the color capability:

```
$ ls
```

Chances are that one or more alias definitions are already defined for you in one of the automatically executed login files. See the sidebar "Bash Auto-Configuration Files" for more information about how many popular distributions make these settings.

The Black-and-White Problem

Now here's the problem that might plague you at times. You want to view a list of files, so you issue the command ls -a. That command lists all the regular and hidden files, and all the files and directories appear in living color. Or perhaps you prefer to use the command ls -al that lists all regular and hidden files in a detailed single column. Once again, the files appear in living color.

When there are many files, the list scrolls off the screen. This is particularly troublesome on a text console that doesn't let you scroll back far enough to see the beginning of the list. What's a geek to do? The intuitive solution is to issue this command:

```
$ ls -al | less
```

This pipes the output of ls -al through the *less* pager, which lets you scroll back and forth through the entire output of the ls -al command.

There's just one catch. All the pretty colors are gone. It is no longer easy to identify compressed files from executable files (and so on...) at a glance.

You don't see colors in the *less* pager for two reasons. First, *less* requires the -R command-line switch to display colors. That won't be enough for most Linux users, however. You can find out for yourself if adding the –R switch is all you need for your Linux distribution by typing this command:

```
$ ls -al | less -R
```

Did you see the list of files in color? Probably not. That's because most Linux distributions set up ls as an alias for the command ls --color=tty or ls --color=auto. These commands output color only when the destination is a terminal screen. When you pipe the output or redirect the output from ls, it turns off the color feature automatically.

There are at least three solutions to this problem.

Solution 1

Here's one way to fix the problem. The ls --color command does not care what the output is, whether it's a terminal screen, a redirection to another file, or a pipe to another program. One or more files in your system contain the commands to set the aliases (see the sidebar "Bash Auto-Configuration Files," which includes information on where these settings are made for various distributions). Find the file on your system where you want to change the way the aliases are set. Look for the line that defines the color as *auto* or *tty* as the default, and change it to this (you might as well add the -R to *less* while you're at it):

```
alias ls='ls --color'
alias less='less -R'
```

By not specifying *tty* or *auto*, the ls command will output color no matter where the output is directed.

There's a catch to doing things this way, so before you edit the file that defines the alias command, try the technique manually so that you can see for yourself what the catch will be. Follow these steps to set the default behavior for both ls and less to support color, and then perform the piped output command to see a listing of files in color:

```
$ alias ls='ls --color'
$ alias less='less -R'
$ ls -al | less
```

There you go—colorized output in the *less* pager.

Now that ls automatically outputs color no matter where the output is directed, try this command to redirect the output of the colored directory list to a file:

```
$ ls -al > directory.txt
```

Now open the file with your favorite editor, and you should see all the codes used to colorize the text. For example, you might see something like this:

```
[[01;34mDesktop[[00m
[[01;31mEiosource-1.1-1.i386.rpm[[00m
[[01;34mGNUstep[[00m
[[00mHello[[00m
[[00mKernel-Win4Lin3-2.6.6.patch[[00m
```

Your editor doesn't interpret the codes to colorize your text. It simply shows you the codes that exist in the output of the command. This is not quite what you want when you redirect output to a file, is it?

So, here's a way to deal with the first solution. You can modify your alias settings so that the following command produces colorized output:

```
$ ls -al | less
```

When you don't want to produce colorized output, such as when you want to redirect the output to a file, you override the alias with a command like this, which specifies that ls should output color only if the destination is a terminal:

```
$ ls -al --color=auto > directory.txt
```

Solution 2

The second solution is precisely the opposite of the first. Leave the alias alone, as it is already set. When you get the hankering to view a long directory list through a pager, override the setting that restricts color output to terminals with this command:

```
$ ls -al --color | less -R
```

Solution 3

Neither of the previous solutions is the "Linux way"; that is, a way to customize and automate everything. So, here's a way to solve the problem like a true Linux hacker would. Define aliases to give you the choices you want while using shorthand commands. Here's one example, but it is by no means the only way to approach this. Edit the file where aliases are defined so that it contains these aliases:

```
alias ls='ls --color=auto'
alias lsp='ls --color | less -R'
alias dir='ls -al'
alias dirp='ls -al --color | less -R'
```

This way, you can issue a command such as ls -al > directory.txt, and the file won't be littered with color codes. Yet anytime you want to page through a full list of your files in living color, all you have to type is the command lsp or dirp.

Bash Auto-Configuration Files

Fedora Core sets default aliases in the */etc/profile.d/colorsls.sh* file to:

```
alias l.='ls -d .* --color=tty'
alias ll='ls -l --color=tty'
alias ls='ls --color=tty'
```

Debian sets default aliases in the */etc/skel/.bashrc* file to:

```
alias ls='ls --color=auto'
```

SUSE uses a complex */etc/bash.bashrc* script that ends up setting the ls alias indirectly to:

```
alias ls='ls --color=tty'
```

Mandrake uses a complex set of files, and sets the default alias in */etc/profiles.d/alias.sh* to:

```
alias ls='--color=auto'
```

Gentoo sets default aliases in */etc/skel/.bashrc* to:

```
alias ls="ls --color=auto"
```

Login Managers
Hacks #16–21

Personal computers are no longer as personal as they used to be. You might have a family computer, for example, and each member of the family uses the computer with his own personal account. In this case, at one time or another you will encounter this conversation, or something like it: "I need to use the computer." "But I'm right in the middle of typing my school report." "This can't wait, you need to log off and let me use it now!"

If you are ever caught in a situation in which you have to relinquish control of your computer to another person, it seems both logical and natural that you should close all your applications and log out before allowing the other person to access the computer. That isn't necessary with Linux. Linux is truly multiuser. You can have two or more people logged in to the same computer at the same time, even running separate graphical desktops at the same time. You don't have to close all your applications and log out. All you have to do to relinquish control to another person is to lock your session (for security purposes), and then let the next person start up his own session.

In some cases, desktop environments, such as KDE and GNOME, provide you with a handy menu option that will let someone start another desktop session. If your Linux distribution doesn't provide you with that easy method, don't worry. The following hacks will show you how you can set up two or more KDE or GNOME graphical login screens, where each user can start up her own session isolated from any other sessions that are running.

I've even provided a method for the staunch power user who resists point-and-click in favor of a command-line approach.

Finally, these hacks introduce a whole new approach to graphical login screens. These screens replace the dull text login prompt with a graphical frame-buffer console prompt that lets you start up anything from plain-text consoles to window managers or desktop environments such as KDE and

GNOME. You can set up as many of these login screens as you want, and each one will start up a separate user session. You can even customize the graphical look and feel of each login screen.

Switch Users Fast

Get two or more people logged in to their favorite graphical desktop at the same time on the same machine.

It's a personal computer. No, it's a family computer. No, it's two...two... two computers in one! Picture this. You're working at home on an important business document when your daughter tells you she needs to use the computer for a while to do research for a school project. Do you have to close all your applications and log out for her to do her work? Nope. The following hack shows you a few ways to let your daughter log in and work with her own desktop without you having to close your applications and log out first.

You can get two or more users logged in and running separate graphical desktops on the same machine in a number of ways. This hack explores the built-in method.

First, a Lesson on Virtual Terminals

You might recall that people used to attach several text-based terminals to minicomputers and mainframes so that many users could access the computer at once. Each person could log in to the computer and work on his separate text console, because he had his own text-based terminal connected to the main computer. Linux simulates that kind of behavior with a single terminal and several virtual consoles. Most Linux distributions provide six text-based virtual consoles and usually three virtual consoles for graphical desktops, although more of both types are possible.

If you have used the graphical interface only on Linux and you're not familiar with virtual consoles, here's a quick way to see what they're all about. Press the key combination Ctrl-Alt-F1. You should see a text-based screen with a login prompt. This is virtual console 1. Press the key combination Ctrl-Alt-F2. This is virtual console 2. You can get back to the graphical desktop by pressing Ctrl-Alt-F7, because the default virtual console for graphical desktops is virtual console 7. If you can start up a second graphical desktop, it will be assigned to the next available virtual console after the previous graphical desktop, which is virtual console 8. You can switch to that desktop by pressing Ctrl-Alt-F8. So, when you achieve your goal of starting up two separate graphical desktops, you can switch between them by pressing Ctrl-Alt-F7 and Ctrl-Alt-F8.

The Built-In KDE and GNOME Way

Some Linux distributions with the latest versions of GNOME or KDE include a menu option to log in as another user on a separate virtual terminal. For example, as of this writing, one menu sequence (on Gentoo Linux) for GNOME is Applications → System Tools → New Login. This brings up a second GNOME-based graphical login screen (GDM), from which a second user can log in and start working with her account. This works only if you started GNOME from GDM. Here's why: after you start a GNOME session, part of GDM is still running in the background waiting for you to exit GNOME. The menu selection depends on this program to be running in the background, so if you didn't start GNOME with GDM, it won't be running and waiting to start another session.

 Fedora Core 2 currently does not offer the option of starting a new login, even though it runs GDM by default. You can still get multiple simultaneous logins with graphical desktops using the other techniques described in this hack.

The latest versions of KDE have a similar option. The menu sequence on my Gentoo system is K Menu → System → New Login. (Beware: I take the risk of running the latest unstable versions of software on my system, so you might not have this option.) Again, this will work only if you logged in to KDE from the KDE graphical login screen, KDM. This launches a second KDM graphical login screen, from which a second user can log in to her own session.

Because your version of GNOME and/or KDE probably lacks these menu options, here are two additional, easy ways to get two or more graphical login screens running at once. The first way sets up multiple login screens for KDM. The second sets up multiple login screens for GDM.

 ## HACK Double Your KDM (KDE) Login Screens
#17   Set up the graphical login manager KDM to run on two different screens when you boot the computer.

If you run the KDE graphical login manager, KDM, you can set up KDM so that one user can log in from one login screen, and if another user wants to jump in and do some work, he can log in from the second login screen. You're not limited to two login screens, but it takes some good horsepower to run more than two sessions at once.

If your Linux distribution runs KDE by default rather than GNOME, it probably uses the KDM graphical login manager to log in. This likely is true even if you're not actually using KDE as your desktop, simply because distributions that favor KDE also favor KDM.

In this case you need to locate the configuration files for KDM to make the changes necessary to enable multiple simultaneous desktop users. The KDM configuration files are located in the same place as your *kdmrc* file. To locate this file, log in as root and type this command:

```
# locate kdmrc
/etc/kde3/kdm/kdmrc
```

In this case, the output tells you that *kdmrc*, and thus the KDM configuration files, are located in */etc/kde3/kdm*. Change to this directory (or whatever directory your Linux distribution uses) and edit the *Xservers* file.

 Your distribution might include support for more than one graphical login manager, in which case it might have more than one *Xservers* file; one for each alternative such as XDM or GDM. Make sure you are editing the *Xservers* file in the directory for the KDM graphical boot manager.

You should see something like the following in the *Xservers* file:

```
:0 local@tty1 /usr/X11R6/bin/X -nolisten tcp
#:1 local@tty2 reserve /usr/X11R6/bin/X -nolisten tcp :1
#:2 local@tty3 reserve /usr/X11R6/bin/X -nolisten tcp :2
#:3 local@tty4 reserve /usr/X11R6/bin/X -nolisten tcp :3
#:4 local@tty5 reserve /usr/X11R6/bin/X -nolisten tcp :4
```

Change the second line in the preceding output so that this section looks like the following:

```
:0 local@tty1 /usr/X11R6/bin/X -nolisten tcp
:1 local@tty2 /usr/X11R6/bin/X -nolisten tcp :1
#:2 local@tty3 reserve /usr/X11R6/bin/X -nolisten tcp :2
#:3 local@tty4 reserve /usr/X11R6/bin/X -nolisten tcp :3
#:4 local@tty5 reserve /usr/X11R6/bin/X -nolisten tcp :4
```

You should remove the # comment mark at the beginning of the second line, and remove the word reserve. Save your changes and exit the editor. That should be all you have to do.

You can make these changes take effect in several ways, but some Linux distributions are stubborn about restarting the login managers. So, the easiest way to enforce the changes is to simply reboot your computer.

Once your system is finished booting, press Ctrl-Alt-F8 to check whether you have two graphical login screens. If you see the same login screen, everything is working as planned. Press Ctrl-Alt-F7 to get back to the default login screen, and proceed to log in and have fun.

If you want to have three graphical login screens, simply edit the *Xservers* file again and change the third line the same way you changed the second. You can get to the third graphical login screen by pressing Ctrl-Alt-F9. Theoretically, you can have several more graphical login screens. The default keyboard settings provide key combinations that will work for up to 22 consoles, including both text and graphical logins, but Linux distributions rarely enable more than 11 virtual consoles, some as few as nine.

HACK #18 Double Your GDM (GNOME) Login Screens

Set up the graphical login manager GDM to run on two different screens when you boot the computer.

This hack will set up GDM to run on two different screens when you boot the computer. One user can log in from one login screen, and if another user wants to jump in and do some work, he can log in from the second login screen. You're not limited to two login screens, but the more sessions you run, the more processor power and memory are needed. Performance shouldn't be a problem on most modern systems, however.

If your Linux distribution runs GNOME by default rather than KDE, or if you're using Fedora, you're probably also using the GDM graphical login manager to log in. This might be true even if you don't use GNOME as your desktop, because distributions that favor GNOME tend to use GDM.

In this case, you need to locate the configuration file called *gdm.conf* to make the changes necessary to enable multiple simultaneous desktop users. Use the `locate` command to find out where *gdm.conf* is located. Type the following command as root:

```
# locate gdm.conf
/etc/X11/gdm/gdm.conf
```

Open the *gdm.conf* file for editing and locate the section that looks something like the following (you can jump right to this spot by searching for the text string [servers]):

```
[servers]
# These are the standard servers. You can add as many you want here
# and they will always be started. Each line must start with a unique
# number and that will be the display number of that server. Usually just
# the 0 server is used.
0=Standard
#1=Standard
```

All you have to do is remove the # comment mark before the line 1=Standard so that this section looks like the following:

```
[servers]
# These are the standard servers. You can add as many you want here
# and they will always be started. Each line must start with a unique
# number and that will be the display number of that server. Usually just
# the 0 server is used.
0=Standard
1=Standard
```

Save your changes and exit the editor. The easiest way to make sure the changes take effect is to reboot your computer. When your computer presents the graphical login screen, you can check to make sure there are two graphical logins by pressing Ctrl-Alt-F8. If you see the same login screen, everything is working. Press Ctrl-Alt-F7 to get back to the default login screen, log in, and have fun.

If you want to have three graphical login screens (and your version of Linux supports at least nine virtual consoles, which is quite likely), simply add another line so that the section looks like this:

```
[servers]
# These are the standard servers. You can add as many you want here
# and they will always be started. Each line must start with a unique
# number and that will be the display number of that server. Usually just
# the 0 server is used.
0=Standard
1=Standard
2=Standard
```

Reboot, and look for the new graphical login screen by pressing Ctrl-Alt-F9. Theoretically, you can have several more graphical login screens. The default keyboard settings provide key combinations that will work for up to 22 consoles, including both text and graphical logins, but Linux distributions rarely enable more than 11 virtual consoles, some as few as nine.

 ## Get Multiple Desktops the Macho Way

#19

Power users don't need no stinkin' graphical login managers, so here's the command-line way.

This hack assumes you're not the type who likes to have graphical login screens running all the time. You want your computer to boot to a text login prompt, after which you're perfectly capable of getting a graphical desktop running. You might still want the ability to have a second person log in and start another desktop. So, here's how.

I'll assume you're the power user who avoids GDM, KDM, and XDM. When your computer finishes booting, it leaves you in a virtual console (virtual terminal 1) with a text login prompt. You log in, and then you start your favorite window manager or desktop using whatever command is most familiar to you. Perhaps you type startkde to start the KDE environment. You could type xinit /usr/bin/wmaker to start WindowMaker. You could also type startx alone to start your default window manager. The default window manager could be defined in various ways, depending on the Linux distribution you're using. In most cases, power users configure the ~/.xinitrc file to define the default window manager, among other things (~/.xinitrc also lets you define other programs to start automatically, etc.).

If you want another user, such as your power-user daughter, to log in and start up a separate desktop, press Ctrl-Alt-F2 to get to the second text console with a login prompt. When she logs in, she can start a new Window-Maker desktop without disturbing your desktop by typing either of the following two commands:

```
$ xinit /usr/bin/wmaker -- :1
$ startx /usr/bin/wmaker -- :1
```

In this case, you add a space, a double-dash followed by a space, then a colon, and then a 1. This tells your system to run WindowMaker on the second virtual console allocated for graphical desktops (the default is 0, so the next available graphical console is 1).

This is a rather inconvenient way to do things because you must be sure display 1 is not in use, and you must know the exact path to the window manager or desktop environment you want to start. Neither of the following simpler commands works, because they do not include the full path to the executables:

```
$ xinit wmaker -- :1
$ startx wmaker -- :1
```

The following script makes this whole process much easier. All you need to know is the name of the executable file that starts your preferred window manager or desktop. Log in as root, or use *sudo* to fire up your favorite text editor, and type in the following script:

```
#!/bin/bash
```

```
screen=nothing
for screen in 0 1 2 3 4 5 nomore
  do
    if [ "$screen" = "nomore" ]
      then
        echo "No more available screens."
        exit 1
```

```
        fi
        [ ! -e /tmp/.X${screen}-lock ] && break
    done

if [ -x "`which ${1} 2>/dev/null`" ]
  then
    windowmanager="`which ${1} 2>/dev/null`"
    echo $windowmanager
    xinit $windowmanager -- -br :$screen
  else
    xinit -- -br :$screen
fi
```

Save it as */usr/local/bin/mstartx*. (I used the name *mstartx* because it is short for *multiple-startx*, but you can name your script anything you want.) Then change the script to be executable with this command:

```
# chmod +x /usr/local/bin/mstartx
```

Now all you have to type to start WindowMaker is this:

```
# mstartx wmaker
```

The script performs two important tasks. First, it finds the first available graphical console. If two people are already using graphical desktops, the script will detect this and automatically run the next session on the third graphical desktop. Second, it automatically locates the full path to the executable file for the window manager you want to start (*/usr/bin/wmaker* in this example). As an added bonus, this script changes the default startup background from a gray mesh to solid black. "Take Your Screens Black" [Hack #22] provides an alternate way to blacken your startup background.

Table 3-1 lists the executable filenames for the most popular window managers.

Table 3-1. Window manager executable filenames

Window manager or desktop environment	Executable filename
KDE	*Startkde*
GNOME	*gnome-session*
WindowMaker	*Wmaker*
AfterStep	*Afterstep*
XFce 4	*Startxfce4*
IceWM	*Icewm*
Enlightenment	*Enlightenment*
qvwm	*Qvwm*
Fluxbox	*fluxbox or startfluxbox*
Blackbox	*Blackbox*

Table 3-1. Window manager executable filenames (continued)

Window manager or desktop environment	Executable filename
Openbox	*Openbox*
Fvwm	*fvwm* or *fvwm2*
XFce 3	*Xfce*
Motif	*Mwm*

No matter which method you choose for launching a second or third user desktop session, you probably want to keep your current session protected. Configure the screensaver for your favorite desktop environment or window manager to lock the screen and require a password to get back to work. When someone else wants to log in with a separate desktop session, start the screensaver (thus locking out anyone without your password) before you allow her to log in on the next virtual terminal.

HACK #20 Scrap X11 for Fancy Login Consoles

Qingy is an attractive replacement for X Windows-based graphical login managers such as XDM, GDM, and KDM.

Qingy is an alternative login screen developed by Michele Noberasco (*http://qingy.sourceforge.net/news.php*). Qingy uses the graphical frame-buffer console capability in Linux to paint an attractive and powerful session login screen on one or more virtual terminals. Unlike XDM, GDM, and KDM, Qingy does not use X11. Despite this, Qingy has as many features as these traditional graphical login screens, if not more (see the sidebar, "Frame-Buffer Versus X11 Graphics"). You can choose your preferred session type, such as KDE, GNOME, WindowMaker, Fluxbox, or just a text console. You can include buttons on the Qingy login screen that will start the screensaver, put your computer in sleep mode, reboot, shut down, and many other options. And of course, you can change the Qingy graphical theme.

Qingy stands for "Qingy Is Not GettY." *getty* is the text-based terminal program that greets you with a login prompt. You have several of these text-based virtual consoles (terminals) on your machine, and you can switch between them by pressing Ctrl-Alt-F1, Ctrl-Alt-F2, Ctrl-Alt-F3, and so on. (You can omit the Ctrl key if you're not switching to a text console from a graphical desktop.) Each desktop is a virtual terminal that uses a version of *getty* as a terminal emulator. Various Linux distributions use alternatives, such as *agetty*, *mingetty*, and others; despite a few feature differences, they all amount to the same thing—a text-based terminal console.

Frame-Buffer Versus X11 Graphics

Put in the simplest terms a *frame buffer* is a block of memory storage that your graphics display card represents on your monitor as pixels (the red, green, and blue dots which combine to make colors from white to black). There are different frame-buffer modes. The higher modes, such as 1280x1024 pixels with up to 64,000 colors, allocate a bigger block of memory for the frame buffer than the lower 800x600-pixel modes with 64,000 colors.

The most common use of frame buffers in Linux is to solve a problem that occurs when you try to use smaller text fonts to cram more text on the screen while keeping your video card in text mode. As you try to put more text on the screen at once, the text starts to get really ugly and hard to read. If you switch the display card into frame-buffer graphics mode, however, higher resolutions automatically present smaller fonts that are rendered dot-by-dot, so even at high resolutions text appears sharper and much more legible.

Frame buffers are ideal for use at boot time, before the Linux kernel loads, because you don't need to know what kind of video card is installed. Frame-buffer usage follows a standard maintained by the Video Electronics Standards Association (VESA). Almost all display cards support one or more VESA frame-buffer modes.

Although you can use frame buffer-based programs such as Qingy to replace the function of an X11-based login screen, comparing frame buffers directly to X11 is an apples-to-oranges comparison. X11 is a much higher-level piece of software. It uses graphics as part of a client/server scheme to provide a rich set of application capabilities.

Admittedly, frame buffer-based X11 drivers do exist that make it possible to use frame buffers as the basis for an X11-based (XFree86 or Xorg) window manager or desktop environment. But frame buffers generally do not take advantage of the special features of your display card, so they are not ideally suited for this use. This is why you generally pick a specific X11 display driver that matches the display card you're using.

For more information on how frame buffers are being used for projects other than boot splash screens and Qingy, see *http://www.directfb.org*. (This web site is also where you'll find more information about the frame-buffer project to run X11 applications.)

Qingy replaces *getty* with an attractive graphical login screen that can automatically launch any one of your favorite graphical desktops or a text console. You can start Qingy on more than one virtual console, which means two or more people can use Qingy to log in and start their own desktops. Qingy also has some built-in security. You can configure Qingy to make it impossible for another user to get to your desktop without knowing your password.

A number of themes are available for Qingy. Figure 3-1 is based on the theme called "biohazard."

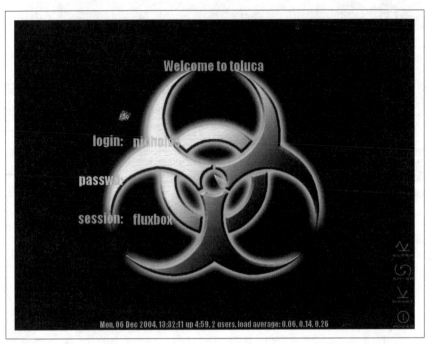

Figure 3-1. Qingy login screen

Prepare to Install Qingy

It is not difficult to install Qingy. First, you must have frame-buffer support and frame-buffer console support compiled into your Linux kernel (you do not need boot splash support compiled into the kernel, however). "Jazz Up Your Debian System Boot" **[Hack #8]** and "Graphics on the Console" **[Hack #9]** include instructions for compiling frame-buffer support and frame-buffer console support into the kernel. Once you have modified your kernel, reboot so that these changes will take effect.

If your system automatically launches a graphical login manager, such as GDM, KDM, or XDM, the first thing you want to do is disable it. You won't need to use it anymore after you have Qingy working.

You can turn off these login managers in several ways. This command is one way you can do it on a Debian system:

```
# update-rc.d -f kdm remove
Removing any system startup links for /etc/init.d/kdm ...
   /etc/rc0.d/K01kdm
   /etc/rc3.d/S99kdm
```

```
/etc/rc4.d/S99kdm
/etc/rc6.d/K01kdm
```

On Gentoo, the command should be as follows:

```
# rc-update del xdm default
```

A generic approach also exists that should work with almost every Linux distribution (it doesn't work for Fedora).

First, check to see what the default run level is for your system. You can do this by examining the file */etc/inittab*. Look for a line that reads like this:

```
id:3:initdefault:
```

This tells you the default run level is 3. For most Linux systems, this means you want to log in as root and change to the directory */etc/rc3.d*. If the default run level turned out to be 5, you would change to the directory */etc/rc5.d*. Then look for any symbolic links to kdm, gdm, or xdm and delete them. For example:

```
# cd /etc/rc3.d
# ls -l *dm
lrwxrwxrwx  1 root root 17 Nov 17  2003 S99xdm -> ../init.d/xdm
# rm S99xdm
```

Install Qingy

If your Linux distribution has a Qingy package, install it via your package manager. If you can install Qingy from a package manager, it will likely place configuration files in the */etc/qingy* directory, place theme files in */usr/share/qingy/themes*, and install the *qingy* program in */sbin*.

> If you download the source code and compile it yourself, it will store configuration files (by default) in */usr/local/etc/qingy*, store theme files in */usr/local/share/qingy/themes*, and place the executable *qingy* in */usr/local/sbin*. Consider these differences when viewing the following examples, which assume that you compiled Qingy for yourself.

If you do not have a Qingy package for your Linux distribution, you have to download and compile the code yourself. Download the latest version of Qingy from *http://qingy.sourceforge.net/news.php*. Log in as root, and change to an appropriate directory (such as */usr/local/src*). Extract the code, change to the source directory, configure, compile, and install the program. (Consider that by the time you read this, a more recent version of Qingy might be available—use that version instead of 0.5.2.) Here is an example of how to perform the preceding steps:

```
$ su -
# cp qingy-0.5.2.tar.bz2 /usr/local/src
```

```
# cd /usr/local/src
# tar jxvf qingy-0.5.2.tar.bz2
# cd qingy-0.5.2
# ./configure
# make
# make install
```

You can specify an alternate prefix when you run **./configure**. The prefix tells the build session where to install the files. For example, if you want Qingy to install in */usr/sbin*, you would type:

```
# ./configure --prefix=/usr
```

The default setting will install the *qingy* program in */usr/local/sbin*, and store the *settings* file in */usr/local/etc/*. This installs the default theme to */usr/local/share/qingy/themes*.

Configure Linux to Use Qingy

If you took the preceding advice, you have already compiled and are running a Linux kernel that supports frame-buffer consoles. This means you can see the immediate results of any changes to your console settings.

To avoid any potential complications, make all of these changes from a virtual console that is not going to be configured for Qingy. For this example, only the first two virtual consoles will be configured as Qingy login screens. If you are logged in to virtual console 1 or 2, press Ctrl-Alt-F1 and log out of the first console, then press Ctrl-Alt-F2 and log out of the second virtual console. If you don't log out of these consoles, the changes you make will not take effect immediately. Then press Ctrl-Alt-F3 to go to the third virtual terminal (which will not run Qingy), and log in as root there.

Now use your favorite editor to edit your */etc/inittab* file. Find the section that looks something like this:

```
# TERMINALS
c1:12345:respawn:/sbin/agetty 38400 tty1 linux
c2:12345:respawn:/sbin/agetty 38400 tty2 linux
c3:12345:respawn:/sbin/agetty 38400 tty3 linux
c4:12345:respawn:/sbin/agetty 38400 tty4 linux
c5:12345:respawn:/sbin/agetty 38400 tty5 linux
c6:12345:respawn:/sbin/agetty 38400 tty6 linux
```

You need to change one or more lines to spawn *qingy* instead of the *agetty* terminal program. (Your Linux distribution might use something other than *agetty*, such as *getty* or *mingetty*. This doesn't matter.) It isn't necessary or even desirable to change every virtual terminal to use Qingy. If something goes wrong, you want at least one terminal to behave normally so that you can log in and diagnose the problem. In this example, change just the first two virtual terminals to use Qingy. Edit the */etc/inittab* file to look more like this:

```
# TERMINALS
c1:12345:respawn:/usr/local/sbin/qingy tty1 --screensaver 0
c2:12345:respawn:/usr/local/sbin/qingy tty2 --screensaver 0
c3:12345:respawn:/sbin/agetty 38400 tty3 linux
c4:12345:respawn:/sbin/agetty 38400 tty4 linux
c5:12345:respawn:/sbin/agetty 38400 tty5 linux
c6:12345:respawn:/sbin/agetty 38400 tty6 linux
```

Obviously, if you installed Qingy from a package that placed the *qingy* executable in the */sbin* directory modify the absolute path to Qingy appropriately. The --screensaver 0 switch at the end of the line turns off the Qingy screensaver. The screensaver is sometimes triggered after a few minutes even if you're actively typing on a non-Qingy console, which can be annoying. Qingy is young yet. Perhaps this quirk will be fixed in a future version.

Save the */etc/inittab* file. Now execute the following commands:

```
# init Q
# killall agetty
```

The first command tells Linux to reexamine the */etc/inittab* file. It does not automatically turn off the *agetty* sessions for any of the virtual consoles, though. That is why you need the second command. This kills every version of *agetty* that might be running except the one you are currently using. Instead of respawning (restarting) *agetty* in virtual consoles 1 and 2, Linux will respawn *qingy*.

If your version of Linux uses something other than */sbin/agetty* for normal terminal sessions, substitute the name of your version of *agetty* in the **killall** command. For example, if your Linux distribution uses *getty*, issue these commands instead:

```
# init Q
# killall getty
```

Press Ctrl-Alt-F1 and now you should see the Qingy login screen. Use the Tab key or your mouse to move from one input field to another. When you select the session field, you can change the session setting by pressing the up and down arrows. Select whichever window manager you prefer or the text console. Once you have typed in your username and password and you've selected your desired session, press Enter. You should see your selected session start up. If you start up a window manager or desktop environment, such as KDE or GNOME, Qingy has to start X11 from scratch. Therefore, you might notice it takes a bit longer to start up than if you were running the KDE or GNOME login manager, which load faster because X11 was already running.

If someone else wants to use the computer and you don't want to close your session, press Ctrl-Alt-F2 to get to the second Qingy login screen. Allow the other user to log in and start her separate session.

You can switch between sessions by pressing Ctrl-Alt-F1 and Ctrl-Alt-F2. Virtual consoles are still available on Ctrl-Alt-F3 through F6.

When Qingy Doesn't Offer Session Choices

One common occurrence is that Qingy doesn't display any window managers or desktop environments in its session field. By default, Qingy looks in the */etc/X11/Sessions* directory for a list of files, each representing a window manager or desktop available on your system. The name of the file appears in the Qingy sessions list. These session files contain a single line, a full path to the executable to the window manager or desktop. For example, the file named */etc/X11/Sessions/KDE* might contain the line */usr/bin/startkde*, and the file */etc/X11/Sessions/WindowMaker* should contain a single line such as */usr/bin/wmaker*.

If you don't see any window managers available from the Qingy login screen, you have one of two problems. Your session files are stored somewhere other than */etc/X11/Sessions* or your system simply doesn't work that way—there is no single directory of session files.

If your system stores the session files somewhere other than */etc/X11/Sessions*, edit the Qingy configuration file */usr/local/etc/qingy/settings* so that it points to the directory where your system keeps its session files. Locate the following line:

```
x_sessions = "/etc/X11/Sessions/"
```

and change it to the absolute path to your *Sessions* directory.

If your system doesn't have a *Sessions* directory, here's an easy way to create one and fill it with session files for each window manager and desktop you have installed. Before you create each session file, check to see if the window manager executable (the file that actually starts up the window manager) exists. If the which command reports back a path to the file you're looking for, create the session file by redirecting the output of the which command to a session file. If the output can't find the executable for a window manager (the following example shows that *blackbox* is not available), don't create a session file for it. Table 3-1, earlier in this chapter, lists the common window manager executable filenames.

You can name the session file anything, so pick a name that is meaningful to you. For example, the WindowMaker executable is */usr/bin/wmaker*, but you can use "wmaker" or "WindowMaker" if you like. The following example shows how to use the which command and command redirection to create your session files:

```
# mkdir /etc/X11/Sessions
# which wmaker
```

```
/usr/bin/wmaker
# which wmaker > /etc/X11/Sessions/WindowMaker
# which twm
/usr/X11R6/bin/twm
# which twm > /etc/X11/Sessions/TabWM
# which blackbox
which: no blackbox in (/usr/bin:/usr/local/bin:/etc...)
# which fluxbox
/usr/bin/fluxbox
# which fluxbox > /etc/X11/Sessions/Fluxbox
# which startkde
/usr/bin/startkde
# which startkde > /etc/X11/Sessions/KDE
# which gnome-session
/usr/bin/gnome-session
# which gnome-session > /etc/X11/Sessions/GNOME
```

These sessions should appear automatically on your Qingy login screen as
you create each session file. There is no need to restart anything.

HACK #21 Personalize Your Qingy Theme

Personalize your Qingy frame-buffer login screens by choosing the theme
that suits you best. In fact, if you run Qingy on more than one terminal, you
can have a different theme for each terminal.

Many themes are available for Qingy. See Figure 3-2 for a look at the default
Qingy login screen.

At the risk of sounding superstitious, some of us are not comfortable with a
start screen featuring a bug. Fortunately, you can download a pack of alternate themes from *http://umn.dl.sourceforge.net/sourceforge/qingy/qingy_0.3_
themepack_1.0.tar.bz2*, and extract it with the following commands:

```
# cp qingy_0.3_themepack_1.0.tar.bz2 /usr/local/share/qingy/themes
# tar jxvf qingy_0.3_themepack_1.0.tar.bz2
```

The j in the tar argument jxvf tells tar to unpack a *bzip2* file (you can tell
this has been packed using *bzip2* because the suffix is *bz2*.) If you find a
theme with a suffix of *tar.gz* or *tgz*, use the command tar zxvf to unpack
the file (z replaces j).

Almost all (if not all) of the themes are optimized for a screen resolution of
1024x768. Keep that in mind when you configure your copy of Linux to use
frame-buffer consoles. If you choose a resolution other than 1024x768, you
might find you have to modify the theme configuration file to get the login
and other prompts to appear in their proper locations. It's not hard to modify Qingy themes for different resolutions, but if you can save yourself the
trouble by sticking to a resolution of 1024x768, why not?

Figure 3-2. Default Qingy login screen

If you prefer a theme other than the default theme, you change the setting in the */usr/local/etc/qingy/settings* file. This line in the settings file controls which theme is used:

```
theme = "default"
```

To use a different theme—the vendetta3 theme, for example—modify the theme value like this:

```
theme = "vendetta3"
```

Save your changes. Then (as root) type the following command:

```
# killall qingy
```

Don't worry; Qingy will restart by itself. That's the purpose of the respawn command in your */etc/inittab* file. Now when your Qingy login screens reappear, they should look something like Figure 3-3.

Personalize Every Terminal

You can assign themes or even screensavers (or not—the screensavers can be quirky) to individual terminals by editing the */usr/local/etc/qingy/settings* file once again. This time add a definition for specific terminals (ttys), like this:

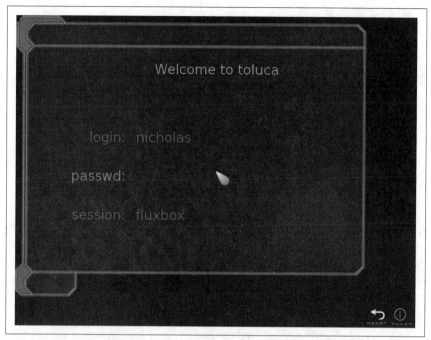

Figure 3-3. The Vendetta3 Qingy login screen

```
tty=2
{
    theme = "fireplace"
    screensaver "pixel"
}
tty=3
{
    theme = "vendetta2"
}
```

Save your changes. Then (as root) type the following command:

```
# killall qingy
```

Don't forget that you have to edit the */etc/inittab* file and make Qingy the default for every terminal for which you assign a theme. If you assign a theme to tty3, but tty3 is still using something such as *agetty* instead of Qingy, your theme assignment won't have any effect.

Once again, Qingy will restart on its own with the appropriate themes for each terminal.

Related to X
Hacks #22–34

The hacks in this chapter are designed to be window manager- and desktop environment-agnostic (that is, they don't depend on any given window manager or desktop environment, such as Fluxbox, WindowMaker, KDE, GNOME, or XFce). For the most part, the hacks simply assume you are running a version of X11.

These hacks range from the relatively mundane (replacing the ugly gray startup background with a black background) to frivolous but exciting changes (customizing your mouse pointer to show animated graphics). You'll also learn two different ways to make your fancy Internet and/or multimedia keyboard work with X11, how to access programs remotely (even if they are running on different platforms), and how to add 3D effects and transparency to your windows.

X11, which also goes by the names X and X Windows, is the client/server graphics engine that runs almost all the desktop environments and window managers on Linux. Almost all Linux distributions used to include XFree86, a free software implementation of X11. However, the folks in charge of XFree86 changed their software license, which led to a political uproar, the magnitude of which led eventually to a fork of the XFree86 code, and a new version of X11 called Xorg or X.org. Xorg has many benefits besides the preferred license. It has built-in support for transparency and drop shadows, and it often takes a better approach to solving problems than XFree86. Virtually all Linux distributions have switched from XFree86 to Xorg, or are in the process of doing so, with the notable exception of Debian.

Most of the hacks in this chapter do not require that you have Xorg installed instead of XFree86, but some of the most visually impressive hacks (transparency, drop shadows, etc.) do require this. The custom-cursor hacks don't require Xorg, but they do require that you have at least version 4.3.0 or better installed if you are running XFree86.

If you are running Xorg, note that a few of these hacks are likely to be more stable on some environments. This is especially true of the hacks that add drop shadows and transparency. This is the first attempt at adding these features to the X Window System, and not all the quirks have been worked out. The Xorg programmers are improving these features very quickly. But don't be surprised if these two hacks crash one window manager and work almost perfectly on another.

Take Your Screens Black

#22 Get rid of the ugly gray mesh that greets you every time you start up an X11 session.

Every time you start up an X11 session, the default background is an ugly gray mesh. Some window managers and desktop environments change this almost immediately, but others leave the background a putrid gray. Here's a tip on how you can make sure the default background is solid black. (In case you're wondering, the choice of colors for the background is like the choice for the Model T Ford—you can make it any color you want as long as it's black.)

The trick behind making the default background black is to add the -br switch to the right configuration file. Which configuration file needs to be modified depends on how you start your window manager or desktop.

startx

If you start your window manager with the startx command, edit the */usr/X11R6/bin/startx* file. Make sure the default server arguments include the –br switch. For example, if the beginning of your *startx* file looks like this:

```
userclientrc=$HOME/.xinitrc
userserverrc=$HOME/.xserverrc
sysclientrc=/etc/X11/xinit/xinitrc
sysserverrc=/etc/X11/xinit/xserverrc
defaultclientargs=""
defaultserverargs="-nolisten tcp"
clientargs=""
serverargs=""
```

Add the -br switch to the definition for either defaultserverargs or serverargs. Just place the switch between the quotes. For example:

```
defaultserverargs="-nolisten tcp -br"
```

Now, when you run *startx* to start a window manager, the default background will be black instead of the gray mesh.

xinit

If you use the xinit command to start a window manager or desktop, add
-- -br to the tail end of the command. For example, if you want to start
the *blackbox* window manager with the xinit command, do it this way:

```
$ xinit /usr/bin/blackbox -- -br
```

If you use the xinit command to start a new window manager or desktop
for a second user [Hack #19], add -- -br after the command and before you
specify the next available virtual terminal. For example:

```
$ xinit /usr/bin/blackbox -- -br :1
```

The Xservers File

One or more of your desktop environments or window managers might use
a file called *Xservers* to determine how to start the X11 engine that drives all
window managers and desktops. In this case, log in as root and locate your
Xservers file with this command:

```
# locate Xservers
/etc/X11/xdm/Xservers
```

If you are using the XDM graphical login manager, this is the file you want
to modify. You can find the *Xservers* file in the directory for the KDE graphical login manager, KDM, or in the directory for the GNOME graphical login
manager, GDM. You might even find *Xservers* files in all three places. You
only need to modify the *Xservers* that is connected to your login manager.
Once you've found it, open the file with a text editor, and you should see a
line that looks something like this:

```
:0 local@tty1 /usr/X11R6/bin/X -nolisten tcp
```

Simply add the -br switch to this line so that it looks more like this:

```
:0 local@tty1 /usr/X11R6/bin/X -br -nolisten tcp
```

Save your work, and that should transform the ugly gray pattern into solid
black.

Spice Up Your Desktop
with Creative Mouse Cursors

**Replace the boring default mouse pointer, resize cursor, wait cursor, and the
rest with colorful custom animated cursors.**

Microsoft Windows lets you change cursor themes easily. Linux doesn't
make it quite as easy (although the KDE desktop environment comes close).
This hack explores how to check if your distribution of Linux supports cursor themes, how to find, download, and install new cursor themes, and how

to set up your desktop to use them. A wide variety of custom cursor themes are available, ranging from the subtle (cursors decorated with a red dot) to the outrageous (a Tux penguin grabbing windows to resize them!).

Does Your Desktop Support Cursor Themes?

You need XFree86 4.3 or later or Xorg (a fork of the XFree86 project) for custom cursors to work. All recently released Linux distributions include one or the other, so it is unlikely that your Linux desktop cannot support custom cursors, but you need to be sure. Type this command to see which version of X you have installed:

```
# X -version
```

If your Linux distribution installed XFree86, all you have to do is make sure the version is 4.3 or higher. For example, look for a string something like the following in the output of the X -version command:

```
XFree86 Version 4.3.0 (or higher)
```

If your Linux distribution is using the Xorg branch of X11, you should see something like this in the output:

```
X Protocol Version 11, Revision 0, Release 6.7 (or higher)
```

If you see anything like either of these strings, it means your version of X supports custom cursor themes.

What Themes Are Available by Default?

Unfortunately, Linux distributions vary considerably as to where they store the default cursor themes. If the documentation for your Linux distribution doesn't tell you where to find these themes, you can use a trick to find out where your particular distribution looks for cursor themes. Generally, the file you want to examine is */usr/X11R6/lib/X11/config/Imake.tmpl*. Check to see if the file exists with the ls command:

```
# ls /usr/X11R6/lib/X11/config/Imake.tmpl
```

If the response is "No such file or directory," you might be able to find the file with the following command:

```
# locate Imake.tmpl
```

If this file does not exist on your system, you're going to have to find another way to locate where your distribution stores globally available cursor themes. A Google search or browsing online forums specific to your distribution are good places to start.

If this file does exist on your system, this command should help you determine the default locations where your distribution stores cursor themes:

```
$ grep XcursorPath /usr/X11R6/lib/X11/config/Imake.tmpl
#  ifndef XcursorPath
#   define XcursorPath "~/.cursors:~/.icons:/usr/local/share/cursors/xorg-
x11:/usr/share/cursors/xorg-x11:/usr/share/pixmaps/xorg-x11"
#ifndef XcursorPath
# define XcursorPath Concat(~/.cursors:~/.icons:/usr/local/share/cursors/
xorg-x11:/usr/share/cursors/xorg-x11:/usr/share/pixmaps/xorg-x11:,IconDir)
        XCURSORPATH = XcursorPath          /* Xcursor cursors path */
```

The useful information is the first line that includes define XcursorPath.
Notice that this particular distribution (Gentoo) defines the XcursorPath to
search the following directories:

```
~/.cursors
~/.icons
/usr/local/share/cursors/xorg-x11
/usr/share/cursors/xorg-x11
/usr/share/pixmaps/xorg-x11
```

 Take note of the order in which your system searches for
cursor themes. It looks first in your home directory, then it
searches directories available to everyone. To install a new
theme for your personal use only (see later for instructions),
you install it in your home directory (under ~/.cursors or ~/.
icons). To install a new theme everyone can use, install it in
one of the remaining directories in the list.

Check all these directories to see if any theme files exist. The first two directories are below your home directory, and few, if any, distributions install
alternate cursor themes there by default. So, you're more likely to find alternate themes in one of the last three directories in the list. Because I'm "in the
know" about Gentoo and therefore have an unfair advantage, I would check
the */usr/share/cursors/xorg-x11* path first:

```
# ls /usr/share/cursors/xorg-x11
Blue  Silver    default  gentoo-blue    handhelds  whiteglass
Gold  blueglass  gentoo   gentoo-silver  redglass
```

There they are. I can choose between any of these cursor themes by referenc-
ing the name of the directory that holds the theme.

Some distributions have the inconsiderate habit of placing the cursor themes in the same directory as icon themes (different types of KDE or GNOME icons for your desktop). If your Linux distribution does this, not all of the theme names you find in the directory will be cursor themes. You'll know you've picked an icon theme by mistake if your desktop starts up with the default mouse cursors rather than a new cursor theme.

Set a Personal Default Theme

Each user can set his own default cursor theme by creating or modifying a file called *~/.icons/default/index.theme* (recall that the ~ represents your home directory). This *index.theme* file is the one that tells your system which cursor theme to use. Create the directories you need with the following command:

```
$ mkdir ~/.icons ~/.icons/default
```

Now use your favorite editor to create the *index.theme* file in the *~/.icons/ default* directory. Place the following two lines in the file:

```
[Icon Theme]
Inherits=whiteglass
```

This example assumes you have a cursor theme called Whiteglass installed on your system (the earlier example showed that it exists on my system, because the directory name *whiteglass* appears in the */usr/share/cursors/xorg-x11* directory that contains all the globally available cursor themes). Obviously, if you don't have the Whiteglass theme on your system, this setting won't do you any good. The next time you start your desktop, you'll see only the default cursor theme, because Whiteglass doesn't exist. If you don't have Whiteglass, substitute a theme name that you do have installed.

Start up your favorite desktop window manager, and *voilà*, you should see a new set of mouse pointers.

If you want to change cursor themes, the best way to do it is to change the setting in the *index.theme* file, and then restart your window manager or desktop. If you don't restart the desktop, you could get unexpected results or no change in cursor theme at all.

Tips for Users of NVIDIA Display Cards

It is not uncommon for people with NVIDIA display cards (such as the GeForce series) to use the accelerated NVIDIA driver available from the NVIDIA web site. If you're using the accelerated driver, not the default driver that comes with X11, your mouse cursors can tend to flicker.

Here's how to fix that problem. Find the Device section for your NVIDIA card in your X11 configuration file. This file is called *XF86Config*, *XF86Config-4*, or *xorg.conf*, depending on the X server you are using, and it is usually found in the */etc/X11* directory. Look for the Device section where you define the video card driver. It should contain these lines, although not necessarily exactly as they appear here:

```
Section "Device"
    Driver    "NVIDIA"
    Option    "HWCursor"    "On"
```

Turn off the HWCursor option so that it looks like the following:

```
    Option    "HWCursor"    "off"
```

The next time you start up your desktop, the flicker problem should be gone.

Get Custom Cursor Themes, Example 1

One popular source of custom cursor themes and other eye candy is a site called KDE-Look (*http://www.kde-look.org*). The URL for cursor themes is *http://www.kde-look.org/index.php?xcontentmode=36*. Find a cursor theme you like and download it. Though this web site is KDE-focused, the cursor themes work on any X server that meets the earlier criteria.

Unfortunately, there's no standard way to package a cursor theme. Different people package their cursor themes in different ways, and not everyone includes a *README* file to tell you how to unpack and install their cursor themes. This makes it impossible to provide you with one set of instructions on how to unpack and install a cursor theme, and to expect those instructions to work for every theme you download.

But there are some simple patterns to look for that make it easy to adapt how you unpack and install cursor themes. For this example, download the Red Dot cursor theme from the KDE-Look site. The URL for this cursor theme is *http://www.kde-look.org/content/show.php?content=4805* and the file (at the time of this printing) is called *4805-RedDot.tar.gz*. Find or create a work directory where you can unpack the file and change to that directory. For example:

```
$ mkdir ~/temp
$ cd ~/temp
```

After you install the cursor theme, you can delete the contents of this work directory. Decompress the file with the following command:

```
$ tar zxvf 4805-RedDot.tar.gz
```

This creates two directories, *RedDot* and *RedDotSource*. For those not familiar with it, the –z option passed to GNU tar will uncompress gzipped files.

In general, once you unpack a cursor theme, the directories that matter are the ones that contain a single subdirectory below them called *cursors*. In this case, the *RedDot* directory has a subdirectory called *cursors*. That tells you which directory you want to install. (For the curious, the *RedDotSource* directory contains all the files the author of the theme used to create the Red Dot theme.)

You can install the Red Dot cursor theme simply by copying the *RedDot* directory and its contents to *~/.icons* (the *.icons* directory in your home directory):

```
$ cp -a RedDot ~/.icons
```

If you want the Red Dot cursor theme to be available to all users, copy *RedDot* to one of the shared directories instead. (Given the previous example of how this Linux distribution is configured, the shared directories are */usr/local/share/cursors/xorg-x11*, */usr/share/cursors/xorg-x11*, and */usr/share/pixmaps/xorg-x11*. They might be different for your system.) You need to log in as root to do this; otherwise, you won't have the privileges necessary to write to these directories.

Now edit the *~/.icons/default/index.theme* file to contain the following two lines:

```
[Icon Theme]
Inherits=RedDot
```

Start up your favorite window manager or desktop environment (or restart the one you're using), and you should see the Red Dot mouse cursors.

Get Custom Cursor Themes, Example 2

As I mentioned before, there's no standard way to package a cursor theme. So, here's another example of how to install a cursor theme that should illustrate that the principles are the same, even if the package is different.

In this case, download the Golden XCursors 3D theme, which (at the time of this writing) is at *http://www.kde-look.org/content/show.php?content=5507* and is located in a file called *5507-Golden-XCursors-3D-0.8.tar.bz2*. Unpack the file with the following command:

```
$ cd ~/temp
$ tar jxvf 5507-Golden-XCursors-3D-0.8.tar.bz2
```

This creates a subdirectory called *Golden-XCursors-3D-0.8*. (If the version of Golden Cursors has changed since the publishing of this book, the filename will be different. Follow these instructions using the new filename.) Change to this subdirectory with the following command, and list that directory's contents:

```
$ cd Golden-XCursors-3D-0.8
$ ls
COPYING  Gold  README  default
```

In this case, the author created a *README* file, but let's ignore it for a moment and use the same reasoning used earlier to identify the relevant directory. Look in the directory called *Gold* by issuing the following command:

```
$ ls Gold
cursors
```

There's the *cursors* subdirectory that we're looking for. So, *Gold* is the directory we want. Copy the *Gold* directory to the *~/.icons* directory:

```
$ cp -a Gold ~/.icons
```

Again, if you want the Gold cursor theme to be available to all users, copy *Gold* to one of the shared directories instead. (Given the previous example of how this Linux distribution is configured, the shared directories are */usr/local/share/cursors/xorg-x11*, */usr/share/cursors/xorg-x11*, and */usr/share/pixmaps/xorg-x11*. They might be different for your system.) You need to log in as root to do this; otherwise, you won't have the privileges necessary to write to these directories.

Edit the *~/.icons/default/index.theme* file to contain these two lines:

```
[Icon Theme]
Inherits=Gold
```

Start up your favorite window manager or desktop environment (or restart the one you're using), and you should see the Gold mouse cursors.

HACK #24 Convert CursorXP Themes for Use with Linux

Convert custom cursor themes meant for Windows for use with Linux.

Want even fancier cursor themes than those currently available for Linux? A company called Stardock has created a product called CursorXP for Windows XP. It allows Windows users to choose from hundreds of fancy animated cursor themes. This hack is a script that will convert these cursor themes for use with X11 under Linux.

A huge repository of publicly available cursor themes are designed for use with CursorXP. You can find these themes at *http://www.wincustomize.com*. The specific URL for the cursor themes is *http://www2.wincustomize.com/skins.asp?library=25*.

You can download one or more of these themes and then use a Perl script to convert them for use with X11, the engine that powers your desktop. Eric Windisch created the original Perl script, which Nicholas Petreley and James Barron have since modified. This hack uses the version of the script called *np-sd2xc.pl*, which you can download from the O'Reilly catalog page for this book: *http://www.oreilly.com/catalog/linuxdeskhks*.

You need to have version 6 or better of ImageMagick installed for the script to work properly. You also need these Perl modules installed:

- `Image::Magick`
- `Getopt::Long`
- `Config::IniFiles`

Once you are sure you have all the prerequisite packages installed, download a cursor theme to convert. For example, download the file *Gear.zip*. Unzip this file to a work directory so that you can perform the conversion. These commands (substitute the name of the zip file you're using for *Gear.zip* if you are using a different theme) use the newly created directory *geartemp* as a work directory:

```
$ mkdir ~/geartemp
$ cd ~/geartemp
$ unzip Gear.zip
```

This expands your zip file into another file, which in this case is called *Gear. CurXPTheme*. Even though this file has the extension *.CurXPTheme*, it's really just another zip file that you can expand with the following command:

```
$ unzip Gear.CurXPTheme
```

Now you're almost ready to run *np-sd2xc.pl*. The `-name` command switch defines the name of the cursor theme when you install it. This theme was originally called *Gear*, but you can use another name if you want. For the sake of frivolity, give this theme a new name, CoolGear, by using this command:

```
$ np-sd2xc.pl -name CoolGear
```

The conversion program can add drop shadows to all the cursors when it converts the CursorXP cursor themes. It's a matter of taste, but I think drop shadows give the cursor a very nice 3D appearance. If you want the cursors to have drop shadows, add the `-shadow` command switch and use this command instead:

```
$ np-sd2xc.pl –shadow -name CoolGear
```

Now you can install the theme (this example installs it in your home directory). The following commands both install the theme and set it as the default theme (the `-R` switch tells the `cp` copy command to recurse through directories so that you'll copy everything below the *CoolGear* and default directories to the destination ~/.icons):

```
$ cp -R CoolGear ~/.icons
$ cp -R default ~/.icons
```

The second command overwrites whatever *index.theme* file you have in your ~/.icons/default directory.

Start up your favorite desktop or window manager (or exit and restart the desktop or window manager you're using), and you should see the cursor theme, formerly designed for Windows, running on your Linux X server-based desktop!

> Not every CursorXP theme converts well. It's possible for a misbehaving cursor theme to prevent you from starting up your window manager or desktop. If you have this problem, switch to a virtual console by pressing Ctrl-Alt-F1. Log in with your normal username. Edit your ~/.icons/default/index.theme file, and change the Inherits parameter to a theme that works.

Use Windows and Mac Fonts

HACK #25

Spruce up your desktop with your favorite fonts from other operating systems.

A major problem that has been leveled at the Linux desktop is a lack of good-quality fonts. This is because font creation is a time-consuming and expensive process that requires a lot of skill. Those who know how to do it are generally not inclined to give their work away for free (a nice contrast to the thousands of open source programmers who do give their code away). You can purchase fonts to use with your Linux system, but it is cheaper to use fonts you already have on another OS.

> When copying fonts from one operating system to another, bear in mind the legal implications of what you are doing. Fonts that are included with proprietary operating systems are sometimes under specific licensing terms that can restrict their use. Before you copy anything, be sure to read the licensing terms for the fonts.

Use Windows Fonts

Linux has full support for the TrueType fonts used by Windows. One method of using the fonts is to simply copy them from Windows and install them either in the X font directories or in *.fonts* in your home directory.

Although this method works, if you have Windows installed on the same computer that runs Linux, it's unnecessary to copy all those fonts when you can use a more elegant solution and access them from one place.

First, you need to ensure that you can mount your Windows partition. To do this you need to have support for the VFAT (or NTFS if you use Windows 2000/XP) filesystem in your kernel. My distribution kernels include this support, but if you compile your own kernels, you need to add support yourself. In your kernel configuration tool, enable support by selecting File systems → DOS/FAT/NT, File systems → VFAT Support or, if you have an NTFS filesystem, File systems → NTFS file system support (read only).

Before you can access the Windows disk, mount the partition. You can do this manually with the following:

```
foo@bar:~$ mkdir /mnt/windows
foo@bar:~$ mount -t vfat /dev/hda1 /mnt/windows
```

Your Windows partition might be located someplace other than /dev/hda1 and you can use a different mount point than /mnt/windows. If you are unsure which partition numbers are available, you can type this command to see a list:

```
foo@bar:~$ ls -al /dev/hda*
```

To make mounting easier, add this mount point to the list of available mount points in /etc/fstab. This file tells the system which disks are available and how they are accessed. You should add one of these two lines depending on whether you have a VFAT- or NTFS-formatted Windows partition:

```
/dev/hda1    /mnt/windows    vfat   rw    0  0
/dev/hda1    /mnt/windows    ntfs   ro    0  0
```

This tells the system that /dev/hda1 is available in /mnt/windows with read and write access and to mount it at every boot. NTFS is mounted read-only (ro), because writing to an NTFS partition is not supported and will cause data corruption.

To use the fonts, you need to access the Windows font directory and run some utilities that will make the fonts usable in X Windows. Although X supports TrueType fonts, it needs some special files to be generated that provide information about the fonts. Windows often keeps fonts in C:\Windows\Fonts, so you should go to /mnt/windows/windows/fonts to run the commands.

The first command is called ttmkfdir. This command creates a special font information file called fonts.scale that displays a list of the fonts and their capabilities in a format the X server can understand; this acts like a reference card that says what each font can do. To create this file, simply run the command inside the font directory:

```
foo@bar:~$ ttmkfdir
```

If your Windows partition is NTFS, you won't be able to run this command because your access is read-only. To get around this, copy the fonts to a directory on your Linux system and run the command. Then copy the file it creates, *fonts.scale*, to media you can access from Windows, such as a floppy disk or USB memory key. From there you can put it in your *C:\Windows\ fonts* directory. You will have to repeat this work each time you add new fonts to your Windows partition that you want to use in Linux, so you have to question if it is really worth it.

You now need to tell XFree86 that this font directory exists and it should use it. You can do this in one of two ways. The first method is to add a FontPath line to your X11 configuration file, which is commonly */etc/X11/ XF86Config-4*:

```
FontPath"/mnt/windows/Windows/Fonts"
```

When you have added this, you will need to restart your X server.

> Remember to use proper capitalization for your Windows files when accessing them from Linux. For example, the main Windows directory is sometimes spelled with all caps: *WINDOWS*. So, you might need to change your font paths appropriately.

An alternative method if you are using the XFS font server is to use the chkfontpath command to add the path dynamically:

```
foo@bar:~$ chkfontpath --add /mnt/windows/Windows/Fonts
```

If you add the directory using this command, you must restart the font server and restart XFree86. You can do this with the following:

```
foo@bar:~$ /etc/init.d/xfs restart
```

Now your fonts should be available.

Use Mac OS X Fonts

Although Mac OS X has support for TrueType fonts, Apple decided to store many of the native system font details in special files known as *data fork resource files*. These files end in the extension *.dfont* and contain a lot more information than is typically found in a TrueType font file. This information is specific to the Mac OS X operating system, so just copying the files over to Linux is not enough as X would not understand what to do with this extra information. Therefore, you need to convert these files to something X can use with the aid of a nifty little tool called Fondu.

Fondu (*http://fondu.sourceforge.net/*) has been developed to extract font information from the *.dfont* files and make usable TrueType font files. Fondu includes not only a converter, but also several other tools to deal with font differences between Unix-type operating systems, such as Linux/BSD and Mac OS X. On the home page is a Mac OS X StuffIt archive that you need to download to your Mac.

When you have downloaded the archive, double-click the icon to extract the software and a .pkg icon will appear on the desktop. When you click this icon, the installation routine will run. Although the installer will require the normal process of clicking Next and selecting where to install the files, you should also set your `PATH` and `MANPATH` environment variables to */usr/local/bin* and */usr/local/man*, respectively, so that the installed files are accessible anywhere in Mac OS X. You can do this in the *.profile* file inside your directory (this file is read each time you log in and sets up any environment settings such as those defined by these variables):

```
PATH = /usr/local/bin:$PATH
MANPATH = /usr/local/man:$MANPATH
export PATH MANPATH
```

Now log off Mac OS X and then log back on, and check that these variables are set by typing the following:

```
foo@bar:~$ echo $PATH
foo@bar:~$ echo $MANPATH
```

To convert the fonts, create a directory in which to perform the conversion:

```
foo@bar:~$ mkdir ~/fontconv
```

You cannot convert the main font files in the system font directory as write access is disabled, so use *fontconv* as a temporary directory. Use this command to copy the fonts from the */System/Library/Fonts* directory into your new directory:

```
foo@bar:~$ cp /System/Library/Fonts/* ~/fontconv
```

Now if you go to the *fontconv* directory, you can perform the conversion with:

```
foo@bar:~$ fondu *
```

When this process is finished you will see a number of *.ttf* fonts in the directory. Create another directory called *macfonts* into which to copy the True-Type fonts, and then make a tarball of them:

```
foo@bar:~$ mkdir ~/macfonts
foo@bar:~$ cp *.ttf ../macfonts
foo@bar:~$ tar zcvf ../macfonts/*.ttf macfonts
```

Now copy these fonts to the Linux machine and extract them into either the system font directory or *.fonts* in your home directory. As outlined in the previous section, be sure to run the `ttmkfdir` tool to create the font information file, and add the font path to XFree86.

Never Miss Another Reminder

#26 Flash your reminders on your desktop on top of any applications you are running.

Did you know you can display pop-up messages on top of X Windows, even if you're using multiple virtual desktops? This trick can come in handy when a pop-up dialog box or messages in a terminal window simply aren't sufficient to get your attention. And it can be fun, too. This hack explores the power of X11 On-Screen Display (XOSD), and then uses it to set reminders that will pop up on-screen at the preset time.

XOSD allows you to print messages, symbols, and even progress bars directly on-screen, on top of anything else you have displayed on your desktop. Think of it as the equivalent of the volume control meter that pops up on many televisions when you adjust the volume.

Use your distribution's preferred installation method to install XOSD. The package name usually includes the term *XOSD*. If you have *yum* set up properly, you can log in as root and install it on Fedora Core (and some other RPM-based Linux distributions) with this command:

```
# yum install xosd
```

On Debian or RPM-based distributions that support *apt-get*, install it with this command:

```
# apt-get install xosd-bin
```

On Gentoo, install it with this:

```
# emerge xosd
```

The distinct advantage of using XOSD is that it is often more likely to get your attention than any other alert technique. That's because the message appears on every virtual desktop, and it appears on top of any applications you are using. You can try out the XOSD program, *osd_cat*, with a simple command, such as the following:

```
$ echo "Hello there, this is osd_cat speaking." | osd_cat
```

You should see the message appear in tiny red text in the upper-left corner of the screen. It's so tiny, in fact, that it's hardly useful. Don't worry; you can do something about that. As long as you see the text (or something red that looks like text) you know *osd_cat* is working.

The Way You Like It

You can add several customization switches to tune how the *osd_cat* command presents text on the screen. The first thing you want to do is increase the text size. Use the –f switch followed by a *font definition* to make *osd_cat* use the font you prefer.

Font definitions, such as the ones used by *osd_cat*, can appear intimidating because they contain so much information littered with dashes and asterisks. Each part of the definition says something about the type of font, the point size, whether the font is bold, etc. It's probably safe to stick with the definitions listed here, but if you want to play with various font definitions, run the program *xfontsel*. This program lets you play with the various parameters that make up a font definition while showing the results in the window. When you come up with a combination you like, you can click the Select button, which will copy the full definition onto the clipboard and let you paste it into your script or program.

If you want a big eye-catching font, you'll probably want to use the following font definition, which is available in almost every Linux distribution:

```
-adobe-helvetica-bold-r-normal-*-*-240-*-*-p-*-*-*
```

If you have the Microsoft TrueType fonts installed [Hack #25], you can get a much broader range of font sizes at the cost of speed. The larger you make the font, the longer it takes for *osd_cat* to render the message. Here's one example:

```
"-microsoft-comic sans ms-*-*-*-*-48-*-*-*-*-*-*-*"
```

You can get some fonts to display text larger than 48 points, but it might take several seconds before you see the text on your screen.

Make sure you enclose font descriptions in quotes if the font name includes spaces. Otherwise, the spaces in the font description will confuse the *osd_cat* program.

Let's try the *osd_cat* test again, this time with a font definition:

```
$ echo "Hello there, this is osd_cat speaking." |
osd_cat -f "-adobe-helvetica-bold-r-normal-*-*-240-*-*-p-*-*-*"
```

If everything works properly, you should see the message in much larger text.

You can use the –c switch to change the color of the text. You can use any color name defined in the */usr/X11R6/lib/X11/rgb.txt* file, but unless you're really picky, it's safe to stick with basic color names, such as blue, green, yellow, cyan, white, black, and magenta. If you really want to branch out into colors, such as PapayaWhip, however, be my guest.

Green is typical of television on-screen displays, so see if it looks good for XOSD:

```
$ echo "Hello there, this is osd_cat speaking." |
osd_cat_-c green \
-f "-adobe-helvetica-bold-r-normal-*-*-240-*-*-p-*-*-*"
```

If you want to get fancy, present the text with a bit of a shadow. Of course, if the message displays on a dark background, you probably won't see the shadow. Add the −s 2 switch to create a 2-pixel shadow for the message:

```
$ echo "Hello there, this is osd_cat speaking." |
osd_cat -c green -s 2 \
-f "-adobe-helvetica-bold-r-normal-*-*-240-*-*-p-*-*-*"
```

Now position the text in the middle of the screen with the -p middle switch (you can choose top or bottom, if you prefer). You might see the message appear at the top of the screen for a moment, after which it shifts to the middle of the screen. This is an occasional idiosyncrasy of *osd_cat* that will probably be fixed as it matures. Finally, you can make the message display on the screen for longer than the default 5 seconds. Add the -d 60 switch to tell *osd_cat* to leave the message on the screen for 60 seconds:

```
$ echo "Hello there, this is osd_cat speaking." |
osd_cat -c green -s 2 -p middle -d 60
-f "-*-helvetica-*-*-*-*-34-*-*-*-*-*-*-*"
```

A number of other switches are also available, such as a switch to indent the text. Browse the manpage for *osd_cat* for a list of the available customization switches.

Scripting the Attention-Getting Reminder

Now that you know what XOSD can do, you can put it to work by writing a script that will cause reminders to flash on the screen at the appointed time. In addition to *osd_cat*, you also need the *at* program installed for this script to work, and you must have the *atd* daemon running. Many Linux distributions install *at* and *atd*, and run the daemon by default. If yours does not, you have to follow the procedure for your particular distribution to install *at* and *atd*, and make sure *atd* starts when you boot the computer.

Now, on to the script itself. Log in as root or use sudo to fire up your favorite editor, create the file */usr/local/bin/remindme*, and type in the bash script from Example 4-1 or fetch the script from O'Reilly's Examples web site for this book.

Example 4-1. remindme bash script

```
#!/bin/bash

# figure out which display we're currently using
```

Example 4-1. remindme bash script (continued)

```
HOST="$(xrdb -symbols | grep SERVERHOST | cut -d= -f2)"
DISPLAYNUM="$(xrdb -symbols | grep DISPLAY_NUM | cut -d= -f2)"
THISDISPLAY=$HOST:$DISPLAYNUM.0

# check to see if the reminders directory exists in the home directory
# if not, then create the directory

if [ ! -e ~/reminders ] ; then
    mkdir ~/reminders
fi

unique=`date +%F-%H-%M-%S`
reminder="reminders/reminder-"$unique
# Now output the reminder script
echo '#!/bin/bash' > ~/$reminder
echo -n 'export DISPLAY=' >> ~/$reminder
echo $THISDISPLAY >> ~/$reminder
echo "echo \"$2 today\" | osd_cat -s 2 -c green -p middle \
 -f -adobe-helvetica-bold-r-normal-*-*-240-*-*-p-*-*-* -d 60" >> ~/$reminder
# Make the reminder script executable
chmod +x ~/$reminder
# Schedule it to run
at $1 -f ~/$reminder
```

Save your work, and change the file to be executable with this command:

```
$ sudo chmod +x /usr/local/bin/remindme
```

Do you need to set a quick reminder to call your boss at 2:00 p.m.? Simply type the following command:

```
$ remindme 2:00pm "Call your boss now."
```

From this command the bash script creates a separate reminder script and schedules it to run at 2:00 p.m. The script it creates will put the message on the screen using on-screen display. That means you won't be able to miss the message, because it will appear on every virtual desktop at the same time.

Here's how it works. The first part of the script determines which X Windows display you are using. Then it adds a line to the reminder file that exports the discovered display setting. The *osd_cat* program does not get that information from the environment, so it must be specified in the script. You can't depend on the user always being on the default display of :0.0, which is why the script has to determine the current display by querying the system with the xrdb command.

Some versions of *osd_cat* are cranky about how the DISPLAY variable is set, and they won't work if you specify the hostname in front of the <:0.0>. Keep that in mind when trying to get this working on your system.

The next part of the bash script creates a unique filename based on the current time. Then it creates the first line of the bash script (#!/bin/bash) and writes it to the reminder file that will run at the proper time.

Next, it adds the on-screen display command, which substitutes "Call your boss now" for the second argument, $2. It makes the reminder script executable, and finally, it schedules the computer to run your reminder program with the at command, which uses the time at which you typed the command as your first argument. The time argument is flexible, by the way. You can type the time as 2:00PM, 2pm, or even 14:00. The script adds today for you, although if you are ambitious, you can rewrite the script to let you create reminders for specific dates in the future.

If you look carefully at the script, you can see that it stores files as something such as *~/reminders/reminder-2004-10-04-05-07-39*. Note that the symbol ~ refers to your home directory, so it is storing all the reminders in the *reminders* subdirectory just below your home directory. If you like this script and use it often, this directory will fill up with those temporary reminder script files. They don't take up much space, so that shouldn't be much of a concern. But if you want to clean out old reminders, you can do so by checking the filenames to see how old they are. Each reminder script includes the year, month, day, hour, minute, and second as part of the filename. This makes it easy to identify expired reminders and delete them.

Note that the year, month, day, hour, minute, and second in the filename represent the time you created the reminder script file, not the time it is scheduled to run. If you create a reminder at 1:00 p.m. that is supposed to run at 3:00 p.m., don't delete the file because it's older than the current time if the current time is sometime before 3:00 p.m. It expires after it was scheduled to run—at 3:00 p.m.—not after the time it was created.

HACK #27 Make Applications Trigger On-Screen Alerts

Many applications can run a program when an event occurs. Use XOSD to make these alerts really grab your attention.

Many of the applications you use daily might give you the option of executing a program when an event occurs. The KMail email client, Jpilot personal information manager, and Swatch log-monitor program are three examples. Each hack in this section takes advantage of XOSD [Hack #26].

KMail

If you use the KDE KMail email client, you can have KMail execute a program when new mail arrives. Here's how you can have KMail display the on-screen new-mail notification "You've got mail!" with XOSD.

First, you need to create a script that displays the on-screen alert "You've got mail!". KMail doesn't allow you to insert the entire echo and osd_cat command line, but it will execute a script that displays the message. Fire up your favorite editor, and enter this script into a file called ~/youhavemail. (This script executes from your home directory, so you don't need any special privileges for it to work.)

```
#!/bin/bash

# figure out which display we're currently using
# then export the DISPLAY environment variable

HOST="$(xrdb -symbols | grep SERVERHOST | cut -d= -f2)"
DISPLAYNUM="$(xrdb -symbols | grep DISPLAY_NUM | cut -d= -f2)"
THISDISPLAY=$HOST:$DISPLAYNUM.0

export DISPLAY=$THISDISPLAY

echo "You've got mail"'!' | osd_cat -s 2 -c yellow -p middle \
 -f -adobe-helvetica-bold-r-normal-*-*-240-*-*-p-*-*-* -d 30
```

 The placement of various quotes in the text for the echo command looks a bit odd, doesn't it? Here's why. The bash shell interpreter will allow you to embed only a single quote in a string that is enclosed by double quotes. If the string "You've" wasn't isolated within double quotes, the echo command would report an error. In addition, the exclamation point (!) has a special meaning in bash. It refers to the command history (a recording of your most recent commands). In this case, you can display the exclamation point only if you surround it with single quotes. This creates a dilemma in the first part of our message because it requires double quotes, yet we have to surround the exclamation point with single quotes. The answer is simple. Break up the message into two parts, the main part surrounded by double quotes followed by the single exclamation point surrounded by single quotes. The echo command handles both strings as part of a single message.

Save your work and change the script to be executable:

```
$ chmod +x ~/youhavemail
```

Now follow these steps to configure KMail to execute the script when new mail arrives:

1. Start up KMail and then click Settings → Configure KMail.

2. Click the button entitled Other Actions at the bottom of the dialog, located right below the Detailed New Mail Notification box, which should be checked by default.

3. Click the More Options button at the bottom of the next dialog box that appears.

4. Check the "Execute a program" box.

5. Enter **~/youhavemail** in the edit field for this selection.

6. Click the Apply and/or OK buttons until you are back to the KMail interface.

Jpilot

You can configure the Jpilot personal information manager (PIM) to run a script that displays an on-screen message when a scheduled event occurs. Fire up your favorite editor, and enter this script into a file called *~/jpilotalert*. (This script executes from your home directory, so you don't need any special privileges for it to work.)

```
#!/bin/bash

# figure out which display we're currently using
# then export the DISPLAY environment variable

HOST="$(xrdb -symbols | grep SERVERHOST | cut -d= -f2)"
DISPLAYNUM="$(xrdb -symbols | grep DISPLAY_NUM | cut -d= -f2)"
THISDISPLAY=$HOST:$DISPLAYNUM.0

export DISPLAY=$THISDISPLAY

echo "You have an appointment scheduled for $1 $2"'!' | osd_cat -s 2 -c
yellow -p middle \
 -f -adobe-helvetica-bold-r-normal-*-*-240-*-*-p-*-*-* -d 30
```

Here is how to set up Jpilot to execute this script and enter the date and time as part of the alert:

1. Select File → Preferences from the menu, or press Ctrl-E to get to the Preferences dialog.

2. Click the Alarms tab.

3. Check the box labeled "Execute this command."

4. Enter the following string of text into the Alarm Command text field: **~/jpilotalert "%d" "%t"**.

Swatch

Swatch is a program that monitors your system logs to watch for certain important keywords in one or more log files. If Swatch finds a keyword, perhaps a word or pattern that indicates someone might be trying to guess passwords and break into your network, Swatch will do whatever you tell it to do to issue the alert.

Normally, when Swatch issues an alert, it simply prints it to the screen where Swatch is running. Swatch can also send you an email alert, but if Swatch detected an attempted break-in, your network could be compromised by the time you check your email. This hack exploits the power of XOSD to give Swatch a better chance of grabbing your attention when something potentially serious is afoot.

Here is an example of how to set up Swatch to tell you when someone tries to log in, but fails (a possible indication that someone is trying to guess a password). Assume that the Swatch configuration file you are using is */root/.swatchrc*, and the log file to be monitored is */var/log/auth.log*, which, for some Linux distributions, is the file that records all login attempts. Here is just one section of a larger file called */root/.swatchrc*, which looks for the word "failure" in */var/log/auth.log*:

```
# Bad login attempts
watchfor /failure/
   pipe "osd_cat -c magenta -p middle \
-f \"-*-arial black-*-*-*-*-48-*-*-*-*-*-*-*\" -d 60"
```

When Swatch finds a new log entry with the word "failure" in */var/log/auth.log*, it prints the suspicious log entry on-screen by piping it through *osd_cat*, which makes the event almost impossible to miss if you're working at the computer. Note that we're using a smaller font than we used for the previous hacks. That's because Swatch messages can sometimes be lengthy, and you don't want to have the most important information hidden off-screen.

H A C K Heat Up Your Keyboard with Hotkeys
#28 Activate those special Internet and multimedia keys on your keyboard.

Hotkeys is a bit antique these days, so it doesn't support all the modern keyboards. But if you are willing to put in some effort, you can get a decent experience from Hotkeys, especially if your keyboard is supported. If your keyboard is not supported, it might take more work than it is worth to you, and you might want to skip ahead to the more modern LinEAK [Hack #29].

First, you must install Hotkeys; you can use your distributions package manager or download and compile it yourself. If your Linux distribution doesn't have a package available, you can find RPM packages for various distributions at *http://rpm.pbone.net/index.php3?stat=3&search=hotkeys&srodzaj=3*, or you can search *http://rpmfind.net*. Just as an example, if you use Debian, get the packages with this command (logged in as root):

```
# apt-get install hotkeys xosd-bin
```

By installing *xosd-bin* at the same time you can take advantage of one of the better features of Hotkeys: the attractive use of on-screen display (Figure 4-1). If you compile hotkeys yourself, be sure to also install the XOSD and XOSD development programs **[Hack #26]** to take advantage of this feature.

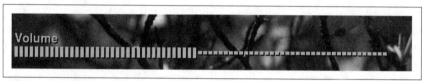

Figure 4-1. The Hotkeys on-screen volume display

Start the process of configuring Hotkeys for your keyboard by copying the default configuration to your personal configuration file. The default configuration file is usually saved as */etc/hotkeys.conf*. You want to create a copy of this file in your home directory, and personalize it to work with your keyboard and perform the actions you want performed when you press the special keys on your keyboard:

```
$ mkdir ~/.hotkeys
$ cp /etc/hotkeys.conf ~/.hotkeys
```

Now look to see which keyboards are supported by default:

```
$ hotkeys -L
Supported keyboards: (with corresponding options to --kbd-list or -l)
    mx2500      - Memorex MX2500 Keyboard
    kbp8993     - Chicony KBP-8993 keyboard
    sk2500      - Fujitsu/Logitech/Trust SK2500 Keyboard / Liteon-ak2500
    sk2505      - SK-2505 Keyboard
    sk2800c     - SK-2800C
    ibook       - iBook Internal Keyboard
    mx1998      - Memorex MX1998 Keyboard
    sk2501a     - Silitek SK5210A Keyboard
    msnatpro    - Microsoft Natural Keyboard Pro
    msnet       - Microsoft Internet Keyboard
    logitech-cfo      - Logitech Cordless Freedom Optical Keyboard
    polypix     - Polypix Keyboard
    sk7100      - Silitek SK7100 Keyboard
    itouch       - Logitech Cordless iTouch/Internet/Cordless Desktop
```

```
hp5181      - HP 5181 Internet Keyboard
msnetpro    - Microsoft Internet Pro Keyboard
acerwl      - Acer Wireless Keyboard
btc9000     - BTC 9000
orktekusb   - ORKTEK USB Hub/keyboard
kb9930      - IBM Rapid Access II Keyboard
mck800      - Process MCK-800
kb9963      - Compaq KB-9963 keyboard
pb5140w     - Packerd Bell Model 5140W
mx3000      - Memorex MX3000 Keyboard
sk9925      - Silitek SK-9925 USB Keyboard
```

This isn't a terribly impressive list, but if your keyboard is there, you're all set. If your keyboard isn't listed, you can use one of the existing Hotkey keyboard definitions as a template to create a new keyboard definition. For example, to create a definition for the Logitech Elite keyboard, log in as root and run these commands:

```
# cd /usr/share/hotkeys
# cp itouch.def lelite.def
```

Now you need to find out what the keycodes are for the Logitech Elite keyboard and adjust the definitions in the file. This is the hardest part of the process. The best way to discover what keycodes your special keys generate is to execute the following command within an X terminal:

```
$ xev
```

You will see a small window appear with a box inside it. Click the window to make sure it's active. Now press the various special keys on your keyboard. As you press each key, information about that key should appear in the terminal from which you launched *xev*. If you press a special key and nothing appears on the X terminal where you started *xev*, you won't be able to assign that key to an action. Also, if you see a result that looks something like this, you probably won't be able to assign that key to an action:

```
KeymapNotify event, serial 30, synthetic NO, window 0x0,
    keys:  4294967222 0   0   0   0   0   0   0   0   0   0   0   0   0
0              0  0  0   0   0   0   0   0   0   0   0   0   0   0   0

ButtonRelease event, serial 30, synthetic NO, window 0x1400001,
    root 0xb6, subw 0x1400002, time 2414137, (35,22), root:(1053,797),
    state 0x200, button 2, same_screen YES
```

However, if you see a result that looks something like the following, you're in luck:

```
KeyPress event, serial 27, synthetic NO, window 0x1400001,
    root 0xb6, subw 0x1400002, time 31223, (44,18), root:(1085,771),
    state 0x0, keycode 162 (keysym 0x0, NoSymbol), same_screen YES,
    XLookupString gives 0 bytes:
    XmbLookupString gives 0 bytes:
```

```
XFilterEvent returns: False

KeyRelease event, serial 30, synthetic NO, window 0x1400001,
    root 0xb6, subw 0x1400002, time 31447, (44,18), root:(1085,771),
    state 0x0, keycode 162 (keysym 0x0, NoSymbol), same_screen YES,
    XLookupString gives 0 bytes:
```

In this example, your keypress generated a keycode of 162. Jot down that keycode and make a note of which key generated it. In the case of the Logitech Elite keyboard, the Play key generates keycode 162.

Given all I could find out about the Logitech Elite keyboard, here is an abbreviated version of the */usr/share/hotkeys/lelite.def* definition file I re-created from the original *itouch.def* file:

```xml
<?xml version="1.0"?>

<definition>

    <config model="Logitech Elite Keyboard">

        <Favorites    keycode="230"/>
        <Shopping     keycode="148"/>
        <PrevTrack    keycode="144"/>
        <Play         keycode="162"/>
        <Stop         keycode="164"/>
        <NextTrack    keycode="153"/>
        <VolUp        keycode="176" adj="2"/>
        <VolDown      keycode="174" adj="2"/>
        <Mute         keycode="160"/>
        <Email        keycode="236"/>
        <Search       keycode="136"/>
        <Sleep        keycode="223"/>
        <Go           keycode="233"/>
        <!-- Media        keycode="129"/ -->
        <userdef        keycode="129" command="/usr/bin/eject">Eject</userdef>
        <!-- My Home    keycode="130   -->
        <userdef keycode="130" command="/usr/bin/xfe">Home</userdef>
        <!-- Go     keycode="233" -->
        <userdef        keycode="233" command="/usr/bin/firefox \
    -remote openURL()"></userdef>

    </config>

    <contributor>
        <name>nicholas petreley</name>
        <email>nicholas at petreley dot com</email>
    </contributor>

</definition>
```

Notice that some definitions begin with userdef. Hotkeys is very strict about the names you define for the available keys on the keyboard. Hotkeys simply refuses to recognize some key names, and therefore you cannot associate those names with a keycode. You can get around the problem by creating a user-defined key definition. In the case of the Logitech Elite keyboard, there is a Media key, a My Home key, and a Go key (among others undefined by Hotkeys). I added these keys along with their functions to the /usr/share/hotkeys/lelite.def file using the Hotkeys userdef command:

```
<!-- Media       keycode="129"/ -->
<userdef        keycode="129" command="/usr/bin/eject">Eject</userdef>
<!-- My Home     keycode="130"  -->
<userdef keycode="130" command="/usr/bin/xfe">Home</userdef>
<!-- Go     keycode="233" -->
<userdef        keycode="233" command="/usr/bin/firefox \
-remote openURL( )"></userdef>
```

Now you're ready to edit the ~/.hotkeys/hotkeys.conf file to define the actions Hotkeys will take when you press certain special keys. Here is a sample configuration:

```
### Specify the default keyboard  (without the .def extension) so you
### don't need to specify -t every time
Kbd=lelite

CDROM=/dev/cdroms/cdrom0

# PrevTrack=xmms --rew
# Play=xmms --play-pause
# Stop=xmms --stop
# Pause=xmms --pause
# NextTrack=xmms --fwd
# Rewind=

WebBrowser=firefox
Email=thunderbird
Calculator=xcalc
FileManager=gentoo
MyComputer=gentoo
MyDocuments=gentoo
Favorites=firefox
Shell=aterm
ScreenSaver=xscreensaver-command -activate
NewsReader=thunderbird -news
Communities=firefox -remote 'openURL(http://slashdot.org,new-tab)'
Search=firefox -remote 'openURL(http://www.google.com,new-tab)'
Idea=firefox -remote 'openURL(http://sourceforge.net,new-tab)'
Shopping=firefox -remote 'openURL(http://thinkgeek.com,new-tab)'
Go=firefox -remote 'openURL( )'
Print=lp
```

```
osd_font=-adobe-helvetica-bold-r-normal-*-*-240-*-*-p-*-*-*
osd_color=LawnGreen
osd_timeout=3
osd_position=bottom
osd_offset=25
```

Some of the actions are simple. The Email key starts the Thunderbird program, so all you need in the file is the line Email=thunderbird. Other definitions require more complex actions, such as opening a new tab in a web browser (if one is already running) and pointing it to a specific web page.

The key definition is Kbd=lelite, which tells Hotkeys which keyboard definition file to use. In this case, it instructs Hotkeys to use /usr/share/hotkeys/ lelite.def.

I confess that most of the keys listed in the configuration file do not exist on the Logitech Elite keyboard, so the definitions are useless. But it's sufficient for my tastes as it enables my keyboard to control the volume, play audio CDs, launch Firefox, and open Google in a browser tab. If you have a keyboard that is officially supported, you can do a lot more.

HACK #29 Get Hotter Hotkeys with LinEAK

LinEAK turbo charges the whole concept of customizing how your Internet/ multimedia keyboard works.

This hack will show you how to adopt the modern equivalent of Hotkeys. LinEAK is a combination of packages, including the main daemon service and several plug-ins. It's a bit quirky and doesn't always launch successfully (at least in this author's experience), but it has support for far more keyboards than Hotkeys. And because Hotkeys hasn't advanced much over the years, it isn't likely to catch up unless someone regains interest in it. LinEAK, on the other hand, is being improved on a regular basis.

As of this writing, you can get Debian packages for some of the programs that make up LinEAK at http://lineak.sourceforge.net/, and you can get the source code for all the packages from the same site and compile the programs and plug-ins yourself. I compiled my own and it was a cinch. The RPM packages at this site are out-of-date but might be current by the time you read this.

Until that time, you can find a variety of RPM packages for LinEAK designed for Mandrake and other distributions at http://rpm.pbone.net/index. php3?stat=3&search=lineakd&srodzaj=3. And you can also search http:// www.rpmfind.net. Make sure you have XOSD and XOSD development libraries installed if you want to enjoy the on-screen display feature. "Never Miss Another Reminder" [Hack #26] provides more information about XOSD.

For example, the volume control shown in Figure 4-2 is one of the nice features LinEAK shares with Hotkeys [Hack #28].

Figure 4-2. LinEAK's on-screen volume display, which is nice-looking as long as you use the built-in volume definitions

The following programs comprise LinEAK as it stands now:

- *lineakd*
- *lineak_defaultplugin*
- *lineak_xosdplugin*
- *lineak_kdeplugins*
- *Media Detect*
- *lineakconfig*
- *Klineakconfig*

At minimum, install *lineakd*, *lineak_defaultplugin*, and *lineak_xosdplugin*. If you can't find packages for your distribution, download the source code and then compile and install the programs using these commands (assuming you place your source code in */usr/local/src*):

```
# cd /usr/local/src/lineakd-0.8.1
# ./configure
# make
# make install
# cd /usr/local/src/lineak_defaultplugin-0.8.1
# ./configure
# make
# make install
# cd /usr/local/src/lineak_xosdplugin-0.8.1
# ./configure
# make
# make install
```

Now log in as a regular user and type the following command to get a list of the supported keyboards:

```
$ lineakd -l
(The complete list is 3 pages long, this is just the first few lines)
LinEAK v0.8.1 -- supported keyboards:

[TYPE]      [Full name]
```

```
A4-KBS21          A4Tech Wireless Desktop KBS-21533RP & Office/Multimedia
Keyboard
A4-KBS8          A4Tech KBS-8
A4-RFKB23        A4Tech RFKB-23
A4-RFKB25        A4Tech RFKB-25 (KBS-2548RP & KBS-2548RPC)
ACE-6512UV        Acer 6512-UV
ACE-TM290        Acer Laptop/notebook Travelmate 290LCi
ACEAKV12          Acer AirKey V (12 keys)
ADEL-9805        Adesso EL-9805
APK7             Apple Pro Keyboard (7 keys)
BEN-AM805        BenQ AM805
```

That kind of beats the tar out of Hotkeys support, doesn't it?

Find your keyboard in the list. For example, the code for the Logitech Elite keyboard is LTCElite. Now type this command to create a default configuration file for your keyboard (substitute LTCElite with the code for your keyboard):

```
$ lineakd -c LTCElite
```

The -c option creates a default configuration file, *lineakd.conf*, for the Logitech Elite keyboard and places the configuration file in the *~/.lineak* directory. Fire up your favorite editor, and customize this file's settings to your heart's content. Here's a sample configuration I created for my Logitech Elite keyboard:

```
# LinEAK - Linux support for Easy Access and Internet Keyboards
#  Copyright (c) 2001,2002, 2003  Sheldon Lee Wen <leewsb@hotmail.com>
#                and Mark Smulders <Mark@PIRnet.nl>
#  http://lineak.sourceforge.net
#
# lineakd configuration file
#
# example key configuration:
#              play               = "xmms --play-pause"
#              eject              = EAK_EJECT
#
# Lineakd supports the following modifier keys:
#    control alt shift mod2 mod3 mod4 mod5

# Normally /dev/cdrom, but UDEV likes /dev/cdroms/cdrom0
CdromDevice = /dev/cdroms/cdrom0
Display_align = center
Display_color = 77FF00
Display_font = "-adobe-helvetica-bold-r-normal-*-*-240-*-*-p-*-*-*"
Display_hoffset = 0
Display_plugin = xosd
Display_pos = bottom
Display_soffset = 1
Display_timeout = 6
Display_voffset = 50
KeyboardType = LTCElite
```

```
MixerDevice = /dev/mixer
Screensaver =
conffilename = /home/nicholas/.lineak/lineakd.conf
keystate_capslock =
keystate_numlock =
keystate_scrolllock =

Arrow =
Email = "thunderbird"
Favorites = "firefox"
Go = "firefox -remote 'openURL( )'"
Media = "cdeject"
Messenger =
Mute = "EAK_MUTE"
MyHome =
Next = "cdplay +"
Play = "cdplay"
Pause = "cdpause"
Previous = "cdplay -"
Search = "firefox -remote 'openURL(http://www.google.com,new-tab)'"
Shopping =
Sleep =
Stop = "cdstop"
VolumeDown = "EAK_VOLDOWN"
VolumeUp = "EAK_VOLUP"
Webcam =
iTouch =
```

Note the use of some built-in commands, such as EAK_MUTE, EAK_VOLUP, and
EAK_VOLDOWN. These are far more preferable when figuring out how to configure a command-line mixer to do the same operations. Unfortunately, Lin-
EAK doesn't automatically insert these as the default settings for the Mute,
VolumeUp, and VolumeDown parameters (it leaves the definitions empty), so
unless you know these generic settings exist, you might waste a lot of time
figuring out how to create a command to mute your sound driver or change
the volume. Well, now that you know they exist, by all means, use them!

Outside of the internal EAK_ commands, the audio CD controls in this example are driven by a command-line package of programs called *cdtool*, created by a host of contributors but currently maintained by Max Vozeler.
You can download cdtool from *http://hinterhof.net/cdtool*. You can choose
any CD player that can be controlled via the command line, but it's nice not
to have an actual graphical CD player clutter the screen when all the controls are already on the keyboard.

> If you decide to try both Hotkeys and LinEAK, restart your
> desktop after using Hotkeys. Even if you kill the Hotkeys
> program, it leaves the desktop in a state that prevents Lin-
> EAK from working properly.

You can thank Mark Smulders (*msmulders@elsar.nl*), the original author, for this fine piece of software. Sheldon Lee Wen (*leewsb@hotmail.com*) is the current maintainer and developer of the latest versions, and wrote plug-ins from the ground up. Phil Woodland (*sir_taco@yahoo.ca*) is the contributions coordinator and maintainer. Finally, Chris Peterson (*rpm@forevermore.net*) does the RPM packaging for LinEAK.

HACK #30 Access Windows and Mac OS X from Linux

No need to move to another computer; just sit put and access them all.

Although you don't need to go far to hear someone extolling the benefits of Linux and free software, many people still need to use other operating systems, such as Microsoft Windows and Apple Mac OS X. Aside from personal choice, other reasons to use non-Linux operating systems include running applications that are available only on a particular OS, an employer mandating that you use a particular platform, or even a need to test software and services across different platforms. For some, the solution is a huge desk set up to accommodate three computers with three monitors and three keyboards/mice; however, there is a better way.

This hack uses a piece of software called Virtual Network Computer (VNC). This useful little tool allows you to essentially redirect your monitor output to another computer on a network, and accept keyboard and mouse input from the remote computer. With this software you can run the VNC server on a Windows machine and view the Windows desktop on your Linux machine. Likewise, you can run the VNC server on your Linux machine and view your Linux desktop on a Windows-based desktop. VNC is available for most Unix-based OSes, such as Linux, FreeBSD, Solaris, etc., as well as Microsoft Windows and Mac OS X. VNC gives you the ability to pull together these disparate operating systems on a single desktop.

Configure a Linux VNC Server

VNC comes in a few different guises, but most attention is focused on the RealVNC and TightVNC variants. Of the two versions, TightVNC appears to be the better performer and you can get it from *http://www.tightvnc.com/download.html*. A number of different packages are available for the supported platforms, and you need both the server (to provide a VNC resource to connect to) and the viewer (to connect to another VNC resource). You should be able to install a recent version of TightVNC using your distributions package manager.

If you run a Mac and want to access your Mac OS X desktop from your Linux machine, you need the OSXvnc package from *http://www.redstonesoftware.com/vnc.html* as RealVNC and TightVNC do not natively support Mac OS X. A VNC client for Mac OS X is also available within the Fink packaging system at *http://fink.sourceforge.net*.

To run a VNC server on Linux you must launch the server and give it a special display number to connect to. This usually starts at 1 and increases by one for each new server created. As an example, if you run a VNC server on a machine with the address 192.168.0.2, you would access the first VNC resource as 192.168.0.2:1. To run the server, specify the screen resolution and color depth with the -geometry and -depth command-line options:

```
foo@bar:~$ vncserver -geometry 1024x768 -depth 24
```

These settings are parameters for your virtual screen, not the real settings of the machine you are running the server on. This means the physical screen might be displaying an image at 1280x1024 in 8-bit color, but you can view it remotely at 1024x768 in 24-bit color. Of course, the machine you are viewing the image on must support your choices.

> You can specify a nonstandard resolution—for instance, 990x745. Doing this allows you to maximize the size of the remote image on your desktop without obscuring your local desktop's toolbars and panels.

When you first run the server, you are prompted for a password. This password is used to ensure that clients are who they say they are, and the password is stored and remains the same each time you use the VNC server (you can change the password later with vncpasswd if you need to). When the password is successfully entered, the server indicates which display number it has been given.

While the server is running, all applications that are used appear on the VNC display as well as the normal screen on the computer (if a monitor is attached). You can also route applications to display only on the VNC server by using the DISPLAY environment variable and specifying the hostname and display number:

```
foo@bar:~$ mozilla -display 192.168.0.2:1 &
```

To stop the VNC server, you need to use the -kill option and the display number assigned earlier when you started the server:

```
foo@bar:~$ vncserver -kill :1
```

Connect to a VNC Server

To connect to the VNC server from a Linux machine, you can use the vncviewer tool that is included with the VNC software. This simple little program is used like this:

```
foo@bar:~$ vncviewer 192.168.0.2:1
```

In this command, you specify the IP address, a colon (:), and then the display number to connect to. When you run the command, you are prompted for the VNC server password and then the VNC desktop is displayed.

Configure a Windows VNC Server

Installing the Windows VNC server is a fairly painless process. Once installed, it can be configured as a Windows Service so that it is always running (like a daemon in Linux). The benefit of running the server as a service is that you will still be able to access the server when the machine is locked or the user has logged out.

Download the Windows installer from the TightVNC web site. It is a typical Windows installer that offers no surprises.

To use the VNC server as a service, tick each box that refers to the VNC Server System Service in the VNC installation routine. When you have done this, the Server Options dialog box will appear, and you must configure at least the Authentication tab to run the server. In this tab, you should select the VNC 3.3 Authentication option and use the Set Password field to define the password for the server. You should never disable authentication unless you are 100% sure the host network is secure.

To start and stop your server, use the standard Windows Services configuration tool to start and stop the service.

Configure a Mac OS X VNC Server

The official VNC distribution does not include support for Mac OS X; however, a VNC server is freely available from Redstone Software (*http://www. redstonesoftware.com/vnc.html*), called OSXvnc. This software is available as a Mac OS X disk image file (*.dmg*). Download the software and then double-click it in the Finder. A window will pop up with the program inside it; drag the program to the desktop. Now if you double-click the icon on the desktop, the VNC Settings dialog will appear. For a quick and easy VNC connection, the defaults are fine, and you can just click the Start Server button to begin the connection.

View Your Desktop in a Web Browser

One intriguing feature of the VNC server is that it includes a small web server that exports the VNC desktop to a browser using a special Java applet. To access your VNC server, connect to port 5801 with a Java-enabled web browser. This port number is appended to the hostname/IP address in the same way as a normal web resource:

```
http://foo.com:5801
```

This port number actually maps to the VNC display you are running. If you are running display number 1, use port 5801; display number 2 is port 5802, etc.

 Some distributions, notably Debian, package the Java applet separately from the VNC server package.

When you are running any server on the Internet, you should take steps to ensure that it is protected with a firewall. A firewall keeps all unwanted traffic away from your server. If you are running a firewall already, you should ensure that ports 5800-5805 are available for use. If you want to be extra secure, only open port 5801 for use and make sure you always run off desktop number 1. Another option is to encrypt your VNC connection with an SSH tunnel [Hack #32].

Run Your Desktop over the Internet
#31
You can access your desktop system and run graphics applications from remote systems at close to full speed, even over dial-up connections.

You might want to access a desktop computer remotely for numerous reasons. Perhaps you are travelling and you forgot an important file on your home machine. You need to edit it, but the application you need isn't on your laptop. It would be nice to connect to your home machine over the Internet, edit the file using software on the desktop, and then transfer the file to your laptop. A number of technologies are available for running applications from remote locations, or remotely sharing desktops; the X Window System has built-in network transparency that allows you to run applications on one machine and display them on another [Hack #32], and the different versions of the VNC protocol allow you to use the desktop on another machine [Hack #30]). Though each method has its purpose and excels at what it does, both also have one drawback—they require significant bandwidth. Remote X applications or VNC desktops are pretty slow, even over a DSL or cable modem connection.

NX, from NoMachine (*http://www.nomachine.com*), is an add-on to X that accelerates remote X applications and can be used to run a full remote desktop at near-native speeds, even over a 56K modem connection. NX works much like a proxy cache for the X protocol, caching and compressing requests and responses to and from the X client and server. This dramatically reduces the network traffic of the X protocol and works in a way that is transparent to the X client. All the NX libraries and components are open source, as is the NX client software. However, the servers NoMachine provides are proprietary, although a free trial period of the personal edition is available, which allows single-client access. In addition, the FreeNX project uses the open source NX libraries to create an open source NX server. The following examples use the personal server and client software from NoMachine.

Installing the NX Server and Client

On the machine on which you want to run the remote session, you need to install an NX server and client. Packages for various flavors of Linux are available from *http://www.nomachine.com*. Download the NX Server Personal Edition for your distribution, along with a client, and install both in the normal way. For example:

```
foo@bar:~# rpm -i nxserver-1.4.0-99.i386.rpm
foo@bar:~# rpm -i nxclient-1.4.0-75.i386.rpm
```

On the machine on which you want to display the remote session, you need to install the NX client. Clients for Linux, Mac OS X, and Windows are available from the same web site as the server.

Setting Up the NX Server

Once NX is installed, you can start the NX server using this command (run as root):

```
foo@bar:~# /usr/NX/bin/nxserver -start
```

Now you need to add user sessions to the server using this command:

```
foo@bar:~# /usr/NX/bin/nxserver --useradd username
```

where username is the name of a preexisting user on the server system. Next you are prompted to set a password for this session. Once that's done, you can connect your client machine to the server using the NX client. Go to a separate machine and run the client using this command:

```
foo@bar:~# /usr/NX/bin/nxclient
```

For the first connection this starts a wizard to collect the connection details. On the second wizard page you can give the session a descriptive name, enter the NX server IP address, and select the type of connection between the client and server.

On the third wizard page, you can choose your protocol type (the NX client is also an RDP and VNC client), the type of desktop session to run the NX server, and the size of the window to display the remote desktop. If there are firewalls [Hack #81] and you only have Secure SHell (SSH) access, check the "Enable SSL encryption of all traffic" box, as this tunnels all communication through SSH (i.e., you only need port 22 open) and has the added bonus of encrypting all the NX traffic. If you don't want to tunnel the traffic over SSH, you'll need to open ports 1000, 5000, and 7000 for the first session, 1001, 5001, and 7001 for the second session, and so on—i.e., three ports for each session started.

Finally, on the fourth wizard page, you can choose to create a desktop shortcut for this session and edit the advanced configuration. Once the wizard is finished, you should have a connection dialog with the Login and Session details filled in.

Now type in the password you set on the NX server and click Login. Once this connects and authenticates you should have a complete remote desktop in a window on your client machine.

Further NX Server Commands

Now that you know how to create a basic connection, a few other useful commands for the NX server might interest you. These commands need to be run as root. To see a list of all NX users, type this command:

```
foo@bar:~# /usr/NX/bin/nxserver --userlist
```

To delete an NX user (this deletes the user from NX, not as a user of the system), issue the following:

```
foo@bar:~# /usr/NX/bin/nxserver --userdel username
```

where *username* is the name of the NX account you want to delete.

—*Paul Cooper*

H A C K #32 Access Your Programs Remotely

The full power of your desktop and its applications never need to be more than a network connection away.

For many years now, the X Window System, which plays host to KDE, GNOME, and other desktops or window managers, has had the ability to support networking in a way that other graphical environments can only dream of. These networking features not only allow you to run an application installed on a remote machine and display it on another machine, but also allow you to access and run an entire desktop from another computer.

Using this feature, you can use any computer capable of running a basic X session to access a desktop environment on a faster computer. Provided your network bandwidth is plentiful, there isn't a noticeable lack of speed running a desktop in this way. In fact, because all the programs run at the speed of the faster remote machine, your performance might be better than it's ever been.

Despite these impressive abilities, the remote networking personality of X is largely ignored by most users. Few regular desktop users seem to experiment with the possibilities of running remote applications over a network, even though these features could save a lot of time in homes or offices with multiple X-based systems. This hack explores some of these features so that you can apply them in your own context and hopefully save some time rushing between different computers.

 The final production work on nearly all O'Reilly books is done by running X applications over the network. Specifically, FrameMaker 5.5.6 is run on a Solaris server and displayed on various Linux, Windows, and Macintosh clients running an X server. All the Linux computers are actually thin clients that run their entire desktop over the network using X.

Access X Programs Securely

Running X applications from another computer is a fairly simple process. You just change the $DISPLAY environment variable (this indicates where the output of X applications should be directed) to point to another computer on the network, such as:

```
foo@bar:~$ export DISPLAY="192.169.0.1:0.0"
```

Now, when you run an application, it is displayed at the new IP address rather than at your local display. Exporting a display like this is the function of the X client. Viewing the display is the function of the X server. For a user sitting at the machine whose address is 192.168.0.1 to see the exported program, he must have a running X server that accepts connections from an outside source. To set up a remote machine to accept X displays from other hosts, use the xhost command:

```
foo@bar:~$ xhost +
access control disabled, clients can connect from any host
```

The plus sign indicates you are willing to accept connections from any computer. Optionally, you can specify a specific host (by DNS name or IP address) in place of the plus sign.

Although you can run remote X applications from anywhere using this technique, the traffic between the two machines is entirely unencrypted and insecure. All this traffic operates on port 6000, and if you want to provide access from outside your network, it means opening another port in your firewall and potentially making yourself vulnerable to attacks. To solve this security problem, I advise you to encrypt your X sessions so that they are as secure as possible. The Secure SHell (SSH) has built-in support for running X applications remotely, and it is simple to turn on and use. Most Linux distributions install SSH by default, but if that isn't the case, use your distributions package manager to install the *openssh* packages.

The first step is to open */etc/ssh/sshd_config* on the machine that will serve X applications and ensure the X11Forwarding option is turned on:

```
X11Forwarding yes
```

In many default installations of the SSH server, this option is added but commented out with the # symbol. If you remove the #, you can enable the option. After you have changed the configuration file, you need to restart the SSH server for the setting to take effect. You can do this with the following:

```
foo@bar:~$ /etc/init.d/ssh restart
```

Now you can run an application on the remote machine by using the -X option to forward the X connection. As an example, you can start the Gimp on 192.168.0.2 by entering this command into your local machine:

```
foo@bar:~$ ssh -X jono@192.168.0.2 gimp
```

To permanently enable X forwarding on your local machine, you need to modify your local copy of */etc/ssh/ssh_config*. Simply add the following line (or uncomment this line if it already exists):

```
ForwardX11 yes
```

What you are doing is telling your local machine to always initiate SSH sessions with X forwarding enabled. This is different from the earlier step where you enabled the remote machine to allow X forwarding. There is no need to restart the *sshd* daemon when you make this change; it will automatically work for all new SSH connections.

If you receive errors when you attempt to run a remote X application, try enabling trusted X forwarding by adding the –Y option when you make your SSH connection. If this works, you can enable this permanently by modifying your */etc/ssh/ssh_config* file to include this line:

```
ForwardX11Trusted yes
```

Access the Entire Desktop

There is no doubt that running X applications remotely is useful, but a truly killer feature is the ability to run the entire desktop from a remote computer on your local machine. To do this, you need to use a feature called the X Display Manager Control Protocol (XDMCP), which is part of X. This protocol allows remote computers to access the GDM/KDM/XDM login program, which then gives access to the remote desktop. If you have a reasonably fast network connection—Ethernet speeds of 10-Mbit or greater are recommended—it is possible for a slow computer to be as responsive as a cutting-edge machine. This is possible because the local box is just a display device, like a television, and all the real work is done on the faster remote machine.

To use XDMCP, you must be running XDM, GDM, or KDM as your login manager on the remote machine. Each display manager has support for XDMCP, and you must turn on that support.

To enable XDMCP in GDM, you need to load the *gdmconfig* tool. Inside this tool is an XDMCP tab. Turn on XDMCP support by setting the Enable XDMCP option. You can use some additional settings on this tab to fine-tune XDMCP support. After you've made your changes, you must restart GDM.

There is no GUI way to turn on XDMCP in KDM, so you need to edit the *kdmrc* file on your system. Both a system-wide file (possibly in */etc/kde3/*) and a per-user file (in *~/.kde/share/config*) exist. Inside *kdmrc* is an [Xdmcp] section where you need to set the Enable option to true. After you save this change, you must restart KDM.

When you have turned on this support, you can return to your local machine and search the network for computers that are allowing XDMCP connections. To do this, ensure that you are logged out of X and run the following command:

```
foo@bar:~$ X -broadcast
```

X will start and the login screen from the remote machine will appear. Now you can log in and use the machine in the same way as if you were sitting in front of it. If you want to connect to a specific machine on the network, you can also run the following command on your local machine (remember to change the IP address to a host that is relevant to your network):

```
foo@bar:~$ X -query 192.68.0.2
```

Add Depth to Your Desktop

#33 Drop shadows add a dimension of depth to every window and pop up on your desktop. The 3D effect is truly mesmerizing.

A composite manager program called *xcompmgr* is available that taps into some of the new features of the Xorg X Window System to create attractive drop shadows for windows, pop ups, menus, and the like. It also gives you the option to make your windows and menus fade in and out instead of the normal behavior of appearing and disappearing instantly.

You can use *xcompmgr* only if you use the Xorg fork of the XFree86 project. You cannot use this with any version of XFree86. And you can use it only if you have a *recent* version of Xorg. Check which X server and version you're using with the following command:

```
# X -version
X Window System Version 6.8.0
```

If you don't see 6.8.0 or higher as the version, this hack is not for you.

Get the Composite Manager

A composite manager taps into the new Xorg features that allow X11 to blend various on-screen elements in ways XFree86 cannot. For example, it allows you to make a window partially transparent by blending the background into the application foreground. You can find some programs that appear to give you this feature, such as X terminals that look partially transparent. But they aren't tapping into the features of Xorg; they are essentially "faking it" with some clever graphics tricks. Faking it might look good, but the difference is speed. The Xorg composite features exist as part of the X11 engine, so the effects are built-in and render much faster.

You'll need to install the *xcompmgr* program to take advantage of these features. You probably won't find this program as a normal package in the standard package repositories for your Linux distribution, because it is experimental and can still be very quirky and unstable at this point. A Google search turned up a number of RPM packages for *xcompmgr* at *http://rpm.pbone.net*.

If this or any other site doesn't have a ready-made package that installs cleanly on your Linux distribution, you will have to compile it yourself. Because this is experimental code there's no guarantee it will compile on your system. You need to connect to a CVS server to download the source code. So, log in as root, change to a directory where you like to keep local source code, such as */usr/local/src*, and run the following commands (you do not need a password, so just press Enter when prompted for one):

```
# cvs -d :pserver:anoncvs@cvs.freedesktop.org:/cvs/xorg login
CVS password: (press Enter)
# cvs -d :pserver:anoncvs@pdx.freedesktop.org:/cvs/xapps co xcompmgr
# cd xcompmgr
# sh autogen.sh
# ./configure
# make
# make install
```

Start Your Desktop or Window Manager

The *xcompmgr* program doesn't play well with every desktop or window manager. In my experience, it does not work well with Metacity, the default window manager for GNOME. Metacity is supposed to have some of the *xcompmgr* capabilities already built-in, but I have not been able to tap into them. Regardless, you can't invoke *xcompmgr* until you have started your favorite desktop or window manager, so do that now.

The manpage for *xcompmgr* explains the various tricks you can do with the program. However, the following combination of command-line switches should please nearly everyone. Open an X terminal and type this command:

```
$ xcompmgr -cCfF -l 0 -t 0 -r 5 -o .6 &
```

If everything works the way it should, the screen should go mostly blank for a moment, after which any open windows will reappear with drop shadows. You should also notice that things such as menus have drop shadows and fade in and out. See Figure 4-3 for an example of this effect.

Here's what the command-line switches do. The -l 0 and -t 0 switches tell *xcompmgr* that 0 pixels (no shadow at all) should appear to the left of the window (-l 0), and no shadow pixels should appear above the top of the window (-t 0). This means you will see drop shadows only to the right of and beneath the windows, as though the light source is up and to the left. Normally, *xcompmgr* creates a shadow around the entire window. This effect isn't too bad, but because many other things that appear on-screen (such as your mouse pointer) have shadows to the right and below, this combination makes the simulated light source consistent.

The -r 5 and -o .6 switches tell *xcompmgr* to give the shadows a radius of 5 and an opacity of 0.6, which makes the shadows somewhat subtle.

Finally, let's pick apart the combination -cCfF. The c tells *xcompmgr* to include shadows and translucency; the C tells *xcompmgr* to try to avoid creating shadows for things such as launch panels. The combination fF tells *xcompmgr* to fade just about everything in and out whenever windows, menus, or other objects change (maximize, minimize, etc.).

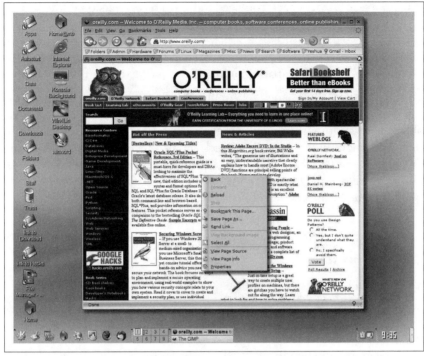

Figure 4-3. Firefox and menu with shadows

 xcompmgr is a work in progress, and as such, things change, so you might have to "go with the flow" if *xcompmgr* works differently by the time you read this. As we go to press, at least one new version is already available that gets its configuration settings from a *~/.xcompmgrrc* file instead of the command line.

Give Your Desktop X-Ray Vision

You don't need X-ray vision to see through the windows of your home, and now you don't need it to see through the windows on your monitor.

This hack won't let you see through anyone's clothes, but it will make your applications translucent so that anything behind the applications shows through, as if you have X-ray vision. You simply issue a command, and then click a window. Poof!—the window suddenly becomes as translucent as you want.

If you want to use this hack you need to have a recent version of the Xorg X Window System, and you need to install *xcompmgr*, as covered in "Add Depth to Your Desktop" [Hack #33]. If you can't get *xcompmgr* to work, you won't be able to get this hack to work, because this hack needs to have *xcompmgr* running in the background.

Once *xcompmgr* is working and running in the background, you need the *transset* program. Once again, this is an experimental program, so you probably won't find it in the regular package repositories for your Linux distribution. You might find that an RPM package for *xcompmgr* includes *transset*, or you might have to find a separate *transset* package. If all else fails, you can always download the program and compile it yourself. Here's how (no password is required, so just press Enter when prompted for a password):

```
# cvs -d :pserver:anoncvs@cvs.freedesktop.org:/cvs/xorg login
CVS password: (press Enter)
# cvs -d :pserver:anoncvs@pdx.freedesktop.org:/cvs/xapps co transset
# cd transset
# make
# chmod +x transset
# cp transset /usr/bin
```

Let's assume you have a window manager or desktop environment running, and you have already launched *xcompmgr* (see the previous hack for a sample *xcompmgr* command). Now, all you have to do is issue the transset command, followed by the degree of opacity you want. For example, open an X terminal and type this command:

```
# transset 0.7
got arg 0.7
d is 0.7
```

You should see the cursor change to a crosshair (or something like one). Click the window you want to make translucent. It is probably best to click the window's titlebar. Now you should be able to see the wallpaper or even other windows behind the window you just clicked. See Figure 4-4 for an example of xterm with a degree of transparency. In case you're not aware of this fact, the *xterm* program has no built-in capability to emulate transparency, so you cannot get this affect with an *xterm* without using *transset*.

Something such as the following text should also appear in the X terminal where you typed the transset command:

```
opacity 0xb3333332
Set Property to 0.7
```

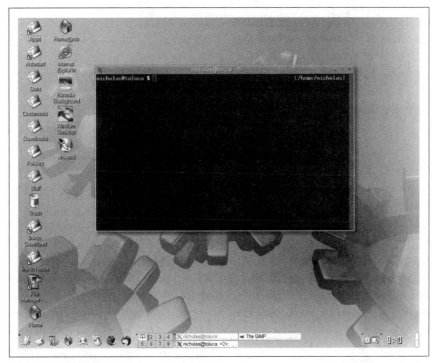

Figure 4-4. An xterm with true transparency

If you want a real thrill (and your window manager has the ability to display the contents of windows while moving, instead of just outlines), move the see-through window around. This is not "fake" translucency, where the window manager has to wait until you have finished repositioning the window for it to redraw the background through the window. It changes in real time, even as you move windows over the wallpaper or other windows.

The *transset* program is at an even more experimental stage than the *xcompmgr* program on which it relies. No fancy features are available for making your window manager know which windows should be transparent, and to what degree. If you want transparent windows, you're going to have to go through the process of making them transparent manually every time you start your desktop.

No doubt this will be made user-friendly in the future. In the meantime, it's not all that difficult to streamline the process of making windows transparent. You can add a menu entry or create an icon on the desktop that executes the **transset 0.7** command. When you want to make a window transparent, just click the icon (or select the menu entry) and then click the target window.

KDE Desktop
Hacks #35–44

The desktop is central to a modern Linux desktop. Traditionally, Linux relied heavily on the command line, and a strong knowledge of the vast portfolio of Linux commands and how they could be strewn together was essential for surviving the Linux way of life. In the last few years, this way of life has changed substantially, and Linux users are becoming less and less reliant on the command line. The command line is still there, but if you want to control and administer your computer in an entirely graphical way with your desktop, you can.

This chapter focuses on the KDE desktop environment. In it you'll find information on how to use the protocol handlers in Konqueror to access remote filesystems, patch KDE with experimental code to improve its appearance and functionality, use desktop enhancements from the *superkaramba* project, and lock down KDE to provide a controlled environment for users.

One point to remember when using the desktop is that it typically provides an interface to the command-line magic that underlies it. The benefit of this is that many of the features and configurations you use in your desktop environment are available in the command line. For example, "Script Hacks with DCOP" **[Hack #39]** shows you how to control your KDE environment from the command line.

The hacks included in this chapter give you insight into the variety of ways you can step in and below the desktop GUI layer to make it behave how you want. The desktop is not just a pretty face.

Make Konqueror a Window
#35 into Remote Spaces

Use the KDE Konqueror file manager to access remote files as easily as local
ones.

It is fairly common knowledge that KDE Konqueror functions as both a file
manager and a browser. What you might not realize is that Konqueror can
load modules that allow it to support many other protocols. Konqueror even
handles the mundane protocols common to most browsers in superior ways.

Konquer Your Remote FTP Sites Using FTP and SFTP

Take FTP, for example. Most browsers support FTP access. Assuming you
have an FTP account on a server, try these steps with Konqueror to see how
it handles FTP access (don't bother trying this with a web browser, such as
Firefox, because it won't work):

1. Open a Konqueror window pointing to your home directory.

2. Maximize the window (optional, but helpful).

3. Press Ctrl-Shift-L to split the window.

4. Click the window pane on the right side to make it the active one.

5. In Konqueror's Location field, enter the URL to the FTP site where you
   have an account (for example, *ftp://<yourserver>*, or if you prefer secure
   FTP [SFTP, which is FTP over Secure SHell, or SSH], use the URL *sftp://
   <yourserver>*).

6. Enter your username and password when prompted for them.

You should see two window panes: the one on the left contains your home
files and directories, and the one on the right contains the files and directories at the remote SFTP server for which you have a valid account. You can
drag files from one pane to the other to move or copy them. You can open
documents on the SFTP site, edit them, and then save your changes. Most of
the operations work just as though both panes point to directories on your
local machine.

You can load a document from the remote server into virtually any program
and modify that document. It doesn't matter if the program you use to modify the document is able to save documents to remote servers. When you
save your changes and exit the program, Konqueror still has a copy of the
modified document in a temporary file. A dialog box will appear asking you
if you want to update the file on the remote server to reflect the changes you
made.

There are some limitations to what you can do between local and remote directories, of course. You can't create symbolic links between the two locations, and some of the built-in Konqueror viewers work only on local files. For example, you can view the contents of a compressed tar archive in the local Konqueror window pane, as if the contents were in folders. If you click a compressed tar archive on the FTP site, you have to open the contents with the Ark application.

> It is not necessary to split the window into two panes if that is not how you prefer to work. In this example, you could open two Konqueror windows, point one to your home directory and the other to the SFTP server, and get the same capabilities.

FISH with Konqueror

FISH works in basically the same way as SFTP in that it uses SSH to exchange information. Simply enter the URL *fish://<yourserver>* and enter a valid username and password for the server, and Konqueror will present you with access to the files almost as if they were local. (The same limitations apply as with SFTP—you cannot navigate compressed archives directly, etc.)

As with SFTP, you can open files, edit them, and save your changes, and Konqueror will ask you if you want to update the remote files.

Browse via LAN Connections with Konqueror

If you enter smb:/ (SMB is the protocol Microsoft Windows uses to share files) in Konqueror's Location field, it will show you the Windows workgroups that are available on your network. When you enter a workgroup folder you should see the servers that belong to the workgroup. From here you can browse to server shares and access remote files. Once again, you can treat the folders and files as if they are stored locally. If you open a file with a word processor, for example, and then you change the contents, save the file, and exit, Konqueror will ask you if you want to save the changes to the remote location. This works when the remote system is a Samba server, a Windows server, or even a Windows desktop that is sharing files.

Open a Konqueror window and type **rlan:/<yourserver>** in the Location field. You should see a number of network access methods, including FISH, FTP, NFS, SMB, and HTTP. This simplifies the various ways to access the remote server. Click the *FISH* folder, and it should ask you for your username and password (unless you've been accessing the site recently and it remembers you are still logged in).

For a more entertaining experience, put an audio CD into your CD-ROM drive and type **audiocd:/** in the Location field. You should see all the tracks represented as individual WAV files. Depending on the plug-ins you have installed, you might also see folders for MP3 and Ogg Vorbis sound files. If you want to convert the songs on the CD to Ogg Vorbis format, simply open the Ogg Vorbis folder, drag tracks from the Ogg Vorbis folder to another folder on your disk, and choose Copy from the pop-up menu. Konqueror will perform the conversion automatically as it copies the files.

> Open the KDE Control Center and click Sound & Multimedia → Audio CDs to fine-tune the settings for your audio CD, how KDE formats the filenames for song tracks, and settings for the available sound formats, such as MP3 and Ogg Vorbis.

Want to locate every filename or directory name on your system that contains the string "Vorbis"? Type **locate:Vorbis** in the Location field and Konqueror will present you with everything it finds.

You can even view and manage your printers from within Konqueror. Type **print:/** in the Location field to get to icons that will let you view your printers and print jobs, manage your printers, and more.

You can find a complete list of the protocols Konqueror supports on your machine by starting the KDE help system and clicking Kioslaves. Then click the protocol for more information. (The list of available protocols Konqueror supports varies according to how your distribution compiles KDE.)

HACK #36   Konquer Remote Systems Without Passwords

Use some of Konqueror's powerful protocol connections without being bothered by password requests.

You might already be familiar with the *KDE wallet system*. The KDE wallet saves usernames and passwords for you so that you don't have to enter them each time you access a site that requires them. You can use the wallet to store your usernames and passwords for use with the various protocols available with Konqueror, including FISH, SFTP, etc. **[Hack #35]**, but you still have to type a password to use the wallet each time.

Here's a better way to save yourself the time involved in typing passwords to access remote sites with the SSH protocols that Konqueror uses (such as FISH and SFTP).

SSH normally requires a username and password. But SSH also supports a public and private key mechanism that lets you bypass the password without opening a security hole. Here is how the two keys are related. Your private key gives you access to any remote accounts that already have your matching public key. But the reverse is not true. Remote users with a copy of your public key cannot use the public key to access your account on your local machine.

Suppose you have an account under the username daggett. Here's how to create an SSH key that can be used to authenticate your user account on other systems:

```
$ ssh-keygen -t rsa
Generating public/private rsa key pair.
Enter file in which to save the key (/home/daggett/.ssh/id_rsa):
Enter passphrase (empty for no passphrase):
Enter same passphrase again:
Your identification has been saved in /home/daggett/.ssh/id_rsa.
Your public key has been saved in /home/daggett/.ssh/id_rsa.pub.
The key fingerprint is:
cd:f5:43:e5:62:16:53:1a:8c:8c:13:3b:5c:28:cc:5b daggett@<yourlocalhost>
```

Press Enter when prompted for information on where to save the key. You'll be asked for a passphrase for the account. Just press Enter all the way through the next series of prompts. This process creates both a private key and a public key. The SSH key is saved to the *.ssh* directory in the example user daggett's home directory.

 You do *not* want to specify a passphrase. Doing so defeats the purpose of this portion of the hack—that is, to get to the remote home directory without having to type in anything to authenticate your user. If you do specify a passphrase in this process, you will be required to enter that passphrase each time you open a Konqueror file manager view of your remote home directory. The fact that you have the private key on your machine is what is truly providing security for the authentication.

Now you need to copy the public key to the server host. The following command makes an SSH connection to the remote server norbert, creates a *.ssh* directory in your user's home directory, and sets read-only permissions on it:

```
$ ssh norbert "mkdir .ssh; chmod 0700 .ssh"
Password:
```

Type in the password for the user account you are connecting with and press Enter. Then copy your public key to the newly created *.ssh* directory and name it *authorized_keys2* with this command:

```
$ scp .ssh/id_rsa.pub norbert:.ssh/authorized_keys2
Password:
```

Once again, type in the password for the user account on the remote system and press Enter.

From this point forward, you should be able to enter your equivalent of the location *sftp://daggett@norbert* in Konqueror, and you should be taken immediately to your home directory on the server without having to enter a password. Similarly, you should be able to enter the equivalent of the FISH protocol, such as *fish://daggett@norbert*, which will take you to your home directory on norbert without asking for a password.

Dealing with Split Personalities

Suppose your username on the remote server is different from your username on your local server. Or perhaps you are an administrator and want to set yourself up with instant access to another user's account.

The procedure to follow in both of these scenarios is almost identical because the principle is the same, regardless of the username on the remote server. As long as the user on the remote server has your public key stored in the *~/.ssh/authorized_keys2* file, you can log in to that account without supplying a password.

The only differences in the procedure are that you must supply the different username during parts of the procedure and—most important of all—you must know the password for the account on the server with the username that is different from your username on your workstation. That is what protects the users on the server from enabling you to plant your public key in their home directories so that you'll have free access to their files.

Even if your username on the server is different from your username on your local machine, you must still create a public and private key using the ssh-keygen -t rsa command, and press Enter when prompted for passwords. If you have already created a public and private key and you intend to give yourself access to another account to which you have the proper rights, you can skip that step.

Here's how to deal with the fact that the username on the server is different from your local username. When you create the *.ssh* directory on the remote machine, specify the remote username in combination with the server name, separated by the @ symbol. Assume your username on the server is oxnard. This is the command to create the directory for oxnard on norbert:

```
$ ssh oxnard@norbert "mkdir .ssh; chmod 0700 .ssh"
Password:
```

Type in the password for the oxnard user account you are connecting with and press Enter. Then copy your public key to the newly created *.ssh* directory and name it *authorized_keys2*. Once again, combine the remote username with the server name, separated by the @ symbol:

```
$ scp .ssh/id_rsa.pub oxnard@norbert:.ssh/authorized_keys2
Password:
```

Now type in the password for the oxnard user account on the remote system and press Enter.

When you want to access the oxnard account using the FISH or SFTP protocol from Konqueror, take the same approach as you did when you used your local username, substituting your remote username. For example, use *sftp:// oxnard@norbert* to use SFTP to connect to your *oxnard* home directory on the remote server without using a password, and use *fish://oxnard@norbert* to use FISH to connect to the remote server without using a password.

Make Remote Konqueror Access a Single-Click Operation

It is possible to create an icon on your desktop to make the entire process a single-click operation. To do this, right-click the desktop and select Create New → File → Link to Application. Give the file a name that suits you. Given the example username and server, an appropriate name might be *Home@Norbert*. Click the icon next to the of the name field to choose an icon image that suits you.

Then click the Application tab, and enter the following into the Command field (substituting your name and your server name, of course):

```
kfmclient openProfile filemanagement sftp://daggett@norbert
```

From now on, whenever you want to manage your home directory files on the server, just click the icon you just created. A Konqueror file manager window should pop up with the remote files ready to be accessed and managed.

kfmclient is actually the program you know as Konqueror. In this case, you are specifying that the profile it should use is the one for file management, after which you supply the starting location. You could just as easily issue a command, such as kfmclient openProfile webbrowser http://www.oreilly.com, and that would open the web browser form of Konqueror and load the location *http://www.oreilly.com.*

Ai Karamba! Flashy KDE Gadgets!

HACK #37

Spiff up your KDE desktop with various information panels and interactive gadgets.

This tip involves two programs, *karamba* and *superkaramba*. The author of the original program, *karamba*, is Hans Karlsson (*karlsson.h@home.se*). The *karamba* project started out as a clone of a Windows program called Samurize, which displayed system information, such as system temperature, network traffic, CPU activity, etc., in attractive ways. The primary function of *karamba* was to display similar information on your KDE desktop, and it did it with such flair and style that it attracted a huge number of hackers to create more inventive and attractive ways of displaying various types of information, such as local weather data and forecasts.

But *karamba* had one notable limitation. The gadgets were pretty, but not terribly interactive. You could configure them and display them, but that was all.

Adam Geitgey (*adam@rootnode.org*), with a little help from his friends, took *karamba* to new heights by creating *superkaramba*. This handy utility introduced the ability to interact with the gadgets, combining the artistic appeal of the *karamba* gadgets with live action. One of the first things hackers did with *superkaramba* was to create much more attractive alternatives to the KDE panel, task switcher, and launcher. Indeed, some *superkaramba* supercharged desktops are so customized that it hardly looks like you're running KDE at all.

Figure 5-1 shows an example of a *superkaramba*-transformed desktop. It replaces the panel with a custom blue kicker (application launcher) and various statistics about your machine (CPU usage, etc.). A separate *superkaramba* applet replaces the taskbar with a subtler version at the top of the screen. In addition, there is a chrome clock and an animated weather applet. Click the cloud or a forecast day to see it will whirl around into a summary of weather for that day.

It is generally easy to find prepackaged versions of *superkaramba* for most Linux distributions. Debian and Gentoo Linux include *superkaramba* as a standard package you can download. You might get the best results by searching the Internet yourself, but you can find a Red Hat 9 *superkaramba* RPM at *http://www.kde-look.org/content/show.php?content=7774*. This package reportedly works for Mandrake, too. You can find a number of SUSE RPMs for *superkaramba* at *http://linux01.gwdg.de/~pbleser/rpm-navigation. php?cat=/Utilities/superkaramba*.

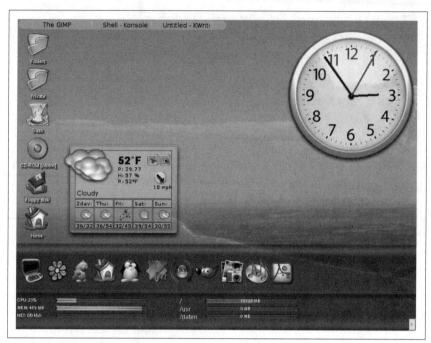

Figure 5-1. KDE with superkaramba

Not all the prepackaged versions are up-to-date, and many of the nicest gadgets require the latest version. If you can't resist some of the latest and greatest gadgets, download the latest *superkaramba* source code from *http://netdragon.sourceforge.net/* and compile it yourself. (You can also find some of the latest gadgets at this site.) Sooner or later, you'll also find the latest RPMs at the SourceForge.net site.

> The *superkaramba* program depends heavily on the Python language (it won't work without Python installed). Many of the gadgets for *superkaramba* employ features available only if you have the Python extensions for KDE and Qt installed, too. I highly recommend that you make sure you have these extensions installed in addition to *superkaramba* itself. They are generally called PyQt and PyKDE, but your distribution might package them under very different names.

If you want to get an idea of the diversity of *karamba* and *superkaramba*, browse the site at *http://www.kde-look.org/index.php?xcontentmode=38*, where you will find pages upon pages of available system monitors, clocks, launch bars, and countless other gadgets. *superkaramba* has been maturing over the years. Many new gadgets now include a configuration menu for customizing the gadget, whereas older gadgets still force you to edit configuration files. I recommend placing your *superkaramba* gadgets in a single location such as *~/gadgets*.

> The one place you should not use as the location for your gadgets is *~/.superkaramba*. This is a special directory that *superkaramba* creates and uses to store settings. If you try to store your gadgets there, *superkaramba* simply will not work.

For this example, download ChromeClock, which you can preview at *http://www. kde-look.org/content/show.php?content=12972*. You can download the file directly from *http://www.kde-look.org/content/download.php?content=12972&id=1*.

Create the *~/gadgets* directory, and then download your gadget (the downloaded file is named *12972-ChromeClock.tar.bz2*) and extract it to *~/gadgets*:

```
$ mkdir ~/gadgets
$ tar jxvf 12972-ChromeClock.tar.bz2 -C ~/gadgets
```

This creates a subdirectory called *~/gadgets/ChromeClock*, which holds the *ChromeClock* files. One or more of the files it creates will have a *.theme* suffix. This is the file you launch with *superkaramba*. If there is more than one theme file, you can try launching each one separately. Each probably represents preconfigured combinations of different features.

Assuming you are currently running KDE, just issue this command to launch this gadget:

```
$ superkaramba ~/gadgets/ChromeClock/ChromeClock.theme
```

A clock should appear on the desktop. (If you don't see it, you might have to switch to an empty desktop!)

Right-click the clock and you should see menu selections to configure the clock, lock it into position, and update the configuration so that it remembers your settings. If you really like the clock once you have it configured to your tastes, you should configure it to start automatically when your desktop loads [Hack #72].

Another way to start a *superkaramba* gadget is to issue the command *superkaramba* with no arguments. This should bring up a screen that looks like the one shown in Figure 5-2.

Click Open... and a KDE file dialog will appear to let you navigate to any directory that contains a *superkaramba* theme.

Now that you've had a taste of *superkaramba*, visit *http://www.kde-look.org/ index.php?xcontentmode=38*, browse through the selections, and try some of the more versatile and interactive gadgets.

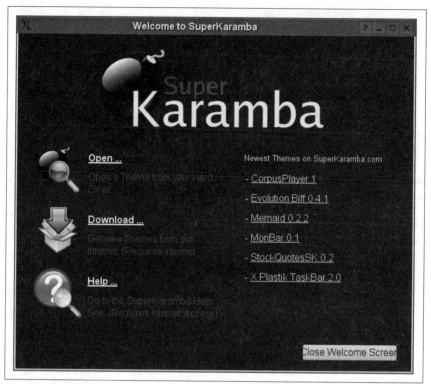

Figure 5-2. SuperKaramba program

Be careful not to download a gadget that requires a later version of *superkaramba* than the version you have installed, unless you are prepared to compile and install the latest version of *superkaramba* itself.

HACK #38   Start Applications in Weird and Wonderful Ways

Start your applications in customized ways to make your programs run exactly how you want them to.

With modern desktop environments, starting applications is a straightforward concept—you either click an application icon or you type in the name of a program. Simple. But if you look under the hood of this simplicity, you'll find a number of tricks and techniques for starting applications in clever and interesting ways. This hack shows you how to make an application start on a particular virtual desktop, load into a particular mode, always appear on top of other applications, or load in full-screen mode.

Starting Programs in KDE

An interesting facility in KDE is a tool called *kstart*. This simple command-line program is used to customize how programs start and display on your screen. *kstart* provides several options that enable you to choose which virtual desktop it appears on, if it starts as a maximized/minimized window, if it has focus and other uses.

As *kstart* is a command-line tool, you can experiment with it from a command-line terminal, such as a konsole, *xterm*, or gnome terminal. To use *kstart*, specify the options that determine how the application is started, and then specify the program name.

To begin with, you can experiment with how you can start applications on different virtual desktops. As an example, if you wanted to start Konqueror on virtual desktop 2, you could use this:

```
foo@bar:~$ kstart --desktop 2 konqueror
```

This command uses the --desktop option in *kstart* with the parameter 2 to specify the virtual desktop on which to start the application. To make Konqueror start on all the virtual desktops (particularly useful for applications that should be visible in all parts of the desktop), use the –alldesktops option:

```
foo@bar:~$ kstart --alldesktops konqueror
```

To extend this functionality a little further, combine the --alldesktops option and the --ontop option to ensure that a specific application always remains visible on every desktop. This is handy for media players such as noatun when you want to control the player at all times:

```
foo@bar:~$ kstart --alldesktops --ontop noatun
```

Another useful modification is to not display the application on the taskbar (the part of the panel that shows which programs are running). You can use the --skiptaskbar option to give the effect of a floating application that is always on top:

```
foo@bar:~$ kstart --alldesktops --ontop --skiptaskbar noatun
```

A final useful switch is the --fullscreen option. This is particularly handy when running an application that should appear like a kiosk [Hack #43]. The benefit of this mode is that you can restrict users from using other applications in kiosk mode. You can run Konqueror in full-screen mode so that it gives you a full-screen kiosk web browser:

```
foo@bar:~$ kstart --fullscreen konqueror
```

Adding Application Options

In addition to the facilities available in *kstart*, you can also combine the options and switches from the program you are running. Each Linux program has accessible options similar to the ones you used in *kstart*, and you can view them in the application manpage. Many programs also have a --help option that will list the different options available:

```
foo@bar:~$ kstart --help
```

As an example of combining these options, you can load Konqueror full screen in web-browsing mode to look at the O'Reilly web site:

```
foo@bar:~$ kstart --fullscreen konqueror --profile webbrowsing http://www.
oreilly.com/
```

In this example you use the --profile option in Konqueror to set the mode of the application to webbrowsing. You also specify the URL of the O'Reilly web site as the site to be loaded into Konqueror when the application starts. It is important to note that the *kstart* options (--fullscreen) are to the right of the *kstart* command and the Konqueror options (--profile webbrowsing *http://www.oreilly.com/*) are to the right of the konqueror command.

Starting Programs Conveniently

Although you have been typing your *kstart* commands into a terminal, you can actually use a desktop icon to run the commands. To do this, add a shortcut by right-clicking the desktop and selecting New Shortcut. In the command box, add the full *kstart* command. Click OK and your shortcut is complete.

Another useful feature in KDE is that you can automatically start applications when the desktop loads. This feature is useful if you use the same programs day in day out and you want them started whenever you load the desktop. If you want to load KMail, Mozilla, the Gimp, Bluefish, and Kopete when you start KDE, this feature saves you from having to click all the program icons each time the environment starts and move the application windows to your preferred desktops.

To do this, use the *Autostart* directory in *~/.kde*. You can access the directory in Konqueror and create normal application shortcut icons inside it by dragging the programs to run into the directory. If you combine the features of *kstart* with the *Autostart* directory, you can enable your desktop to start up exactly how you want it to with the right applications running in the right part of the desktop.

Script Hacks with DCOP

Use the KDE scripting tool of choice to tweak your desktop for maximum flexibility.

For most users, interaction with the desktop is a simple process that is limited to clicking buttons and typing things in from the keyboard. Although fine for most cases, this normal form of interaction limits what you can accomplish with an application, because you are restricted to the program elements that the GUI has been designed to show, and because complex or repetitive tasks require the user to input every command himself. Many programs can be augmented with a scripting tool to overcome traditional input methods.

Within the KDE feature set is a special tool called the Desktop COmmunications Protocol (DCOP). This facility can access a number of so-called "hooks" in KDE applications that can allow programs to communicate with other applications either remotely, with a scripting language, or from the command line. DCOP essentially provides a means for you to hook together graphical programs in the fine tradition that Unix and Linux command tools can be connected with pipes.

DCOP is a tool that typically resides in the developer's toolbox, out of sight from most users. But DCOP is also a tool that you can use in everyday desktop practice. Although hackers are animals that enjoy wallowing in reams of code, a little GUI application is available, which nonhackers can use as an interface to DCOP to facilitate the process of writing DCOP programs. It is called KDCOP and you can start it by typing **kdcop** into a console or in the Run application dialog box (Alt-F2).

DCOP and Processes

Each KDE application that you are running on the system has a number of DCOP "interfaces" that provide methods for learning information about the application and adjusting how it works. When you run KDCOP, each interface is displayed and you can play with them inside the program. For example, run KDCOP and then load a Konqueror browser. You will see Konqueror added to the list of applications in the KDCOP window. You should also see a number to the right of the entry, such as konqueror-1377. This number relates to the process number of the application. This number is added, because often more than one process is running for each program at any one time. If you click the Konqueror entry you are presented with a list of categories that contain DCOP interfaces.

To test an interface, look in the category called KonquerorIface and double-click the entry DCOPRef createNewWindow(QString url), as shown in Figure 5-3.

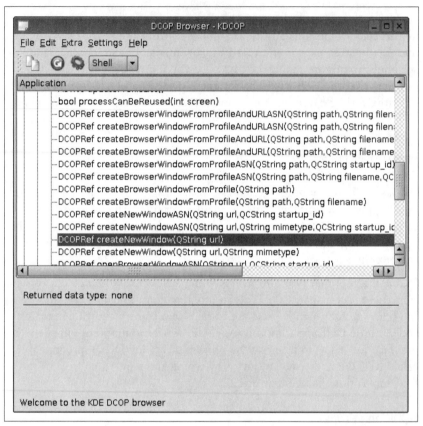

Figure 5-3. Browsing DCOP interfaces with KDCOP

Not surprisingly, this string creates a new window. The QString url part in brackets means you can pass the interface a web address or file location and the interface will display that resource in the window. When you double-click the interface, you are prompted for this value and then Konqueror opens a new window with the requested URL.

You can tie DCOP functionality into a number of places. For example, you can access a similar DCOP interface from the command-line shell with:

```
foo@bar:~$ dcop konqueror-1377 KonquerorIface openBrowserWindow http://www.
oreilly.com/
```

Notice how you need to specify the process number of the application within the application name (your process number might be different from mine). This is so you can probe the correct Konqueror process and open a new browser window.

Write a DCOP Shell Script

The true power of DCOP comes into its own when you start writing shell scripts. As an example, imagine that numerous applications are in use across all your virtual desktops. Things are getting a little messy on these desktops and you want to tidy up. You can solve this problem by writing a little script that switches to each desktop and runs the cascadeDesktop interface, which organizes the windows in a cascaded order.

To create this script, create a new file called *cascade.sh* and add the following code:

```
#!/bin/bash
for i in seq 1 5:
do
    dcop kwin KWinInterface setCurrentDesktop $i
    dcop kwin KWinInterface cascadeDesktop
done
```

This code creates a bash for loop that loops four times (for the number of desktops). Inside the loop, it sets the current desktop to that of the loop number, and then it issues the cascadeDesktop interface command.

To run the script, you need to turn on the execute bit on the file:

```
foo@bar:~$ chmod a+x cascade.sh
```

Then you can run the script with:

```
foo@bar:~$ ./cascade.sh
```

As another example, say you want to receive an email when your friend Nick logs on to your instant messenger network. This could be particularly useful if you leave Kopete (the KDE instant messenger) running at home and you want to know when someone is online while you are at work. You can accomplish this with the following script:

```
#!/bin/bash

nick=$1;
echo Waiting for $nick
while ((`dcop kopete KopeteIface reachableContacts | grep -c $nick` == 0))
do
sleep 10
done
echo Sending message
mail -s "$nick is online" you@foo.com
```

Save this script to a file such as *immail.sh* and run it, like so:

```
foo@bar:~$  ./immail.sh bob
```

This script works by first making the command-line argument available as the $nick variable. After this, a while loop is started that uses grep to search for the chosen *nick* in $nick within the output of the reachableContacts interface in KopeteIface. Nick is not online, so the process will just sleep for 10 seconds. When Nick does come online, an email is sent to *you@foo.com* using the mail command.

HACK #40 Create Your Own KDE Right-Click Menu Actions

Create custom menu actions for when you right-click a file, directory, or group of files and/or directories.

When you use KDE, do you ever find yourself having to click too many times to do a simple operation, or resort to opening up a terminal to do a task at the command line that should have been a no-brainer feature of KDE? Now you can add your own features to KDE context menus. Right-click a file and click Action → Make Executable to make the file executable. Right-click an empty space in a folder and click Action → Create a new Bash Script to open an editor and fill in the first line. This is a very cool hack because you can create a context menu to launch scripts or programs written in any language. It is especially powerful if you learn DCOP scripting [Hack #39]. That way you can use the context menu selection to control KDE programs.

Remember all the times you wrote a dandy new bash script and created an icon to launch it, but when you clicked it, it didn't run? Instead, it popped up in an editor, because you forgot to make the script executable. With this hack, you can create a script to make your file executable by right-clicking its icon and selecting Actions → Make file executable (see Figure 5-4). It takes much less time than traditional methods.

All you have to do to create the context menu that will make a file executable is create a text file formatted very much like an application link, and then drop it in a special directory. We'll start by creating a file called *make_executable.desktop*. Start up your favorite editor, and enter the following text:

```
[Desktop Entry]
Encoding=UTF-8
ServiceTypes=application/x-shellscript
Actions=MakeExe
```

```
[Desktop Action MakeExe]
Name=Make file executable
Exec=chmod +x %f
Icon=kfm
```

Save your work. The action this file takes is defined by the entry Exec=chmod +x %f. KDE substitutes the name of the selected file for %f. If you want to make this feature available to everyone who uses KDE on this computer, place the file here:

```
# cp make_executable.desktop <path to kde>/share/apps/konqueror/servicemenus
```

Depending on your Linux distribution, the path might not be tied to your KDE directory. It might be */usr/share/apps/konqueror/servicemenus*.

If you simply want to make this feature available to yourself, place the file here (assuming your KDE settings are kept in *~/.kde*; your distribution might use *~/.kde3.3* or something similar):

```
$ cp make_executable.desktop ~/.kde/share/apps/konqueror/servicemenus
```

> The *ServiceTypes* field in the file is set to the mime-type *application/x-shellscript*, which means the menu option will be available only when you right-click a shell script file.

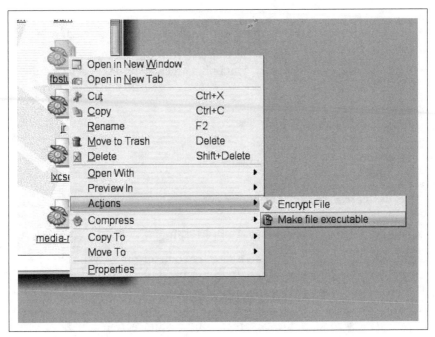

Figure 5-4. Context-sensitive Actions menu

Symbols Available for Menu Actions

Konqueror passes the names of selected URLs, selected files, and other selected elements to your custom menu actions through the use of symbols. Symbols exist for single files, multiple files, single URLs, and more. The right-click action that allows you to change a file to be executable works, because it substitutes the name of the selected file for the symbol %f. Here are some other symbols available to you, and how they work.

%f

A single filename, even if you select multiple files. In general, you use this only when you intend to select a single file. In some cases, you can use this to select several files for use by a program that knows how to launch a separate instance for each filename.

%F

Multiple selected files. Use this for programs that can act upon several files at once.

%u

A single URL.

%U

Multiple URLs.

%d

The single directory that contains the selected file represented by %f.

%D

A list of the same directory containing an entry for every selected file in that directory (%F).

%n

A filename without a path.

%N

Multiple filenames without paths.

%k

A file represented as a URI.

Create an Action to Jump-Start Script Writing

Here's another hack to give you a taste of some of the power behind KDE custom menus. This time, you will exploit three powerful features of KDE. The first is the ability to create submenus. You will create a general menu selection that lets you choose between two actions that appear as sub-menus. The second is the fact that your custom action can be a script instead of a simple command, such as the chmod +x command we used in the previous example. Finally, the script will exploit the ability to use DCOP to manipulate KDE applications [Hack #39].

To get started, create the file */usr/local/bin/CreateBashScript.desktop*. Use your favorite editor to put the following contents into that file:

```
[Desktop Entry]
ServiceTypes=inode/directory
Actions=CreateBashScript;CreatePythonScript
X-KDE-Submenu=Create Script

[Desktop Action CreateBashScript]
Name=Create a bash script
Icon=kfm
Exec=/usr/local/bin/writeBashScript
[Desktop Action CreatePythonScript]
Name=Create a Python script
Icon=kfm
Exec=/usr/local/bin/writePythonScript
```

In this case, the ServiceTypes definition of inode/directory tells KDE that the submenu entry Create Script will appear under the Action menu selection only if you are pointing to a folder or to an empty area within the Konqueror file manager (which represents the currently open folder). When you select this action, it will give you the choice of creating a bash or Python script. If you choose Action → Create Script → Create a bash script, it will launch the shell script */usr/local/bin/writeBashScript*. Use your favorite editor with *sudo* (or log in as root) to create the *writeBashScript* file, with the following contents:

```
#!/bin/bash

cd ~/bin
kwrite &
sleep 2
kwid=`dcop | grep kwrite | sort | tail -n 1`
echo $kwid
dcop $kwid EditInterface#1 insertText 0 0 '#!/bin/bash'
dcop $kwid EditInterface#1 insertLine 1 ''
dcop $kwid EditInterface#1 insertLine 2 ''
dcop $kwid ViewCursorInterface#1-1 setCursorPosition 2 0
```

Here's how it works. First, it changes to the user's directory where the user keeps his personal *~/bin* scripts. This is totally arbitrary, and it assumes you want to place all your personal shell scripts in this directory. Replace this directory with whatever directory you prefer (and one to which you have read, write, and execute access). Then it launches *kwrite* followed by an ampersand to let it run in the background while the *writeBashScript* shell script finishes. Again, the use of *kwrite* is arbitrary, but it is a good example of how to use DCOP to automate actions, because it is a KDE editor with DCOP capabilities. Then the script sleeps for 2 seconds (you can set this to a higher number if your system is always slow and busy) to make sure *kwrite* is running before it starts issuing DCOP commands to it.

The next line is a bit tricky. Each time you launch an instance of *kwrite*, it gets a DCOP listing with a number attached to it. You want to address the most recently launched copy of *kwrite*, so the script runs *dcop* to list all DCOP applications, finds all the applications that match "kwrite," sorts the list, and picks the last entry. That entry's name is assigned to the variable $kwid. This works even if this is the first instance of *kwrite* you have launched.

Then the script issues a few DCOP instructions. It automatically enters the first line of a typical bash script, *#!/bin/bash*, after which it enters two more blank lines and moves the cursor to the last blank line.

Now create the bash script that gets you started writing a Python script. The only difference between */usr/local/bin/writeBashScript* and */usr/local/bin/writePythonScript* is that you will insert the first line as the full path to your Python interpreter instead of #!/bin/bash. That line of code should look like this:

```
dcop $kwid EditInterface#1 insertText 0 0 '#!/usr/bin/python'
```

Obviously, there's no limit to the kinds of templates you can create for various scripting languages.

These examples barely scratch the surface of what you can do. You can create a single menu entry that lets you select a half dozen directories, tar and compress them, and burn them to a multisession CD, all in one fell swoop. And you have the flexibility to do this as a bash script, as a Python script, or in any method you prefer. You'll be surprised at how much more you rely on the GUI interface of KDE once you have customized menu features for your personal convenience.

Make KDE Even Easier to Use

HACK #41   Beautify and enhance the usability of KDE by patching it with experiment code.

This is actually a combination of code hacks that improve KDE in several ways. Some of the changes are purely cosmetic, but some enhance the usability of KDE, especially the sidebar in the Konqueror file manager and web browser. This collection of hacks makes the practically indecipherable design of the sidebar thoroughly intuitive. It also makes selecting files a more pleasant experience and spruces up a few parts of the KDE interface.

André Moreira Magalhães (*andrunko@yahoo.com.br*), a 24-year-old computer science graduate from Brazil, has provided a pack of incredibly cool KDE hacks via *http://www.kde-look.org* for KDE 3.3.1. Some of André's patches are modified and ported from hacks written by Aviv Bergman (*aviv_brg@yahoo.com*).

As I write this, KDE 3.3.2, a bug-fix release to KDE 3.3.1, is being launched. I have downloaded and applied the patches to the KDE 3.3.2 source code, and they apply cleanly (though occasionally you might receive a message that the patch was offset by a few lines, which is a warning you can usually ignore). So far, the patches seem to work fine with KDE 3.3.2, although I have not had the time to give KDE 3.3.2 a thorough workout. It is possible, and even likely, that an updated patch set for KDE 3.3.2 will be available on *http://www.kde-look.org* by the time you read this.

KDE 3.4 is due to be available by mid-March 2005, and that release might incorporate some of the hacks documented here. If not, keep an eye on *http://www.kde-look.org* for new patches for these features.

Figure 5-5 shows what Konqueror looks like before the enhancements, and Figure 5-6 gives you an idea of most of the changes these hacks will make to KDE 3.3.1 Konqueror.

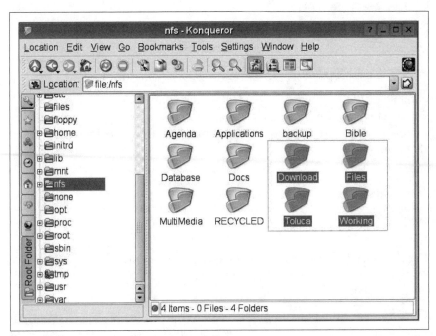

Figure 5-5. Konqueror without enhancements

I assume you already compiled and installed KDE 3.3.1. If you still have the source code on your hard drive, this will make things easier. If not, get the source code for the following portions of KDE, and unpack it where you will

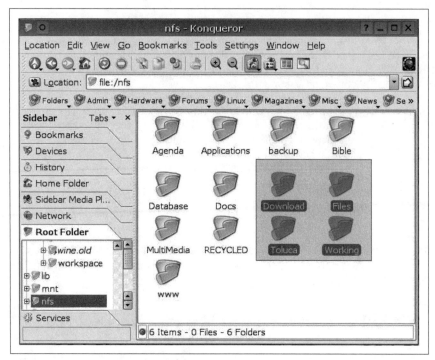

Figure 5-6. Konqueror with enhancements

compile it. For this example, I am assuming you will work in the */usr/local/ src* directory. You need to have the source code installed for the following packages, which are listed in the order in which you will compile and install them:

- *Qt 3.3.3*
- *kdelibs 3.3.1*
- *kdebase 3.3.1*
- *kdeartwork 3.3.1*

For more detailed instructions on how to build and install all of KDE 3.3.1, see *http://www.kde.org/info/3.3.1.php* and/or "Run KDE on the Bleeding Edge" **[Hack #44]**.

Once you have the preceding source code ready, download the hacks from *http://www.kde-look.org/content/show.php?content=16962*. You want to download the *16962-patches-1.0.0.tgz* file.

Keep in mind that things change quickly. From the time I wrote this hack to the time I made the first set of revisions (just weeks later), the URL stayed the same, but the file I download changed from *16962-patches-0.5.5.tgz* to *16962-patches-1.0.0.tgz*. The URLs on *www.kde-look.org* tend to stay the same as versions of a single package change. If URLs printed here don't work, go to the main page, *http://www.kde-look.org*, find the category on the left side of the page (KDE Improvements, in this case), and page through the packages until you find the correct package. Because KDE 3.3.2 was just released at the time of this writing, it is likely that the version of this patch set will change again when it is adjusted for KDE 3.3.2.

André provided a number of downloads to make it easier to patch specific Linux distributions, but this example assumes you will download and apply the hacks to the source code for Qt 3.3.3 and KDE 3.3.1, which works for any Linux distribution with the proper development tools. You need to log in as root, create a patch directory, and unpack this file in the patch directory. For this example:

```
$ su -
Password:
# mkdir /patches-1
# mv 16962-patches-0.5.5.tgz /patches-1
# cd /patches-1
# tar zxvf 16962-patches-0.5.5.tgz
Changelog
README
TODO
kdeartwork-3.3.1.diff
kdebase-3.3.1.diff
kdelibs-3.3.1.diff
qt-x11-free-3.3.3.dif
```

As noted earlier, this procedure assumes you have already unpacked the necessary Qt 3.3.3 and KDE 3.3.1 source code in the */usr/local/src* directory. These patches are guaranteed to work only with Qt 3.3.3 and KDE 3.3.1, so apply them to other versions at your own risk.

Here are the commands for patching, compiling, and installing Qt, *kdelibs*, *kdebase*, and *kdeartwork*:

```
# cd /usr/local/src/qt-x11-free-3.3.3
# cat /patches-1/qt-x11-free-3.3.3.diff | patch -p0
# ./configure <your configure preferences>
```

```
# make
# make install
# cd /usr/local/src/kdelibs-3.3.1
# cat /patches-1/kdelibs-3.3.1.diff | patch -p0
# ./configure <your configure preferences>
# make
# make install
# cd /usr/local/src/kdebase-3.3.1
# cat /patches-1/kdebase-3.3.1.diff | patch -p0
# ./configure <your configure preferences>
# make
# make install
# cd /usr/local/src/kdeartwork-3.3.1
# cat /patches-1/kdeartwork-3.3.1.diff | patch -p0
# ./configure <your configure preferences>
# make
# make install
```

These commands assume the names of the directories for your Qt, *kdelibs*, *kdebase*, and *kdeartwork* source are:

- */usr/local/src/qt-x11-free-3.3.3*
- */usr/local/src/kdelibs-3.3.1*
- */usr/local/src/kdebase-3.3.1*
- */usr/local/src/kdeartwork-3.3.1*

The names of the directories in this example, such as *qt-x11-free-3.3.3*, might not match yours, depending on where you get your source code. Just substitute your directory names for the ones in the examples.

Take note of **<your configure preferences>** following every ./configure command. This is where you can specify the destination directory prefix, along with other configuration parameters you find necessary. As for the prefix, some people like to install KDE under the */opt/kde* directory, others like */usr*, and so on. It's up to you, but you should stick with whatever prefix you used when you installed KDE 3.3.1, before making this modification. If you installed it with the prefix */usr*, the command would look like this:

```
# ./configure --prefix=/usr <other preferences>
```

Make sure to run ./configure --help before you actually run ./configure as part of the build process. This command tells you about options that might be important to your installation of KDE 3.3.1.

Provided everything has gone smoothly so far, all but one of the enhancements should automatically be enabled and work. You have to make one more change to enable the fancy new sidebars in addition to the new rubber-banding effect for selecting icons. Use your favorite editor to edit the configuration file *konqsidebartng.rc*. This file is located in the default configuration directory for KDE 3.3.1, and a copy of it is located in a subdirectory of your home directory. Assuming you have installed KDE to */opt/kde*, you want to edit */opt/kde/share/config/konqsidebartng.rc* if you want the changes to affect everyone who uses KDE. If you simply want to change the sidebar for your own use, edit the configuration file in your home directory. Assuming the home KDE configuration directory is *~/.kde*, the file you want to edit is *~/.kde/share/config/konqsidebartng.rc*. The contents of the file should look something like this:

```
HideTabs=false
OpenViews=services.desktop
SavedWidth=241
ShowExtraButtons=true
ShowTabsLeft=true

[filemanagement]
HideTabs=false
OpenViews=root.desktop
SavedWidth=200
ShowExtraButtons=true
ShowHeader=true
ShowTabsLeft=true
SidebarStyle=0
SingleWidgetMode=false

[webbrowsing]
HideTabs=false
SavedWidth=207
ShowExtraButtons=true
ShowHeader=true
ShowTabsLeft=true
SidebarStyle=0
SingleWidgetMode=false
```

Note that the SidebarStyle is set to 0 for both web browsing and file management. The 0 sets the sidebar to the default style, which is what you are trying to replace. To change it to the new hacked style, change 0 to 1. You can change to the new sidebar look for the file manager, web browser, or both:

```
SidebarStyle=1
```

Start up KDE, and enjoy the new sidebar and the new look for selecting icons.

Give Depth to Your KDE Windows

HACK
#42

Create a 3D effect with drop shadows for all open KDE Windows.

You can give your application windows and other on-screen elements (such as menus and dialog boxes) a really nice 3D effect if you add drop shadows to them. The active window seems to pop right out at you, and you don't even need geeky cardboard and plastic glasses for this trick to work.

Although it is also possible to create drop shadows if you use the *xcompmgr* utility with Xorg-X11 6.8.0 or higher instead of XFree86 **[Hack #33]**, *xcompmgr* is still a work in progress. The *xcompmgr* program crashes a lot, and sometimes it takes down the window manager with it.

The only real disadvantage to this hack is that it is most useful on fast machines, especially if you have an accelerated X driver for your video card. But apart from speed and convenience, these patches have the distinct advantage of saving you time restarting after a window manager crash caused by *xcompmgr*.

These instructions assume you are using KDE 3.3.1; you can combine these instructions with the KDE improvements in "Make KDE Even Easier to Use" **[Hack #41]**.

As I write this, KDE 3.3.2, a bug-fix release for KDE, is being launched. The patches described here do not apply cleanly to KDE 3.3.2, although if you are an experienced programmer, you might be able to fix the areas where the patches fail.

Figure 5-7 shows what the drop shadows look like, as well as proof that this hack and the previous sidebar and icon hacks work well together. Notice also from Figure 5-7 that you can configure this hack to give inactive windows a smaller drop shadow to make them look like they've receded into the background.

I assume you already compiled and installed KDE 3.3.1. If you still have the source code on your hard drive, this will make things easier. If not, get the source code for the following portions of KDE, and unpack it where you will compile it. For the purposes of this example, I am assuming you will work in the */usr/local/src* directory. You need to have the source code installed for the following packages, which are listed in the order in which you will compile and install them:

- *kdelibs 3.3.1*
- *kdebase 3.3.1*

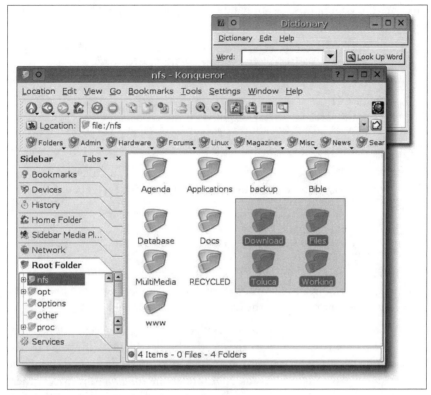

Figure 5-7. KDE windows with drop shadows

For more detailed instructions on how to build and install all of KDE 3.3.1, see *http://www.kde.org/info/3.3.1.php* and/or "Run KDE on the Bleeding Edge" [Hack #44].

Download the hack (*http://www.kde-look.org/content/show.php?content=15781*). The file you want should be named *kwin_shadow-patch.tar.bz2*. Log in as root, and then enter the following commands to put the patches in the */patches-2* directory:

```
# tar jxvf kwin_shadow-patch.tar.bz2
# cd kwin_shadow/kde-3.3.1
# cp kdebase.kwin-kwin_shadow-3.3.1.patch /patches-2
# cp kdelibs.kdefx-kwin_shadow-3.3.1.patch /patches-2
```

Now you are ready to apply these patches to the KDE source code.

If you are working with source code that has already been patched to include the KDE improvements described in this hack, you will see some messages that the patches were applied at various offsets (2 lines, 52 lines, etc.). These messages are harmless.

Here are the commands for applying the drop-shadow patches, then configuring and installing *kdelibs* and *kdebase*:

```
# cd /usr/local/src/kdelibs-3.3.1/kdefx
# cat /patches-2/kdelibs.kdefx-kwin_shadow-3.3.1.patch | patch -p1
# ./configure <your configure preferences>
# make
# make install
# cd /usr/local/src/kdebase-3.3.1/kwin
# cat /patches-2/kdebase.kwin-kwin_shadow-3.3.1.patch | patch -p1
# ./configure <your configure preferences>
# make
# make install
```

These commands assume the names of the directories for your *kdelibs* and *kdebase* source are:

- */usr/local/src/kdelibs-3.3.1*
- */usr/local/src/kdebase-3.3.1*

The names of the directories in this example, such as *kdelibs-3.3.2*, might not match yours, depending on where you get your source code. Just substitute your directory names for the ones in the examples.

Take note of *<your configure preferences>* following every ./configure command. This is where you can specify the destination directory prefix, along with other configuration parameters you find necessary. As for the prefix, some people like to install KDE under the */opt/kde* directory, others like */usr*, and so on. It's up to you, but you should stick with whatever prefix you used when you installed KDE 3.3.1 before making this modification. If you installed it with the prefix */usr*, the command would look like this:

```
# ./configure --prefix=/usr <other preferences>
```

Make sure to run ./configure --help before you actually run ./configure as part of the build process. This command tells you about options that might be important to your installation of KDE 3.3.1.

If all went smoothly, you should be able to start up KDE, but you won't see any drop shadows yet. To set up the drop shadows, open the KDE Control Center and click Appearance & Themes → Window Decorations. Then click the Shadows tab, which should look something like the picture in Figure 5-8. From here, you can choose to draw drop shadows on active or inactive windows, determine how big a drop shadow you want on each, set the opacity (how much you can see through the shadow), and more. Experiment until you get the effect you like best.

This hack has a long list of credits. Karol Szwed started the process, and David Sansome wrote some decoration code, some of which was converted

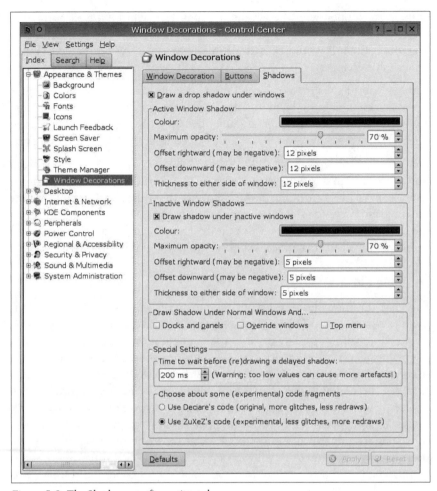

Figure 5-8. The Shadows configuration tab

for use in this patch. Thomas Libking added a lot of work to make the drop shadows for different applications interact. Bernardo Hung pulled it all together, and then Heiko Przybyl (*zuxez@uni.de*) ported the latest version of the code for use with KDE 3.3.0 and KDE 3.3.1.

HACK #43 Lock Down KDE with Kiosk Mode

Control exactly what your users can tinker with, and what they can't change at all.

System administrators typically spend a lot of their time fixing trivial problems for users who have accidentally changed their settings in some way. When an inexperienced user moves a desktop icon into the trash or sets a mime-type to open with the wrong program, he might be unable to reverse his changes. Calls to the system administrator for help are a poor use of everyone's time. It would be better if the user had never been able to make undesirable changes.

Perhaps you just want to set up a Linux desktop for your grandmother but she keeps changing the layout of the application toolbars without meaning to. The new look confuses her so much that she calls you all the time asking for help, or worse, she gives up on Linux or computers. Wouldn't it be great if you could protect your grandmother from herself?

For computers in a public setting such as an Internet café or library, problems such as these turn into more than just timewasters; they can prevent others from using the machine or cause distress for users. Have you heard the common anecdote of the script kiddy who has changed the background wallpaper on all the machines in a library to pornographic photos?

Enter the Kiosk

KDE has traditionally been one of the most configurable desktop environments available, but KDE 3.2.3 pushed the fold and added the Kiosk framework, which allows for any or all of the configuration options to be marked as unchangeable. With Kiosk you can create profiles that are attached to users or groups of users. A profile can define any KDE setting, but usually includes the contents of the desktop, panel, and K Menus, as well as the choice of wallpaper, default fonts, and widget style. You can also specify important system settings, such as the network proxy and file associations. Most importantly, all these options can be set to be unchangeable by the user. This means grandma will never accidentally delete her web browser icon, and a bored teenager can't change the library's computer wallpaper to something that will give grandma a heart attack.

The easiest way to set up a Kiosk profile is to use the Kiosk Admin Tool. Some distributions include this by default or include a package for it. If you need to, you can download the source from its web site at *http://extragear. kde.org/apps/kiosktool.php*.

Start the Kiosk tool (as a normal user; there's no need to run as root) by selecting K-menu → System → Kiosk Admin Tool, or with the kiosktool command, and click Add New Profile. Give this profile a name such as "locked-down" and click OK to save. When prompted, provide your root password to save the new profile. Now click Manage Users and add a user policy to link a user to your new locked-down profile. You can also add Linux user groups to the policy. The Kiosk tool links to */etc/group*, which is where you should manage group membership. To configure a profile, select it in the list and then click Next. The next screen presents numerous modules, each with specific configuration options in it. Ticking an option will lock down its corresponding feature. The settings will be saved when you click Back.

Some of the modules offer graphical setup for their settings. For example, under the Desktop Icons module you can load a temporary desktop to replace your normal one. Switch to a different virtual desktop (Ctrl-F2) if you have windows covering your background. You can add, remove, and move any of the icons on the temporary desktop. When you click Save in Kiosk Admin Tool, the settings for this desktop will be saved and your normal desktop will be loaded again. This makes configuring the setup for your Kiosk profile as easy as configuring your own desktop.

A general breakdown of the types of settings you will find in the most important modules follows:

General
> Contains the settings that control the global properties for all KDE programs and includes the ability to run commands, log out, or move toolbars. Disabling Konsole removes not only its entry from the K Menu, but also the embedded Konsoles in Konqueror and Kate.

Desktop Icons
> Settings to prevent users from moving or deleting desktop icons.

KDE Menu
> Controls which programs are available from the K Menu.

Themeing
> Prevents users from changing the widget style, color, or font settings.

Konqueror
> Stops the user from being able to browse outside his home directory.

Menu Actions
> Turns off standard menu actions such as open, print, paste, settings, etc., from all KDE applications.

File Associations
> Ensures that files can be opened only with the specified programs.

Network Proxy
> Enforces the use of your web proxy. Uses a web proxy to restrict which web sites a user can browse.

Panel
> Used to lock down the panel, prevents users from adding or removing the items you place here, and enables you to prevent panel context menus from working.

The Kiosk framework has been used in large enterprise deployments of KDE. Administrators report that it cuts the time taken up by user support by half, because it reduces the number of small but time-consuming problems users have. If you are considering using Kiosk in a public setting you might want to make yourself familiar with the KDE configuration file format. Browse through */etc/kde-profile* to see the settings made by the Kiosk Admin Tool. Adding [$i] to a configuration option, group of options, or file makes them unchangeable by users.

Kiosk is not a substitute for using Unix filesystem permissions or other security settings. You should also make sure you set X to not be killable with Ctrl-Alt-Backspace, and prevent users from changing to a text console. Finally, make sure the login manager does not allow users to log in to any other desktop environment that has not been locked down.

—Jonathan Riddle

Run KDE on the Bleeding Edge

Explore the underground world of KDE by compiling development code.

Of all the free and open source projects, KDE is possibly the fastest-growing, as evidenced by the large and active community of developers, features that go from the drawing board to computer in record time, and the constant stream of additions being committed to the KDE source code. The rapid pace of development means something new or interesting is always in the development code. This hack shows you how to compile and run all the newest code in advance of official binary releases.

The first thing to be aware of when you are going to play with development software is that most likely it will not work the first time you try it. Some things will work, and some things won't, and you might even lose data and information to crashes, bugs, and other nasties that are part and parcel of development code. In this hack, you will download some code and compile it, but I recommend you back up any important data first.

To get a basic desktop up and running, you need to compile the following KDE CVS modules, in this order:

- *qt-copy* (you need this only if you do not have the latest copy of Qt installed on your system)
- *arts*
- *kdelibs*
- *kdebase*

Details on getting code via CVS are discussed in "Grab the Latest Source Code" [Hack #86]. The anonymous CVSROOT for the KDE code is:

```
:pserver:anonymous@kde.org:/home/kde
```

You need to grab the *qt-copy*, *arts*, *kdelibs*, and *kdebase* modules from CVS. Compile the modules in the order in which they appear in the earlier list.

Compiling the Code

When you have checked out the code for each module, you need to go into each module directory, and issue a number of commands to configure and compile the software. The first command is:

```
foo@bar:~$ make -f Makefile.cvs
```

This performs some special logic on the files in the module so that it is suitable for compiling. You need to use this command only with a CVS copy of KDE and not normal, stable, packaged versions. Next, you need to configure the module. This means running a special script called *configure*, which checks that you have everything needed to compile the code (such as a compiler, linker, etc.) and finalizes the code and makes it ready for compilation. You can normally run *configure* like this:

```
foo@bar:~$ ./configure
```

Although this is fine, *configure* has a few options that can be useful. The first is the --prefix option that can be used to specify where the compiled software will be stored. As an example, to store your CVS version of KDE in */opt/kde*, use the following command:

```
foo@bar:~$ ./configure --prefix=/opt/kde
```

If you do use --prefix on your configure command, you also need to add your prefix to your PATH environment variable so that your system can find the compiled software. You can set your path to PATH=$PATH:/opt/kde/bin, for example. One other note to make is that the *qt-copy* module needs quite a few arguments to be passed to its configure script. You can find information on this in the *INSTALL.qt-copy* file in the module. If you get any errors while configuring a module, you need to fix them before you can continue.

With a module configured, it is time to compile it by running:

```
foo@bar:~$ make
```

Now grab some coffee and eat some flapjacks; your module will take quite a while to compile. When it has finished you are returned to the prompt. At this point you can install it with:

```
foo@bar:~$ make install
```

You might need to be root to run this command when you are installing it to a normal system binaries directory, such as */usr/bin*. If you used the --prefix command in the configure script, your files are installed to that directory instead. Remember that you will need to run each command for each module you want to compile.

Running KDE

With your new development version compiled, it is advised that you back up your existing KDE configuration before you run the new version; it is not uncommon for new development code to eat previous configuration files. KDE stores its configuration in the *.kde* directory within your home directory. A simple way to back up this directory is to rename it to another name. When you start your new development KDE version, the *.kde* directory will be re-created with the new configuration files.

To run KDE, set your PATH environment variable to include the path where KDE is installed (as discussed earlier), and then edit your *.xinitrc* file and add exec startkde to it. This will load KDE when you run startx.

GNOME Desktop Hacks

Hacks #45–48

Though Linux users have plenty of choices as to which desktop environment or window manager they use, the reality is that the vast majority of them choose KDE or GNOME. Chapter 5 was about KDE, and this chapter is focused on GNOME.

GNOME has become the default desktop for Fedora and Red Hat, is the only desktop for Sun's Java Desktop System, and is currently fighting it out with KDE to become Novell's preferred corporate desktop. Since the introduction of the 2.0 series GNOME has moved to a time-based release schedule, with new major versions out every six months. This has led to rapid development of the core environment, advanced features, and even wider acceptance as a desktop than it previously enjoyed. Combine this with outstanding applications such as Evolution and Gaim (which look more at home on the GTK-based GNOME desktop than the QT-based KDE desktop) and developers' adherence to the GNOME Human Interface Guidelines, and you have a desktop environment that is loved by many.

This chapter provides a few hacks to help you customize your GNOME desktop even further, and one hack to keep you up-to-date with the latest development releases.

Randomize Your GNOME Wallpaper

#45 Periodically change the wallpaper to a random image.

Like many Linux enthusiasts, you spend hours each day staring at your computer screen. You're lucky to have nice graphical interfaces sprinkled with pretty pictures to make all the work you do seem more interesting, but after a time, things can still get dull. To spice up your daily working grind, it would be nice to have the GNOME desktop periodically change to a random image. With a collection of suitable wallpaper this could add a little more sparkle to your desktop.

Unfortunately, a default option for performing this kind of randomized wallpaper adjustment does not exist. Therefore, you will write a small script in this hack to accomplish this. After a little time preparing the script, not only will you have a randomized wallpaper set up, but also you will have a deeper understanding of how GNOME can be scripted.

Selecting a Random Image

With a small bash script, it is possible to randomly select an image from a directory and change the current GNOME wallpaper to that image. It's easy to forget just how powerful bash can be; more than just a simple command shell, bash has a whole host of features that make it well-suited for even complex programming tasks.

To begin this hack, you need to have a directory full of wallpapers somewhere. Assume this directory is located at */home/foo/Images/Wallpapers/*. This script will take an image from that directory and set it as the current wallpaper. Here's the first part of the script:

```
#!/bin/bash
export DIR='/home/foo/Images/Wallpapers/'
export NUMBER=$RANDOM
export TOTAL=0
```

The first line is a standard piece of code that says which program should be used to run the script (in this case *bash*). After this line is the location of the directory containing your images, stored in the $DIR variable for future use. Next, you store a random number, which is generated by the built-in variable named $RANDOM. You also set $TOTAL to 0 to begin with; this variable stores the total number of images in the directory.

> If you get an error when running this script that reports a "Bad Interpreter" or something similar, you should check the documentation for your distribution and make sure the path to the *bash* binary is correct (*/bin/bash* should be correct on most distributions).

After this initial code, you need to create a loop that counts the number of images in the directory using the output of the ls command. Because this script doesn't check file types, it is important that you store only images in this directory. Here is the loop:

```
for f in `ls $DIR`
do
    let "TOTAL += 1"
done
let "NUMBER %= TOTAL"
```

The line let "NUMBER %= TOTAL" is the part that actually selects which image will be used. This line divides the randomly generated number by the number of images in the directory and stores the remainder of this division in the $NUMBER variable. If you're wondering how this works, the remainder must be between 0 and 1, minus the number of images, and because in the next part the script starts counting from 0, it is possible for any image to be selected with this method.

The final part of the script simply counts through each image to see if it is the one that was selected. When it finds the correct image, it modifies the *GConf* setting that stores the filename of the wallpaper using the gconftool command (this might be gconftool-2 on some systems). Nautilus notices this change immediately and updates the wallpaper. So, here's the final script:

```
#!/bin/bash
export DIR='/home/adam/Images/Wallpapers/'
export NUMBER=$RANDOM
export TOTAL=0
for f in `ls $DIR`
do
    let "TOTAL += 1"
done
let "NUMBER %= TOTAL"
export CURRENT=0
for f in `ls $DIR`
do
    if [ $CURRENT = $NUMBER ]
    then
        /usr/bin/gconftool-2 -t string -s /desktop/gnome/background/picture_
filename $DIR/$f
        break
    fi
    let "CURRENT += 1"
done
```

Save the script somewhere convenient such as */home/foo/setbg.sh*. Also make it executable by running the following in a terminal:

```
foo@bar:~$ chmod +x setbg.sh
```

Now when you run this script your wallpaper will be changed.

Automating the Task

Using *cron* you can run this script automatically at set times. "Automate Your Life with cron" [Hack #70] discusses how to use *cron*. Another option is to use GNOME's session manager to have the script run when you log in. You can even add a launcher to your panel so that you can change the wallpaper with one click. Just enter */home/foo/setbg.sh* as the program name.

—Adam McMaster

Grow Your GNOME with gDesklets Steroids

HACK
#46

Spiff up your GNOME desktop with various information panels and interactive gadgets.

gDesklets are GNOME's answer to KDE's *karamba* and *superkaramba*. You can set up and use *gDesklets* that place system information, clocks, and other information on your desktop. Some *gDesklets* provide more interactive functions. Even though they are associated primarily with GNOME, gDesklets are not GNOME-only programs. The *gDesklets* system runs reasonably well with other window managers, even KDE.

Like the KDE gadget programs, *gDesklets* depend heavily on Python and Python interfaces to GNOME. Here are the minimum requirements for *gDesklets* to work (some sensors might have extra requirements):

- Python 2.3 or higher
- *pygtk 2.0.0* or higher
- *libgtop2*
- *librsvg*
- *GConf*
- *gnome-python 2.0.0* or higher
- GConf support for *gnome-python* (plus the extra package *gnome-python2-gconf* on Red Hat Linux)

The web site for *gDesklets* is at *http://gdesklets.gnomedesktop.org/*, but you won't find RPMs there. Your best bet is to search *http://rpm.pbone.net/index.php3* for RPM packages for Fedora, SUSE, Mandrake, and others, and you'll also find some RPM packages at *http://www.rpmfind.net*. Debian and Gentoo provide packages you can download through their Internet installers, *apt-get* and *emerge*, respectively.

Although both *superkaramba* and *gDesklets* provide a user interface for selecting gadgets (called displays), the one for *gDesklets* is the only one worth using. In most cases, you should be able to start up the *gDesklets* Display selector by choosing gDesklets from the GNOME → Applications menu, although the location of the selection varies considerably from one Linux distribution to the next.

Once you find the selection and start *gDesklets*, it launches itself as a daemon that runs in the background, after which it presents the gDesklets interface to select from a variety of displays (Figure 6-1). Double-click a display selection on the right to start up that display.

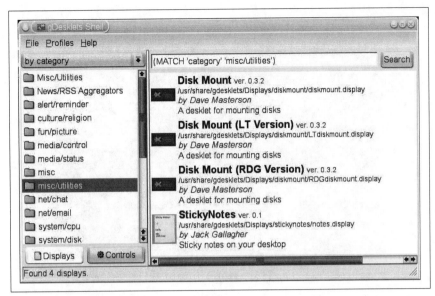

Figure 6-1. gDesklets selector

In my past, personal use, the *gDesklets* selector shell (which launches the daemon) often failed to start a display, or the shell interface crashed before I had a chance to select a display. Recent updates to GNOME seem to have fixed this problem. Regardless, if this happens to you, you can usually bypass the launcher and start up a display directly from the command line. The trick is to use the --no-config switch for it to work (*gDesklets* is evolving and changing rapidly, as are the rules for its use, so even that switch might not be necessary at some point). For example, to launch the clock display, use this command:

```
$ gdesklets --no-config /usr/share/gdesklets/Displays/Clock/osXclock.display
```

Of course, launching from the command line gives you the ability to auto-launch a *gDesklets* display each time you start GNOME [Hack #72]. Figure 6-2 shows both the clock and the weather display.

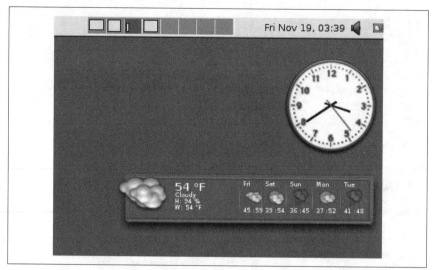

Figure 6-2. Two gDesklets on the GNOME desktop

Create Your Own GNOME Right-Click Actions
#47

Create custom menu actions in the Nautilus file manager.

GNOME and its file manager, Nautilus, have a custom menu feature similar to KDE/Konqueror. This hack shows you how to exploit that Nautilus feature, add your own menu selections, and get around some of the limitations of Nautilus.

The Nautilus approach and the KDE approach to adding custom menu selections differ in that you can't make the Nautilus menu selections context-sensitive so that they appear only when they would be useful. This means you can create menu actions that are useless in the wrong context. For example, there's no reason why you would want to click a spreadsheet and then select "convert to PNG image" from a custom menu. Yet, if you create a script that converts a file to a PNG image, that menu option (along with all the other script menu selections you have created) will appear even when you select files where such a conversion would be nonsense.

The only way to make a script context-sensitive is to associate the script with a type of file by using the GNOME File Types and Programs applet. After that, the script will appear as one of the ways to "Open" the file.

Adding a Scripts Option to the Nautilus Menu

You run custom scripts from the Nautilus File menu or by right-clicking and selecting the Scripts option. You might notice your current Nautilus menu doesn't contain a Scripts option. This simply means you haven't defined any scripts yet. Once you define a script, the option to run scripts will appear (along with the option to open the scripts folder where you can add, change, delete, or edit your scripts).

Place your scripts in the ~/.gnome2/nautilus-scripts directory. If you find you are adding so many scripts that the menu gets confusing, you can divide them into categories and place them into subdirectories of ~/.gnome2/nautilus-scripts. For example, you can put all your file conversion-related scripts in the ~/.gnome2/nautilus-scripts/Convert directory. This will place all the conversion scripts in a submenu so that you can select Scripts → Convert → Your Script to run one of those scripts.

Image Conversion Script

This sample script takes an image file and converts it to the GIF format. It uses the convert command that comes with the ImageMagick package. This command is capable of converting images from just about any format to just about any other format.

Create the ~/.gnome2/nautilus-scripts/Convert2Gif script. Use your favorite editor to enter the following code, and then save the file:

```
#!/bin/bash

convertprg=`which convert`

while [ $# -gt 0 ]; do
    picture=$1
    newfile=`echo "$picture" | cut -d . -f 1`
    $convertprg "$picture" "$newfile".gif
    shift
done
```

Make the script executable with this command:

```
$ chmod +x ~/.gnome2/nautilus-scripts/Convert2Gif
```

Now you're about to find out if Nautilus scripting works in your version of GNOME. Use Nautilus to navigate to a non-GIF image file in a folder where you have permission to create new files. Right-click the image file and select Scripts → Convert2Gif. If scripts work in your copy of Nautilus, you should see a new file appear in GIF format.

Checking File Types

The one time you can easily get into trouble with Nautilus scripts is when you run a script against the wrong kind of file. It's easy to find the type of a file, but it's not that easy to narrow it down to something usable in a script. The following script has some additional code that checks to make sure the file is an image:

```
#!/bin/bash

convertprg=`which convert`

while [ $# -gt 0 ]; do
    picture=$1
    filetype=`file $picture | cut -d ' ' -f 3`
    if [ $filetype = "image" ]
    then
        newfile=`echo "$picture" | cut -d . -f 1`
        $convertprg "$picture" "$newfile".gif
    fi
    shift
done
```

This additional code runs the file command against the target image. The file command returns a string of text describing the type of the file. Then it uses the cut command to find the word "image" in the text output of file. The word "image" should be the third field if you separate the words with spaces. If this command returns the word "image," the script attempts to convert the image; otherwise, the file is skipped. The second field would identify the type of the image (JPEG, for example), but if we used that field we would have to compare it against a long list of image types. It is much easier to simply identify the file as an "image."

One final tip: the preceding script doesn't care what kind of image it is converting. That makes the script easily adaptable to become a conversion script to any other format that the ImageMagick convert command can handle. All you have to change is the file extension of the target file. In short, change *.gif* to *.png* and then save the file as *Convert2Png*, and now you have a script that converts images to PNG format. Place *Convert2Png* in the *scripts* directory, and off you go.

Environment Variables

Nautilus scripts automatically recognize the following environment variables which you can use in your scripts.

NAUTILUS_SCRIPT_SELECTED_FILE_PATHS
> This environment variable includes the names of all the selected files, separated by newline characters (\n). This works only if the files are local, not if they are accessed over a network.

NAUTILUS_SCRIPT_SELECTED_URIS
> This environment variable returns newline-delimited URIs for the selected files.

NAUTILUS_SCRIPT_CURRENT_URI
> This environment variable returns the current URI, regardless of whether it is local.

NAUTILUS_SCRIPT_WINDOW_GEOMETRY
> This environment variable stores the position and size of the current window.

If you're interested in Nautilus scripts, you can find an excellent collection at *http://g-scripts.sourceforge.net/*. This site also includes some tutorial information on scripting for Nautilus.

 Compile a Bleeding-Edge GNOME Desktop

#48   Why wait for your distribution to play catch-up? Get your GNOME fix now.

The use of binary packages has transformed Linux into a convenient system in which the software you need is readily available in RPM or Deb form. Although these packages are perfectly fine for the majority of users, they have a few limitations. The first issue is that binary packages are generically built for the widest range of hardware, which means they are not as optimized for your computer as they could be. Another issue is that availability of the latest software in binary form depends on your distributor and how quickly they can build the packages. The solution to these two common problems is to use the source and compile the code yourself. Although the idea of compiling code might send a shiver down the spine of even the bravest user, the method of compiling the latest version of GNOME is actually surprisingly simple.

The process of compiling GNOME used to be fraught with difficulties, and the great many modules took time, effort, and patience to compile. As more developers came on board, a few sensible hackers realized the process needed to be improved and created a GNOME compilation tool called GARNOME (*http://cipherfunk.org/garnome*), which provides a simplified method of compiling the code. GARNOME has been actively developed for a few years now, and you can compile a lot of GNOME software using it.

Prepare Your System

Before you install and configure GARNOME, first you should install the build tools required to compile the main GNOME desktop. You probably already have most of these tools, but for the sake of thoroughness, here is the complete list:

- A shell (preferably bash)
- *wget* (required to download the tarballs)
- *gzip* and *bzip2* (required to extract the tarballs)
- *binutils*, *gcc*, *g++*, and make (required to compile)
- *bison*, *flex*, *gettext*, *diff*, and patch
- *autoconf*, *automake*, and *libtool*

Besides these tools, you need to obtain some additional software if you want to use certain packages that are available in the GARNOME system. These tools include:

- *fam* (required to compile *gnome-vfs*)
- *bzip2-devel* (required to compile *gnome-vfs*)
- *samba* (required to compile *gnome-vfs*)
- *libpng*, *libjpeg*, and *libtiff* (required to compile Nautilus)
- *db4-devel* (required to compile Evolution)
- *krb5-devel* (required to compile Evolution)
- *openldap-devel* (required to compile Evolution)
- *gnutls* (required to compile *vino*)

With this software installed, you should download the latest stable version of GARNOME from the projects web site and unzip it into a directory on your disk. Inside this directory is a main configuration file called *gar.conf.mk*. This file has a lot of possible settings, each well documented in the file itself. Most of the settings relate to different ways the packages can be built. For even more specific configuration, you can also edit the makefiles inside the different subdirectories in the GARNOME source directory.

Compile the Code

Within your GARNOME directory are a number of subdirectories such as *desktop*, *fifth-toe*, *hacker-tools*, *mono*, and *office*. Each directory contains scripts that will build the relevant software. For example, the main GNOME desktop is present in the *desktop* directory, Mono is in the *mono* directory, etc. The *README* file included with GARNOME explains the contents of these modules in detail.

To compile the code, enter the directory of your choice and run make. As an example, to compile the main GNOME desktop, do the following:

```
foo@bar:~$ cd desktop/
foo@bar:~$ make paranoid-install
```

GARNOME downloads the required source code and compiles it in the right order. This process can take quite some time, depending on the speed of your computer. When it is complete, the compiled software is installed in a *garnome* directory created inside your home directory. If you prefer the installed software to be located elsewhere, you can edit the main_prefix setting in the *gar.conf.mk* configuration file to specify a new location.

The final step is to launch your new GNOME desktop. To do this, you need to write a small script that you can call to set up your environment variables and log you in to the desktop. Add this script to a file called *garnome-session* and save it to your home directory, such as *~/garnome-session*:

```
#!/bin/sh GARNOME=$HOME/garnome
PATH=$GARNOME/bin:$PATH
LD_LIBRARY_PATH=$GARNOME/lib:$LD_LIBRARY_PATH
PYTHONPATH=$GARNOME/lib/python2.2/site-packages
PKG_CONFIG_PATH=$GARNOME/lib/pkgconfig:/usr/lib/pkgconfig
XDG_DATA_DIRS=$GARNOME/share
GDK_USE_XFT=1
export PATH LD_LIBRARY_PATH PYTHONPATH PKG_CONFIG_PATH
export GDK_USE_XFT XDG_DATA_DIRS
exec $GARNOME/bin/gnome-session
```

Now you can call this script by adding the following to *.xinitrc* in your home directory:

```
#!/bin/sh exec
garnome-session
```

This ensures that when you type startx, the new desktop will be started. If you use GDM as a graphical login manager, you need to place these two lines to *.xsession* in your home directory.

If you want all users on the system to have access to the installation, ensure that the main_prefix setting in the *gar.conf.mk* configuration file is a generic file path that all users can access (such as */opt/gnome*).

CHAPTER 7

Terminal Empowerment
Hacks #49–54

Linux distributors are anxious to shed the idea that Linux is too complex and to prove you can do anything in Linux from a graphical desktop without having to resort to entering a single command at a command line. Fedora Core doesn't even include a terminal icon on its launcher panel, as if to communicate the message that only outdated geeks and power users need to resort to command-line tools.

Linux users "in the know" recognize that an easy-to-use graphical interface is ideal only for some users and some tasks. Other tasks, however, demand the power of the command line and/or text command scripts.

In addition, some of us simply like some text-based applications. I, for one, still often use the text-based Mutt email client simply because Mutt supports macro commands that help you plow through the stacks of new mail more quickly than with any graphical email client.

So, whether you're an outdated geek and proud of it, a power user, or someone who simply likes using text-based programs, this chapter is for you. Indeed, this chapter assumes you not only like to use X-based terminals, but you prefer to use the lightweight terminals instead of the GNOME and KDE terminals, which consume far more resources.

The last three hacks, "Display PDF Documents in a Terminal" [Hack #53], "View Microsoft Word Documents in a Terminal" [Hack #52], and "View Word and PDF Files from Within Mutt" [Hack #54], are not only useful in an X terminal, but are ideal if you don't use X and work strictly from a virtual text console (preferably a frame buffer-based console). Indeed, I struggled with the decision as to whether to include these hacks in Chapter 2, which is dedicated to consoles, or here, where we discuss X terminals. It was just as difficult to decide to put the three hacks "Put Your Command Prompt on a Diet" [Hack #13], "Simplify Changing Directories" [Hack #14], and "Colorize Files in Your Pager" [Hack #15] in Chapter 2, because those hacks work perfectly well in X terminals, too. I encourage you to try out all these dual-personality hacks in both virtual consoles, and X terminals and see for yourself how well they work in both cases.

Share Applications and Monitors with screen

#49 Work together and collaborate on the console.

Although doing clever things with X gets most people's attention, you can perform some cool tricks with the console using a tool called *screen*.

screen is a window manager for your terminals. It provides the following nice features:

- Multiple screens
- A scrollback buffer
- Copy and paste buffers

Although this sounds like a fairly boring list—after all, you can do this with multiple X terminals—bear in mind that these features are provided within the terminal. You don't need to be using X; *screen* works just as well (or better) from one of the Linux virtual terminals or even on a remote machine. For more advanced use, it also provides the ability to detach and share the output of a process. *screen* is a GNU tool and is available for most Unix-based platforms, including Linux. Most, if not all, distributions provide a package for it, or alternatively it can be downloaded from the GNU web site and compiled.

You can access *screen*'s functions via the control key combination Ctrl-A. Pressing this, and then the question mark (?) key, displays a list of some of the commands you can use.

(Dis)connected

One of the most commonly used features of *screen*—besides its support for running multiple applications—is its ability to continue running applications while detached. When you run *screen*, it creates a new process separate from your current terminal. Then you can close that terminal (or log out), open a new one (or log back in), and reattach to your screen. This is useful for running long background jobs (such as compiling a kernel) that you don't want to accidentally "break" by closing the terminal or logging out. And it's especially useful if you're performing that job on a remote computer where there is a distinctive risk of your connection dropping.

To begin, simply run *screen* without any parameters:

```
foo@bar:~$ screen
```

Now press the control key combination Ctrl-A; then press D. You'll be returned to your original console with the following message:

```
[detached]
```

To see a list of your running screens, type:

```
foo@bar:~$ screen -ls
```

You'll see something like this:

```
There is a screen on:
        25091.pts-3.foo        (Detached)
1 Socket in /var/run/screen/S-user.
```

Now you can reattach to your screen with:

```
foo@bar:~$ screen -r
```

If you've got multiple screens listed, you can select which one to connect to with this:

```
foo@bar:~$ screen -r n
```

Here you should replace n with the number shown by screen -ls (e.g., 25091), as shown earlier.

Mirror, Mirror

Another useful feature is the ability to attach to an already attached screen. This is often used for rescuing an uncleanly detached session (e.g., your connection dropped), but you also can use it to mirror applications.

IRC is a good example for this. People running several machines at once (e.g., laptop and desktop) might want to have their IRC channels open on both machines, but don't want to be signed in twice. With screen you don't have to!

From a shell, enter the following:

```
foo@bar:~$ screen irssi
```

This launches *screen* and loads *irssi* (a console IRC client) onto screen 0 (you don't always have to use an interactive shell).

From another shell (local, or remotely in an SSH shell), enter the following:

```
foo@bar:~$ screen -ls
```

This will give you a list of sessions like these:

```
There is a screen on:
        3483.pts-0.foo        (Attached)
1 Socket in /var/run/screen/S-user.
```

Using this session number, enter the following:

```
foo@bar:~$ screen -x 3483
```

Now you are sharing your screen session; go ahead, try it from multiple shells. You can attach as many sessions as you want, but when you exit the application (assuming you launched the application directly like you did for *irssi*, not from a screen shell), that screen terminates.

It's Good to Share

It is also possible for multiple users to access a single screen instance—e.g., to collaborate on a document or some code. For this to work, the following must apply:

- *screen* must be compiled with "multiuser" enabled (most packages are).
- *screen* must be suid root (chmod +s /usr/bin/screen).

To do this as user1 and assuming *screen* is running, press Ctrl-A and then type **:multiuser on**. Still as user1, press Ctrl-A and then type **:acladd** **username**, where *username* is the user you want to be able to access your screen. For this example, use user2.

As user2, launch *screen* with:

    foo@bar:~$ screen -x user1/

At this point you should be connected to user1's *screen*. Besides acladd, you also have the aclchg, acldel, and aclgrp commands for controlling who can access your *screen*, and what they can do (e.g., you can make them read-only). To see who's connected to your session press Ctrl-A. Then press the asterisk (*) key.

To prevent people from (temporarily) editing all your windows, press Ctrl-A and then type **:writelock on** to lock editing and **:writelock off** to remove the lock. If people have write permissions, they can "steal" writelock from you. To prevent someone from editing any of your windows, press Ctrl-A and type **:aclchg username -w "#"**.

—*David Murphy*

Stop Using Terminal Command-Line Switches
#50
Power users switch window managers almost as often as "Alias" character Sydney Bristow changes hairstyles. Here's a way to deal with the fact that each window manager starts up X terminals differently.

GNOME and KDE are terrific in terms of ease of use, and their terminals (gnome-terminal, konsole) make it easy to save your preferences. But when you want to do something that sucks up computer resources (such as a large compile), you can free up resources by using a more minimalist window manager, such as Fluxbox, WindowMaker, ION, or any of several dozen others that are available. Also, some people who like to use a graphical desktop simply prefer these lightweight window managers, because they run better on older hardware.

If you're going to use a minimalist window manager to conserve system resources, it doesn't make much sense to use the fancier terminals available for GNOME and KDE, which might need to load a lot of libraries just to run. If the point of using a minimalist window manager is to save resources, it makes sense to use a lean terminal emulator, such as *xterm*, *aterm*, or *rxvt*. This hack shows you how to start up any of these terminal programs without having to use command-line switches to make them appear the way you want them to.

Here's a scenario that involves the hard way to make a terminal such as *xterm* launch with your favorite settings in different window managers. You want to give Fluxbox a try, so you fire it up as your window manager. You launch an *xterm* from the menu, and up it comes with the default settings. And for *you*, the default settings are wrong, wrong, wrong. So, what do you do? You create a ~/.*fluxbox* directory, find the default menu file (a file appropriately named *menu*, usually found in */usr/share/fluxbox*), copy it to your ~/.*fluxbox* directory, and start customizing the commands that launch terminals. For example, if you want to start an *xterm* with a predefined size, a white foreground, a black background, a font size of 10x20, the ability to remember 4,000 lines after they've scrolled off, etc., you have to create a menu entry that reads something like this:

```
[exec] (xterm) {xterm -fn 10x20 -fg white -bg black -geometry 120x40
-sb 4000}
```

Now, what happens when you have set up all your terminal menu options for Fluxbox, and then you decide you prefer to use WindowMaker? You can't just insert a copy of the preceding line of code into the file WindowMaker uses to construct its menus, because WindowMaker uses a different format for menu command entries.

Fear not. There is an oft-forgotten file in which you can set your preferences once, and then just start xterm with the simple *xterm* command and no arguments, and aterm with the *aterm* command and no arguments, and these terminals will pop up just the way you want them to. It even simplifies menu entries. Here's all you need for the Fluxbox entry:

```
[exec] (xterm) {xterm}
```

The crucial file is located in your home directory, and it is called .*Xdefaults* (some distributions prefer to use .*Xresources*, but all distributions seem to check and respect .*Xdefaults*). Few programs these days care about the settings in ~/.*Xdefaults*, but most of the lean, mean terminal programs still use it.

Here is a sample *~/.Xdefaults* file that customizes the look and feel of *xterm*, *aterm*, and *rxvt* with the same settings used earlier in the Fluxbox menu file to define an *xterm*, and even more. All three terminals tend to respect the following XTerm definitions (or at least the definitions for which *aterm* and *rxvt* have equivalent features), but sometimes you might need to define some separate settings for *aterm*, *rxvt*, and other terminals.

```
XTerm*scrollBar: on
XTerm*rightScrollBar: on
XTerm*title: XTerm
XTerm*font: 10x20
XTerm*savelines: 4000
Xterm*geometry: 120x40
XTerm*background: black
XTerm*foreground: white
XTerm*colorMode:  on
XTerm*dynamicColors:  on
XTerm*underLine:  off
XTerm*colorBDMode: on
XTerm*colorBD: cyan
XTerm*colorULMode:  on
XTerm*colorUL: magenta
XTerm*customization: -color
XTerm*reverseWrap: true
XTerm*color0: #000000
XTerm*color1: #b21818
XTerm*color2: #18b218
XTerm*color3: #BE5F00
XTerm*color4: #6D85BA
XTerm*color5: #b218b2
XTerm*color6: #18b2b2
XTerm*color7: #b2b2b2
XTerm*color8: #686868
XTerm*color9: #FF5454
XTerm*color10: #54FF54
XTerm*color11: #FFFF54
XTerm*color12: #73A5FF
XTerm*color13: #FF54FF
XTerm*color14: #54FFFF
XTerm*color15: #FFFFFF
```

More options are available for each terminal program mentioned. The best way to find out which options you can control is to view the manpage for each terminal and view the section entitled RESOURCES. As this method of controlling the look and feel of programs is going out of style, some of these resources are not very well documented. You might have to play around with various settings until you get the look you like best.

Ultimate Terminal Transparency
You want a lightweight terminal, but you want it to look cool.

You can set a number of terminal programs to have their own graphics back-grounds or to be "transparent," so that your wallpaper shows through, which really makes the terminal look good. Transparency seems to be the trendy look these days.

The only problem with true transparency is that you need to stick with monochromatic wallpaper for it to work. If you have wallpaper with both bright and dark patterns, you're in trouble (Figure 7-1). It doesn't matter if you set your text color to black or white. Depending on where the text shows up on your colorful wallpaper, you'll be able to read some text, and other text will blend into the background and disappear.

Figure 7-1. A hard-to-read transparent terminal

Sure, Figure 7-1 looks pretty, but one could go blind trying to read the text. Heavyweight programs such as KDE Konsole or a GNOME terminal solve this problem nicely. But it seems counterproductive to run a lightweight window manager only to load heavyweight terminals just to get a cool tinted transparency. Xorg (a fork of the XFree86 X Windows project) has experi-mental transparency features [Hack #34] that will solve this problem for all ter-minals, but it is currently unstable. Until Xorg works out the bugs, *aterm*, *urxvt*, and some settings in *.Xdefaults* come to the rescue.

Tint Your urxvt

At least two relatively lightweight terminals—a Unicode version of *rxvt*, called *urxvt*, and *aterm*—provide the ability to tint the transparent background. A project called *mrxvt* that lets you open multiple terminals in a single window also offers this feature. But the *mrxvt* project is such a quickly moving target I cannot recommend any settings until it matures further.

In the case of *urxvt*, the terminal will still be transparent so that it shows the desktop wallpaper as its background. But *urxvt* can modify the background by applying a colored tint to adjust the view of the desktop wallpaper. You define the color of the tint and the level of shading of the tint, and you can do it all in your *.Xdefaults* file **[Hack #50]** so that you never have to remember the command-line parameters. Starting with *urxvt*, here are the settings to add to your *~/.Xdefaults* file to get the results, as shown in Figure 7-2.

```
urxvt*inheritPixmap: True
urxvt*tintColor: green
urxvt*shading: 70
urxvt*fading: 70
```

The added green tint with a shading value of 70 makes a huge difference in the legibility of the text, doesn't it?

 Here are two more tips: I find it very useful to set the *termName* to *rxvt*. Some versions of Linux do not recognize *urxvt* as a valid terminal type and therefore do not format text properly. Also, *urxvt* has a resource setting called *fading* that determines how much the text will fade when the window loses focus.

aterm Is a Beautiful Thing to Tint

The terminal shown in Figure 7-2 is *urxvt*, but *aterm* looks identical with the suggested settings. Here's all you have to do to get the same useful transparency from *aterm*. Fire up your favorite editor, add these settings to your *.Xdefaults* file, and then run *aterm*:

```
Aterm*transparent: true
Aterm*tintingType: true
Aterm*tinting: green
Aterm*shading: 80
```

If you have your system set up to use multiple text colors, one of those colors might be difficult to read no matter what color you pick for a tint. Pick dark green, and the dark green text is hard to read. Pick dark blue, and the dark blue text is hard to read. I simply tweak the shading values to make the tint lighter or darker until I find a happy medium where I can read all the text colors. I recommend you do the same if you like this effect.

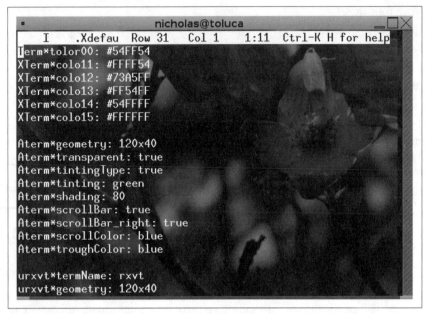

Figure 7-2. Transparent and tinted urxvt terminal

View Microsoft Word Documents in a Terminal

#52

Avoid the load time of OpenOffice.org and view Microsoft Word documents in a terminal.

The simplest way to view a Microsoft Word document in a terminal is to use the catdoc command. But catdoc turns a Word document to plain text, which does little or nothing to preserve the format of the original Word document. Obviously, it's nearly impossible to view a Word document in a terminal exactly the way it would look in Word. Heck, competing word processors have trouble importing Word documents without upsetting the format, and they have the advantage of being a graphical desktop application. But this hack is still a vast improvement over the popular *catdoc* program, because it preserves at least some of the formatting of the original document by converting the Word document to HTML.

You'll need both the *wvWare* set of file conversion utilities and the hybrid web browser/pager *w3m*, along with a little scripting magic to view Word documents in a terminal or console while retaining at least some of the original formatting.

wv, the All-Purpose Word Converter

There is a way to retain at least *some* of the original formatting while print-ing the document to the screen. For this, you need a set of utilities under the name of *wvWare*. You can find the home page for *wvWare* at *http://wvware. sourceforge.net*. Packages of *wvWare* are readily available for almost all Linux distributions, although the package name is usually just *wv*. For example, if you don't already have it installed on your system, you can install *wv* in Debian Linux with this command:

```
# apt-get install wv
```

Users of the *yum* package can get the RPM version of *wv* with this command:

```
# yum install wv
```

w3m, the All-Purpose Web Browser/Pager

That's not all you need for this hack. You also need a popular pager/browser called *w3m*. Packages of *w3m* should be available for most Linux distribu-tions, and the package name is usually *w3m*. For example, you can install *w3m* in Debian Linux with this command:

```
# apt-get install w3m
```

Users of the *yum* package can get the RPM version of *w3m* with:

```
# yum install w3m
```

The *w3m* program is rather unique in that it is a web browser that works like a pager—that is, you can pipe text into *w3m* and use *w3m* to simply page back and forth through the text. Some versions of *w3m* even render graphics in a frame-buffer console without having an X Windows desktop running.

You can combine the two utilities to get the desired result of viewing a Word document in a terminal. Use *wvWare* to convert a Microsoft Word document to HTML format, and then pipe the output into the *w3m* pager to view it. Here's the full command you need to make it work (this command assumes *wvHtml.xml* is stored in the */usr/lib/wv* directory, which might not be the case on your Linux system):

```
$ wvWare -x /usr/lib/wv/wvHtml.xml document.doc | w3m -T text/html
```

That's a lot of typing every time you want to view a Word document, so turn it into a script called *viewdoc* to make it easier to use in the future. Log in as root and use your favorite editor to create the following script:

```
#!/bin/bash

wvWare -x /usr/lib/wv/wvHtml.xml $1 2>/dev/null | w3m -T text/html
```

Note the one subtle addition, *2>/dev/null*. This simply redirects any error messages to the twilight zone so that they do not interfere with the presentation of the Word document. Store it as */usr/local/bin/viewdoc* and make the script executable with this command:

```
# chmod +x /usr/local/bin/viewdoc
```

Now all you have to do to view a Word document in a text console or terminal is issue this command:

```
$ viewdoc document.doc
```

Not only does this technique preserve at least some of the formatting of a Word document, but also, hyperlinks are live and you can activate them to visit the URL from within the w3m viewer you're using to view the document. Figure 7-3 shows an example of a Word document viewed with *w3m*. Note both the bold headings and the live link to *http://www.bootsplash.de/files*.

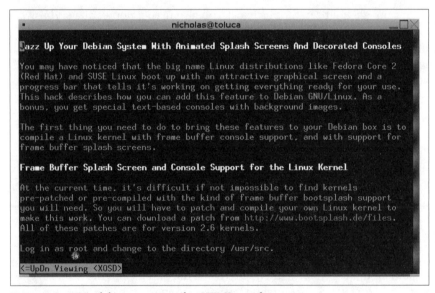

Figure 7-3. A Word document viewed in HTML text format

Display PDF Documents in a Terminal
HACK #53

You can view PDF documents in a terminal or console; no graphical desktop is required.

This hack is similar to the previous one, which converts Word documents into HTML. But this hack shows you how to convert PDF documents into HTML. Then you view the HTML version with a text-based browser or pager called *elinks*. (The previous hack used the *w3m* text browser, but *elinks* works better than *w3m* with this hack.) With a little scripting magic and help from two programs, you can view the contents of a PDF file in a text terminal or console.

This time you need to convert a PDF document to HTML before you run it through the *elinks* pager. There's a fine utility for doing just that, and it's called (appropriately) *pdftohtml*. You can find the home page for *pdftohtml* at *http://pdftohtml.sourceforge.net/*. If *pdftohtml* isn't already installed in your distribution of Linux, or isn't on your CD set, it's commonly available for Debian and RPM-based distributions, such as Fedora, SUSE, and more. The *elinks* program is also easily available if it isn't automatically installed in your distribution. For example, you can install *pdftohtml* and *elinks* in Debian Linux with this command:

```
# apt-get install pdftohtml elinks
```

Users of the *yum* package can get the RPM version with this command:

```
# yum install pdftohtml
```

Now you can view a PDF document with the following command. This particular command has one drawback. The output will not include frames (PDF files generally have a frame on the left that lets you jump to different pages).

```
$ pdftohtml -q -noframes -stdout document.pdf | elinks
```

If you want the left frame of page numbers, you can always use the following command instead:

```
$ pdftohtml -q document.pdf ; elinks document.html
```

You can write a script to save you all this typing each time you view a document. Use *sudo* or log in as root to create the */usr/local/bin/viewpdf* script and enter the following code:

```
#!/bin/bash

pdftohtml -q $1 ~/temp.html
elinks ~/temp.html
```

This code assumes it's OK to store the temporary HTML file in your home directory. You can use another location if you prefer.

Now save your work and make the file executable:

```
$ sudo chmod +x /usr/local/bin/viewpdf
```

Figure 7-4 shows an example of what a PDF document will look like when you use *viewpdf*.

```
ELinks - thy                                    ▀□╳
                                /nfs/Docs/pdf/temp_ind.html (1/33)
Outline       Issue Date
Page 1        Org. Code
Page 2        NATIONAL WEATHER SERVICE
Page 3        Program
Page 4        Section
Page 5        07/07/00 W/0S032
Page 6        Engineering Handbook
Page 7        EHB-13
Page 8        3.0
Page 9        Ser II
Page 10
Page 11       SOFTWARE NOTE INDEX
Page 12       AWIPS
Page 13       Software Installation Instructions . . . . . . . . . . . . .
Page 14       . . . . . . . . . . . . . . . . . . . . . . . . . . . 3.1
Page 15       Software Release Notes . . . . . . . . . . . . . . . . . .
Page 16       . . . . . . . . . . . . . . . . . . . . . . . . . . . 3.2
Page 17       Software Patch Modification Notes . . . . . . . . . . . .
Page 18       . . . . . . . . . . . . . . . . . . . . . . . . . . 3.3
Page 19       Lessons Learned . . . . . . . . . . . . . . . . . . . . .
file:///nfs/Docs/pdf/temps.html#1                        [------]
```

Figure 7-4. A PDF file shown in elinks

View Word and PDF Files from Within Mutt

HACK #54

View Microsoft Word documents and PDF files you receive as attachments in email right inside the email client as part of the body of the message.

Mutt is an extremely powerful terminal-based email client that supports IMAP, POP, and much more. No graphical email client can come close to the configurability of Mutt. That's why a lot of hard-core Linux users still use Mutt in spite of the myriad GUI-based email clients.

It is certainly possible to launch a GUI application such as OpenOffice.org or Acrobat Reader to view Word and PDF email attachments in Mutt. But Mutt users aren't always using a graphical desktop, so it's handy to be able to view these documents as text, right inside the message itself.

Here's how to do it. First, you need to edit the Mutt configuration file. The default configuration file is usually */etc/Muttrc*, but you'll most likely want to create your own even if you do it by copying the default and modifying it. Mutt lets you define your user configuration file as either *~/.muttrc* or *~/.mutt/ muttrc*. Modify your personal Mutt configuration file to point to a custom mailcap file. For example:

```
set mailcap_path="~/mailcap.mutt"
```

Then edit the *~/mailcap.mutt* file to include these two lines:

```
application/pdf; pdftohtml -q -stdout %s | w3m -T text/html; copiousoutput

application/msword; wvWare -x /usr/lib/wv/wvHtml.xml %s 2>/dev/null | w3m -T
text/html; copiousoutput
```

Now all attached PDF and Microsoft Word documents will appear within the text of the email. Granted, the formatting isn't as pretty as when you view Word or PDF documents **[Hacks #52 and #53]**, because all the output is piped into Mutt's own display, and not in a specialized pager, such as *elinks* or *w3m*. But you can still read the content of the attached file. And if it interests you enough to read it in a better format, you can save the file and read it with whatever program you want—including one of the scripts in the previously mentioned hacks.

CHAPTER 8

Desktop Programs
Hacks #55–69

This truly is an odd collection of hacks that represents the diversity of things a user might do with her desktop. It is not an attempt to be a definitive solution to any particular set of common problems a Linux user might experience. You won't find any KDE-, GNOME-, or X-specific hacks here, as those were covered in the previous three chapters.

The first hack covers how to load the OpenOffice.org office suite faster, and the last hack explains how to create a PPTP connection to a Microsoft VPN. The rest of the hacks focus primarily on things you can do over the Internet. Half of the hacks deal with your email or web browser, while a couple of others cover how to make free long-distance phone calls or set up a video conference call.

 HACK #55 Reduce OpenOffice.org Startup Time

Preload some of the OpenOffice.org office suite so that you can launch any of the OpenOffice.org applications without the typically long startup times.

OpenOffice.org might seem like it is composed of separate productivity applications, such as a word processor and spreadsheet, but it actually is closer to being a single large application with different faces, one being a word processor, another a presentation manager, etc. That's why it takes so long to start the first OpenOffice.org application you decide to use. When you launch the first OpenOffice.org application, such as the word processor, you can run out to the nearest Starbucks for coffee and get back in time to see the opening splash screen finish loading. OK, that's a bit of an exaggeration, but sometimes it *seems* like it takes that long to start an OpenOffice.org application.

Yet, did you ever notice that if you leave the word processor running, you can open a spreadsheet application very quickly? That's because the behemoth engine behind the spreadsheet was already loaded into memory when you started the word processor.

The obvious solution to providing quick launches of OpenOffice.org is to preload the bulk of OpenOffice.org when you first start your window manager or desktop, before you launch your first application.

OOOQS, I Did It Again

A utility is available for KDE that does just that. It preloads much of OpenOffice.org, and then makes it possible for OpenOffice.org applications to start up almost immediately. The utility is called OpenOffice.org Quickstarter, or *oooqs*, and it was created by Christian Nitschkowski.

Quickstarter places an icon on the KDE panel. You right-click the icon, and from a menu, select what you want to do with OpenOffice.org, such as start a new text document or open an existing document. Depending on the speed of your computer, the application can appear on-screen almost immediately.

Many Linux distributions make the OpenOffice.org Quickstarter package readily available. You can get the Debian version over the Internet by logging in as root and issuing this command:

```
# apt-get install oooqs-kde
```

An RPM package is available for Fedora Core, SUSE, and other RPM-based distributions and goes under the name *oooqs*. You can retrieve this package from a number of sites, including *http://www.rpmfind.net*. Chances are that if you are running *apt* or *yum*, you can simply install it with either of these two commands:

```
# apt-get install oooqs
# yum install oooqs
```

You can also download an RPM package of the latest version from *http:// developer.berlios.de/project/showfiles.php?group_id=366&release_id=1620*. Finally, if you prefer to roll your own software, you can download the source code from *http://kde-apps.org/content/show.php?content=10156* or from *http://segfaultskde.berlios.de/index.php?content=oooqs*.

Depending on how you or the package manager installed the program, either *oooqs* starts automatically and makes an icon appear in the KDE panel, or you might have to start it manually from the KDE menu the first time, after which it will start automatically from then on.

The OOQSTART-GNOME of Antiquity

A similar hack is available that preloads some of OpenOffice.org and then places an icon on your GNOME panel. It is called *ooqstart-gnome*, and it was written by Kumaran Santhanam. If it works at all for your Linux distribution, it works basically the same way *oooqs* works. You right-click the icon to launch any of the OpenOffice.org applications quickly, avoiding the typically long startup times.

The problem is that this utility has remained basically unchanged since 2002, which makes its usefulness and compatibility questionable. It seems to work well with Debian, even the unstable branch, which has the most up-to-date software (for Debian, anyway). Debian users can install the program with this command:

```
# apt-get install ooqstart-gnome
```

You can also find an RPM package of *ooqstart-gnome* at *http://sourceforge.net/ project/showfiles.php?group_id=47895*. When I tried to install it in Fedora Core 2, the installer complained about unmet dependencies. I took the dangerous path and forced RPM to ignore package dependencies, using this command:

```
# rpm -i --nodeps ooqstart-gnome-0.8.3-1.i386.rpm
```

Surprisingly, it installed and worked fine. Then I tried the same thing with Fedora Core 3, the latest version. It didn't work at all. (What did work, mysteriously enough, was the KDE *oooqs* program. It appeared in the GNOME panel just as it would in the KDE panel.)

Alternative Methods to Quick-Start OpenOffice.org

GNOME problems aside, what about all the other window managers? If you're used to using WindowMaker or XFce 4, you're unlikely to benefit from a program such as *oooqs*.

It so happens that OpenOffice.org has a feature called *quickstart*, which works fine with any desktop or window manager. You activate it with this command:

```
$ ooffice -quickstart &
```

Once you issue this command, the bulk of the OpenOffice.org engine starts up invisibly in the background and remains there—sort of (more about this in a moment). This makes it possible to start up Writer, Calc, or other OpenOffice.org applications very quickly. Of course, no pretty icon appears in the panel, so you have to use the regular KDE or GNOME menu icons, or another means of starting the word processor, spreadsheet, or other OpenOffice.org applications.

Now let's get back to the "sort of" part of the equation. First you start *ooffice -quickstart* manually, or have it launched automatically when you start your window manager or desktop [Hack #72]. Then you start up your OpenOffice.org productivity applications, do a little work, and then close the applications.

As soon as you close the last OpenOffice.org productivity application, the background *quickstart* process automatically exits, too. Unlike the methods employed by *oooqs*, *quickstart* interprets the closing of the last application as an indication that you're done with OpenOffice.org for the day. So, the next time you open the word processor, it's back to "trip to Starbucks" time again. (Well, not necessarily. If you ran the OpenOffice.org application recently, much of it might still be in memory, and it will start quickly.)

Respawn Trick to the Rescue

Here's where the respawn method I describe later in "Don't Let Elvis Leave the Building" [Hack #73] comes in really handy. Log in as root, start up your favorite editor, and create a file called */usr/local/bin/oostay*. Type the following text into the file:

```
#!/bin/bash
# Restart ooffice -quickstart every time it exits
instances=`ps ax | grep -e -quickstart | grep -v grep | wc -l`
if [ $instances == 0 ]; then
while true; do ooffice -quickstart ; done
else
exit 1
fi
```

Save your work and make the file executable with this command:

```
# chmod +x /usr/local/bin/oostay
```

Now execute oostay instead of ooffice -quickstart whenever you want OpenOffice.org's *quickstart* feature to keep running no matter how many times you open and close OpenOffice.org applications. Best of all, this trick is completely window manager- and desktop-agnostic. It doesn't work any better or worse for KDE, GNOME, WindowMaker, Fluxbox, or any other environment you like best. You can start up */usr/local/bin/oostay* automatically when you start your window manager [Hack #72].

Read Yahoo! Mail from Any Email Client
#56
Use your Yahoo! webmail account in a normal email client.

A few years back webmail exploded onto the scene. It was new, it was cool, and it enabled you to read your email from any computer with Internet access. In an age when people were increasingly using computers at work, school, and home, webmail was a natural progression for email access.

Despite the benefit of reading your email on any computer with a web browser, the very fact that the browser is your client is a tad limiting. Aside from the issue that webmail is slower than a normal email program, deleting and moving mail with webmail is a tedious process that involves selecting lots of checkboxes and waiting while the web site slowly updates your mailbox. Therefore, many people have opted to use alternative methods to access their webmail accounts using traditional email clients. However, not all webmail accounts allow access methods, such as POP3 and IMAP, so users have to use clever workarounds. This hack covers one such method to retrieve email from a Yahoo! email account.

Using FetchYahoo

To solve the problem of getting your email from the Yahoo! server into your own mailbox, the *FetchYahoo* script was written to screen-scrape the information from the web site. This screen-scraping involves connecting to the Yahoo! site, picking out the right bits of information from the HTML, and sending them back to your computer in the form of usable email. When combined with a few other tools, *FetchYahoo* is an invaluable piece of software.

To begin, grab *FetchYahoo* from *http://fetchyahoo.twizzler.org/*, and extract the tarball:

```
foo@bar:~$ tar xcvf fetchyahoo-x-x-x.tar.gz
```

The directory that is extracted will have the version number in it, so you should rename it to a simpler directory name (this is useful if you create a cronjob later, as you can upgrade the script without having to update the cronjob entry):

```
foo@bar:~$ mv fetchyahoo-x-x-x fetchyahoo
```

You need to replace *fetchyahoo-x-x-x* with whatever directory name is extracted from the tarball.

Configure the Script

The *FetchYahoo* script needs to have a properly configured *fetchyahoorc* configuration file that specifies your login details and configures certain options in the script. A *fetchyahoorc* file is included within the main tarball, and you can configure it by loading it into a text editor. You can locate this file anywhere on your system as you will call it with an absolute path later, but keeping personal configuration files in your home directory is always a good idea.

The most important parts to configure are at the top of the file. Like many other Linux configuration files, each option has the format option_keyword = setting. For example, username = johnsmith sets the username option to johnsmith. To get started, you need to set the username and password options to your Yahoo! account settings (you don't need to put these settings in double quotes, as with other configuration files). It is also advisable that you set use-https = 1 to ensure secure communications between your computer and the mail server.

The spool option is another important setting. This indicates where your *mail spool* (the place where your mail is stored) is located on your Linux system. Most distributions place this in a file with your account name inside the */var/spool/mail/* directory. As an example, the user bob would have his mail spool at */var/spool/mail/bob*. To check this, have a poke around */var/spool/mail* and see if the username exists in there—every user should have a mail spool file. If you don't have a mail spool (such as if your mail client cannot read mail from a spool), you can have the mail stored in *maildir* format by adding a slash (/) to the spool setting (e.g., */var/spool/mail/*); this directory will contain the mailbox.

A variety of other options are in the configuration file, and each one is documented inside the file itself. These options control how much mail is delivered, if attachments are delivered, whether to empty the bulk mail directory, and other useful functions.

It is recommended that when you first use *FetchYahoo*, you should set no-delete = 1 so that your Yahoo! mail won't be deleted when running the script. When you are confident the script is working, set no-delete back to 0 so that it will delete the mail on the server, once it has been successfully received.

Run the Script

With the configuration file set up, execute the script by simply running:

```
foo@bar:~$ fetchyahoo --configfile=fetchyahoorc
```

The first time you run the script against a Yahoo! account containing lots of email messages, you might find the script downloads only some of the mail before exiting with an error. This is usually because the Yahoo! server is set up to deny malicious requests that bombard it with traffic, and it misinterprets your use of the *FetchYahoo* script as one of these malicious programs. If you get an error such as this, visit the web interface to Yahoo! mail, and if you cannot log in, this is likely what happened. To resolve this problem, simply leave the server alone for a few minutes and then try to access the web interface again—if you can log in, the server has recovered and you can run *FetchYahoo* again. It might take a number of runs to get all your email transferred to your computer. You do not encounter this problem when downloading only a few emails at regular intervals.

Automate FetchYahoo with cron

Most people who use email want to check it regularly. With this in mind, you ideally want to run *FetchYahoo* every few minutes to update your mail spool with new emails, but you don't want to have to manually rerun the command every time; repetitive tasks such as this are what computers are for. To solve this problem, use *cron* to automate running the script [Hack #70]. First, you should edit your crontab:

```
foo@bar:~$ crontab -e
```

If you want to run the fetchyahoo command every three minutes, you can use the following cronjob:

```
*/3 * * * * /sources/fetchyahoo/fetchyahoo --configfile=/sources/fetchyahoo/
fetchyahoorc
```

In this cronjob, you are running the script every three minutes on every day, month, and year. It includes a full path to the location of the script because you have not installed the *FetchYahoo* script to your path, so you need to specify its path to the system. You also need to give a full path to the location of the configuration file.

H A C K   Encrypt Your Email
#57   Because you have a right to privacy.

We all seem to take email for granted these days. Although we are using it for more and more things, we rarely stop to think about its security, and regularly include telephone numbers, home addresses, and even credit card details inside email without a second thought. So, it's worth reminding ourselves that email is sent in plain text and that anyone between you and the recipient can read this directly off the network very easily.

Two main methods are available for encrypting your email. One uses certificates and the other uses Pretty Good Privacy (PGP) or GNU Privacy Guard (GPG). This hack is about the latter. It assumes you are using a graphical mail client, such as Thunderbird, Mozilla Mail, or Evolution, but the concepts apply equally to text-based email clients that support encryption, such as Mutt.

GPG uses public/private key technology to secure communications. This dual-key approach could use a quick explanation. You might want to read this bit through a couple of times if public/private key technology is new to you.

One of the first things you will do is generate a keypair that is unique to yourself. As the name suggests, two keys will be generated. One (the public one) will be distributed to all your friends, and the other (the private one) you must keep safe. Anything that is encrypted with your public key (the one you distribute) can be decrypted only by your private key (the one you have for safekeeping).

Here's how the system works. When someone sends you an email message, she encrypts it with your public key. When you receive the message, you decrypt it with your private key. If anyone along the way intercepts the encrypted email, they won't be able to read it, because they don't have your private key. Likewise, when you send email to your friends, you should encrypt the message with their public key. This is why it is important that you share your public key with as many people as possible so that they can send you encrypted email. You can also upload your public key to a key server. These servers host public keys and give them to users who request them so that they can send you a message.

In case you are wondering, by the way, the public and private keys are mathematically related, but having one doesn't mean you can reverse-engineer it to become the other. This fact is mathematically proven and is the heart of any public/private key system. You can, and should, give everyone your public key and even put it on a public key server. The only thing people can do with this key is encrypt stuff for you. So long as you keep your private key secret, you will be secure.

What You Need

Email clients require the first of the following two items to encrypt email; Thunderbird also requires the second item.

GPG
> The GNU Privacy Guard, which performs the encryption/signing of your messages. It is available at *http://www.gnupg.org/download/*.

Enigmail
> A nice plug-in for Mozilla-based mail clients such as Thunderbird. It is available at *http://enigmail.mozdev.org/download.html*.

Creating Your Keypair

As I stated earlier, most distributions come complete with GPG these days, so your first step is probably to create a keypair for each email account that you want to use. The process is quite straightforward, and although the Enigmail plug-in can do some of this for you, I think it's prudent to be able to configure GPG from the console.

To begin, you need to run the gpg command with the --gen-key switch to generate a key:

```
foo@bar:~$ gpg --gen-key
Please select what kind of key you want:
   (1) DSA and ElGamal (default)
   (2) DSA (sign only)
   (4) RSA (sign only)
```

You are asked which type of key you want to generate. The default is DSA and ElGamal, and that is a good choice as the other two options allow for only signing, not encrypting and signing.

```
DSA keypair will have 1024 bits.
About to generate a new ELG-E keypair.
              minimum keysize is  768 bits
              default keysize is 1024 bits
    highest suggested keysize is 2048 bits
What keysize do you want? (1024)
```

Next, you are asked what size you want the keys to be. Your answer really depends on your level of paranoia. The default of 1024 is fine, but it doesn't hurt to use 2048.

```
Please specify how long the key should be valid.
         0 = key does not expire
      <n>  = key expires in n days
      <n>w = key expires in n weeks
      <n>m = key expires in n months
      <n>y = key expires in n years
Key is valid for? (0)
```

Now you are asked how long you want this key to be valid. Here I suggest you don't accept the default (which is that it doesn't expire). It is best practice to change keys occasionally, so I suggest you choose either one or two years. To do this you simply type:

```
Key is valid for? (0) 2y
```

This sets the key lifetime to two years. After two years you will need to generate a new set of keys.

```
You need a User-ID to identify your key; the software constructs the user id
from Real Name, Comment and Email Address in this form:
    "Heinrich Heine (Der Dichter) <heinrichh@duesseldorf.de>"
```

```
Real name: Joe Blogs
Email address: joe.blogs@foobar.com
Comment: optional comment
```

Once you have confirmed the key lifetime you are asked for your name and email address. Note that the output of the program is somewhat confusing here. It states that you need to enter the information in a specific way, all on one line. This is not true; you need to enter this information on three separate lines, and press Enter after you enter each value. The comment field is optional.

```
You selected this USER-ID:
    "Joe Blogs <joe.blogs@foobar.com>"

Change (N)ame, (C)omment, (E)mail or (O)kay/(Q)uit?
```

Here you are asked if you want to edit any of the fields, or type O to continue or Q to quit.

```
Enter passphrase:
Repeat your passphrase:
```

Finally, you are asked to type in a passphrase to protect your secret key. The thing to remember here is that it is a pass*phrase*, not a pass*word*. A passphrase typically consists of a sentence such as "I love eating cheese," and the longer the passphrase, the better. When you have added it, you are asked to confirm it by typing it twice. Then your keys are created and saved in your GPG keyrings that are located in *.gnupg* in your home directory. You have two keyrings, because one contains only other people's public keys and one contains only your private key. It's a good idea to back up your secret keyring (*.gnupg/secring.gpg*) to a safe place because if you lose your private key, you can't re-create it and you will not be able to access encrypted messages that have been sent to you.

> It's critical that you choose a very strong passphrase: using a key with a high level of encryption with a short passphrase is like building a bank vault but securing the door with only a piece of string. If your passphrase is weak, you leave your private key vulnerable to brute-force dictionary attacks if it ever falls into the wrong hands.

Publish Your Key to a Server

Now that you have your key, it's a good idea to send it to a public key server. A *key server* is a public resource that will provide a means for you to distribute your public key to those who need it to encrypt email to you. It is also a place where you can download their public keys, should you need to encrypt email to them. You have to upload it to only one key server, because the key servers replicate with each other. Here is the command to upload your key:

```
foo@bar:~$ gpg --keyserver wwwkeys.pgp.net --send-key joe.blogs@foobar.com
```

> To save some typing, store values for options such as the key server name in *~/.gnupg/options*.

Enigmail supports a number of key servers by default:

- *wwwkeys.pgp.net*
- *random.sks.keyserver.penguin.de*
- *pgp.dtype.org*
- *keyserver.kjsl.com*
- *ldap://certserver.pgp.com*

Installing Enigmail in Thunderbird

Download copies of the Enigmail and Enigmime modules, for your version of Thunderbird, from *http://enigmail.mozdev.org/download.html*. Enigmail handles the basic encryption and decryption while the Enigmime enables PGP/MIME-formatted email. (Later versions of the Enigmail plug-in for Thunderbird move all this into one module.)

From within Thunderbird, select Tools → Extensions and click Install. Now browse to the Enigmail and Enigmime modules and select them.

You need to close and reopen Thunderbird before Enigmail will work.

Configuring Enigmail

Now that you have Enigmail installed, you just need to configure it. Inside Thunderbird, select Tools → Account Settings and then select OpenPGP Security under each account for which you have a key. Then check "Enable OpenPGP support (Enigmail) for this identity." You don't need to change anything else (unless you want to); the defaults are fine.

Now you can sign your own emails, which is how you can start distributing your public key to people you correspond with.

To send an encrypted email to someone, that person will need to have her own keypair, and you will need a copy of her public key. You can ask her to either put it on a key server or send you a signed email (which includes her public key).

To receive encrypted email, people will need your public key first—again, they can get this off the key server or you can sign an email to them.

Configuring Evolution

Evolution has support for GPG built in: once you install GPG and have created a key for yourself, you can select Tools → Accounts → Your default account → Security, where you will see options that allow you to tell Evolution to do things, such as always sign messages by default.

You will also see a field where you can enter your PGP/GPG key ID. Type in the email address associated with your key so that Evolution knows which key to use.

Keysignings

You can do many more interesting things with GPG, such as determine if a person you never met is really who she says she is. To learn more about key-signings and other GPG-related events, browse to *http://www.keysigning.org*.

—Adrian Bradshaw

HACK #58 Reclaim Your Email with procmail

Manage your email automatically without depending on your email client.

Email is the Internet's killer app. Everybody uses it, everybody loves it—even those who feel like their lives are controlled by it. The volume of email in our lives has increased exponentially the last few years, and I'm not refer-ring just to spam. With email's acceptance as a mainstream communica-tions medium, it has become increasingly important for users to manage their volume of email efficiently. Most GUI email programs provide numer-ous features to help manage email, including searching, filters, and spam-checking. But for some users these features aren't enough. They have found it best to augment their email client with the Swiss Army Knife of email pro-cessing, *procmail*. This email tool allows you to define what you do with your mail, where it goes (if it goes anywhere), and how it should be stored using a simple, albeit terse, rule-based syntax. This hack explores how to use *procmail*.

To get *procmail*, use your distribution tools to search for and install it. For instance, on Debian, use:

```
foo@bar:~# apt-get install procmail
```

If your distribution doesn't come with *procmail*, you can always download it from *http://www.procmail.org* and compile it yourself.

Configure Your MTA to Use procmail

procmail is typically used on computers that have a Mail Transfer Agent (MTA) running, and as such, before you use *procmail* you must configure your MTA to use it. The majority of distributions include a default MTA that, although sometimes not installed by default, can be installed at a later time. An example of this is Debian, which includes the Exim MTA as the default server. You will need to ensure that your MTA is able to send and receive mail before you can begin configuring *procmail*.

Along with the many different MTAs available are many different ways to configure them to use *procmail*. Despite the mass of potential options, an almost foolproof method is to use a *.forward* file in your home directory. This file contains rules that, when followed, invoke *procmail* for all incoming mail. The following command enables *procmail* for most MTAs:

```
foo@bar:~$ echo '|exec /usr/bin/procmail' > ~/.forward
```

If your MTA complains, you might have to use just |/usr/bin/procmail instead.

Using procmail

procmail rules, better known as recipes, are defined in the *.procmailrc* file in your home directory. Although a full treatment of the recipe syntax is beyond the scope of this hack, a simple example shows the basic format. Add the following to your *.procmailrc* file:

```
:0
*
```

This simple recipe delivers all mail addressed to you to your default system mailbox file (usually */var/mail/$USER*). The :0 indicates the beginning of a rule and the * indicates that all mail should be handled by this rule. This recreates what your MTA usually does by default. If you use the *maildir* format (the preferred format of the *qmail* MTA and the KMail client), *procmail* can move all mail to a directory with a recipe, such as this:

```
:0
*
Mail/
```

This delivers your mail into a *maildir*-formatted directory (*$HOME/Mail* by default). If you prefer standard mailbox format (*mbox*), you can use this:

```
:0
*
mbox
```

This recipe delivers all your mail to *$HOME/mbox* by appending all new mail to the same file. Although these examples are trivial and do no more than your MTA, they are the most basic recipes *procmail* uses. These simple concepts form the basis behind more complex *procmail* recipes.

Standard procmail Usage

Now that you know how *procmail* works, you can use it to do some processing. Say you want to store mail from your friends Bruce (*bruce@foo.org*) and Steve (*steve@bar.com*) in a different mailbox file or *maildir* directory. You can use the following recipe:

```
MAILDIR=$HOME/Mail

:0
* ^From.*(bruce@foo.org|steve@bar.com)
friends/
```

Any mail from Bruce and Steve will be stored in the *maildir*-formatted directory *$HOME/Mail/friends*. *maildir* format is denoted by the trailing / in the rule; if you don't use the /, the mail will be delivered to a standard mailbox file named *friends* in your *$HOME/Mail* directory. The regular expression in the second line of the recipe conforms to the usage of egrep, so anything that egrep can use as a regular expression can be used in *procmail* rules. Consult the manpage for egrep for more information.

You can also use this format to separate mail sent to a mailing list into a specific directory. This is shown in the following recipe:

```
:0:
* ^TObugtraq
bugtraq
```

This recipe stores all mail sent to the bugtraq mailing list in a *bugtraq* mailbox in your *$HOME* directory. The second : in :0: tells *procmail* to use a default lock file to prevent multiple instances of *procmail* from trying to write to the mailbox at once. The ^TObugtraq regular expression is shorthand that expands to a more complex regular expression that catches all mail sent to an address containing a specific word (*bugtraq* in this case).

Now let's look at something fun. If you have *festival* (a text-to-speech system that is freely available on most distributions), you can have it speak to you when new mail arrives, using this recipe:

```
:0
*
{
    SUBJECT=`formail -xSubject:`
    FROM=`formail -xTo:`

    :0 c
    Mail/

    :0 W
    | echo "Incoming mail from, ${FROM}. Subject is: ${SUBJECT}" \
      |/usr/bin/festival --tts -
}
```

The {} allow you to combine more than one rule. The formail utility that is bundled with *procmail* allows you to grab various headers and, in this case, put them in variables for use in the second rule. The c in :0 c indicates this rule works on a copy of the incoming message, and the message will continue on through the various rules that follow.

Other potential uses for *procmail* include sending all mail through Spam-assassin to root out all the junk and prevent it from entering your mailboxes.

See Also

- *procmailex* manpage
- *procmailrc* manpage
- *egrep* manpage

—Adam Garside

 Convert Your Mailbox

Convert Your Mailbox

Don't let your old email become stranded in a format that your new mail program can't read.

Switching email clients, MTAs, or mail servers can be a traumatic process. And getting used to the different interface of an email client and its way of working can be awkward. Aside from the cosmetic changes, you might have a far more serious problem if the new client stores its mail differently.

This hack takes you through the steps of converting between the two most popular formats on Linux: *mbox* and *maildir*. This can often be a daunting and confusing process, but with this hack by your side, you will be converting your mail in no time.

The most common reasons to switch mailbox formats are as follows:

Switching email clients
Not all email clients support both mailbox formats. If you really want to use a client that doesn't support your current format, you need to covert your old mail to a format that is supported.

Switching your local delivery agent
Many Linux users run an MTA on their desktops to handle mail delivery to local users. Like email clients, not all email servers support each mailbox format. When switching servers, it might be necessary to convert your mail from one format to another.

Switching mail servers
This is like switching your local MTA, only on a larger scale. If you administer users on a mail server, it might be necessary to convert their mailboxes when you switch MTAs.

Generally, the mailbox format is dictated by the MTA, and you choose your client accordingly. Of course, if you want a particular client for its unique feature, you might need to switch (or reconfigure) your MTA. You might also decide to switch between the two based purely on technical merits, so here is a brief rundown of the differences.

mbox Versus maildir

mbox is the older of the two mail storage formats. It is actually the generic name for a family of related formats. Although the formats are slightly different, they both store multiple messages within a single file. These multiple formats came about because of different Mail User Agents (MUAs) implementing their own variations of the original format. Although they are very similar, they are generally not compatible between MUAs. Because of the single file format, there can be problems with file-locking and storage on networked filesystems such as NFS, which might cause the mail file to be corrupted.

maildir, on the other hand, stores one message per file. This removes the locking problems of *mbox*, which means it should be your first choice is your mail is stored over NFS. Because of its relative youth compared to some of the MUAs that support it, there are no variants of the format, so your mail should be portable between clients.

Generally, *maildir* is considered to be superior to *mbox*.

Converting mbox to maildir

You can convert between the two formats with the *mb2md.pl* Perl script, which you can find at *http://batleth.sapienti-sat.org/projects/mb2md*. To use this tool, you need to have both Perl and its TimeDate module installed, but packages of the script are available for various distributions that should take care of these dependencies for you.

First, you need to know where your mail is coming from. Your *mbox* mail is normally stored in two locations: */var/spool/mail/$user* for new mail and an *mbox* file in your home folder for read mail, although the paths and filenames can be distribution-dependent. If you sort your mail into folders, each folder is represented by a single file within your mail directory.

When run, *mb2md.pl* discovers your new and read mail locations automatically, but you need to point it at any other folders containing *mbox* files. If necessary, you can also point it at specific files. The following examples assume you've downloaded the script from its site.

To convert your new and read mail into a *newmaildir* folder:

```
foo@bar:~$ perl mb2md.pl -m
```

To send the output to a different folder:

```
foo@bar:~$ perl mb2md.pl -m -d somefolder
```

To tell it where to convert the files in a specific folder:

```
foo@bar:~$ perl mb2md.pl -s sourcefolder
```

To convert the files in a folder recursively (for nested folders):

```
foo@bar:~$ perl mb2md.pl -s sourcefolder -R
```

Converting maildir to mbox

The main conversion from *maildir* to *mbox* is achieved in a much more hack-ish way, by writing a small shell script that uses the formail tool to filter input into *mbox* format. Create a file called *md2mb.sh* in you home folder, making sure you replace maildir with your own mailbox. Insert the following text into the file:

```
#!/bin/bash
for file in `find maildir/.$1/cur/ -type f`
do
    cat $file | formail -a Date: >> mbox
done
```

Make the script executable with:

```
foo@bar:~$ chmod +x md2mb.sh
```

Then run it with:

```
foo@bar:~$ ./md2mb.sh
```

To process a particular folder, run it with:

```
foo@bar:~$ ./md2mb.sh foldername
```

This appends any email in the *maildir* folder to an *mbox* file that can be read with mail or your favorite MUA.

—David Murphy

Configure Firefox Under the Covers

HACK #60

To keep the Firefox GUI preferences simple, some of the more interesting but less common options were moved under the covers by the developers.

Almost every application allows you to customize it to some extent. For most graphical programs, these configuration options are available through dialog boxes and settings menus, whereas console programs usually store these options in a series of configuration files. In either case, the options are clearly visible and available to be configured.

Firefox is a little different. Instead of bombarding the user with every potential option and setting for the program within the settings dialog boxes, Firefox puts only the most commonly needed options in the main Preferences dialog box. Everything else it hides away. This has the benefit of making Firefox simple to use for most users, whereas power users can jump under the covers to tweak many different settings.

Entering Configuration Mode

Firefox has a number of different modes that give information about how the browser is running. To see one such mode, type the following into the address bar and press Enter:

`about:plugins`

This page gives you information about the plug-ins that are configured for the browser. There are a number of modes, including about:mozilla, about: credits, about:, and most interestingly, about:config, the main Mozilla configuration interface.

When you enter about:config, you see a number of lines listed down the page. Each line refers to a different setting that can be configured. As an example, one of my lines is:

`browser.startup.homepage user set    string    http://www.jonobacon.org/`

This setting simply sets the default home page that is loaded when the browser is started. The status column refers to this as user set, because this option was configured in the dialog box in Firefox. The type column refers to this setting as a string because the setting browser.startup.homepage requires text strings as a value. The final value column actually states the desired page for the setting. You can see that most of these settings follow the same format, and most have their status set to default. Here are a couple of examples on how to use these settings to configure Firefox to do things you can't otherwise control from the Preferences page.

Teach Firefox to Lie

When you connect to any web site on the Internet, your web browser leaves a small fingerprint with the web server that gives some details about which browser and operating system you are running. This information is called the *user agent*.

Many web sites use this information to cater their content to specific browsers. This has traditionally been the case with web sites that have not been coded to run in every browser (as they really should be) and are instead designed specifically around Internet Explorer. This causes a problem for anyone using a different browser, and even if the site was to work correctly in Firefox, the user agent would probably trigger a "This site requires IE" access-denied page. Luckily for the Firefox faithful, you can use about:config to change your user agent to anything you want. This means you can lie about your browser to web sites you visit, so you can get around their stupid IE-specific coding practices.

By default Firefox sets a sensible user agent string for you, and you can see it when you select Help → About Mozilla Firefox. On Linux the default user agent is:

```
Mozilla/5.0 (X11; U; Linux i686; en-US; rv:1.7) Gecko/20040914 Firefox/0.9.3
```

To override this setting you need to set the general.useragent.override setting. By default this setting is not available, so you need to add it. To do this, right-click the about:config page, select New → String, and in the box that appears, type:

general.useragent.override

In the box that pops up, enter a new user agent string such as:

Mozilla/4.0 (compatible;MSIE 5.5;Windows 98)

Restart Firefox and select Help → About Mozilla Firefox to see the new user agent string. Now you can access web sites that require IE in Firefox!

Loading Web Pages Faster

You can use the about:config screen to tweak Mozilla's performance by increasing the maximum number of connections to different aspects of the network. Here are the settings to change, along with their values:

```
network.http.max-connections                          128
network.http.max-connections-per-server                48
network.http.max-persistent-connections-per-proxy      24
network.http.max-persistent-connections-per-server     12
```

These values are only guidelines for some sensible settings.

> You should bear in mind that the higher the values in these settings, the greater the load on the web site server your connection will cause. Therefore, don't increase these values too much.

Eliminate Annoying Browser Stalls
H A C K
#61   Here's a method to short-circuit the part of the web page that is stalling your browser.

It doesn't happen often, but every once in a while, you visit a web page that seems to take forever to load, or simply hangs and never finishes loading. The problem often occurs because the web page includes a picture, a button, an advertisement, or some other web element from another server that your browser cannot reach or cannot reach quickly.

These resources are slow to respond for a few reasons. Sometimes there's a bottleneck on the Internet itself. Sometimes a link to a button, picture, or ad points to an Internet site that is overloaded and having trouble responding.

Sometimes a link to an off-site graphical element is pointing to an address that is inexplicably difficult to resolve. You see, for every domain name, such as *oreilly.com*, there are one or more numeric Internet protocol (IP) addresses. Your browser needs to ask a domain name server (DNS) for that IP address, and that server might have to pass the request on to another server, and then to another. Sometimes there's a bad link in the chain, and your browser simply gets hung up waiting to find out the numeric IP address.

This hack refers to a problem with a specific link or site. When Internet access in general seems slow, one thing you can do is go to *http://www.internethealthreport.com/* to see the current status of various Internet access and router points. The poor performance could be caused by a router outage somewhere. It might have nothing to do with the speed of your personal access method to the Internet.

But when you visit a web page again and again for weeks and notice that it consistently stalls, that's a sign that one or more identifiable elements, such as a graphic or advertisement, might be causing the stall. For this hack, assume the problem is with a graphical button. In this case, the web site you are trying to view does not contain the graphics file needed for that button to be displayed. Instead, the web page includes an HTML instruction to get the graphic for that button from another site. You can run into trouble if the browser has trouble finding the IP address for the site that contains the graphic. Or perhaps your browser doesn't have fast access to the site that provides the graphic, or your browser is blocked from accessing that site. The bottom line is that your browser can stall when loading the web page simply because it cannot get the graphical element from a remote site. Some browsers might even refuse to finish loading the page until the problem is resolved.

You can short-circuit this process so that it never has to contact the problematic web site. The trick revolves around how your computer translates domain names, such as *oreilly.com*, to IP addresses.

The */etc/nsswitch.conf* file determines how your computer tries to resolve the address of a domain name. Examine your */etc/nsswitch.conf* file, and look for the line that starts with the label hosts. For example, it might look like this:

```
hosts:      DNS files
```

This tells your computer to check the DNS first, and if it cannot find the IP address from the DNS, to try looking up the IP address in your local file called */etc/hosts*.

If the line looks more like the following, it checks the local file */etc/hosts* first, and then checks with a DNS if it can't find the IP address from your local file:

```
hosts:      files DNS
```

In most cases, browsers are slow to load pages or stall on something such as a graphical element, because the DNS is having trouble resolving the domain name into an IP address.

Short-Circuit the DNS Request

You can short-circuit this process in a few steps. First, make sure the line in your */etc/nsswitch.conf* file looks like the latter example, where files precedes DNS. If your */etc/nsswitch.conf* file places something other than files first, rearrange the order to make sure files comes first.

Next, determine the domain name that is causing your browser to load a page slowly or get stuck loading a web page element. Here's how to track down the troublesome site. Keep your eye on the status bar in your browser. If you are experiencing the kind of problem I've been describing, the status bar usually reads something like "Looking up *www.someadvertisementsite.com*" or "Waiting for *www.someadvertisementsite.com*" while is it slow or stuck. The status message won't change until it can find or contact that site. (Be careful not to move the mouse while you are waiting for the site to load, or you might inadvertently clear this status message even though the problem continues to exist.)

Suppose your browser is getting stuck loading a page, because it is having trouble trying to figure out the IP address of a host such as *www.someadvertisementsite.com*. That's because it cannot find the IP address in your */etc/hosts* file, and it has to resolve the address using DNS.

Now edit your */etc/hosts* file and add a line that defines the problematic web site so that it points to the IP address for your *localhost* (your own machine):

```
127.0.0.1 www.someadvertisementsite.com
```

That's all you need to do. The next time you browse the web page, your browser will assume the graphic, button, advertisement, or other problematic element resides on your own machine. It will fail (quickly) to find what it needs, and then move on to finish loading the page.

You can also use this technique to block advertisements. Many domain names are dedicated exclusively to serving advertisements. If you list those domain names in your */etc/hosts* file and make them point to your own machine, your browser won't load the advertisement. I don't recommend doing this, however. This ad-blocking technique isn't nearly as effective as it once was. For one thing, many advertisers have figured out how to get around this short-circuit technique, and it simply won't work. For another, ads are often useful instead of annoying. But if you're determined to block advertisements, plenty of more-effective methods are available, such as ad-blocking extensions for various browsers, or other ad-blocking tools that run in the background.

HACK #62 Get Browser Plug-ins Working

Liven up the Web with a plug-in or two.

The Web has long moved beyond its humble beginnings as a text-based medium. Now it is filled with dynamic content that includes animations, interactivity, video, sound, and other types of media. Special software, known as plug-ins, is usually required to use this new content. Getting plug-ins to work in Firefox can be a little difficult, so this hack explores how to get the two most common plug-ins working: Macromedia Flash and Java.

Use the Macromedia Flash Plug-in

The Macromedia Flash plug-in enables you to view animations on dynamic web sites. A few years back, installing Flash was a difficult and error-prone process, but luckily, the process has improved. First, download the Linux Flash plug-in from *http://www.macromedia.com*, and unzip it into a directory. Once it is extracted, you will see a number of files, including a file called *flashplayer-installer*. This file automates the process of installing Flash.

Before you can run the installer, you must change its permissions so that it is executable:

```
foo@bar:~$ chmod a+x flashplayer-installer
```

To run the installer and have it install the plug-in for you, type the following command:

```
foo@bar:~$ ./flashplayer-installer
```

Once you have run through this installation routine, load up Firefox and type the following into the address bar:

```
about:plugins
```

This page tells you the plug-ins Firefox has installed. Once you've installed the Flash plug-in, you should see two entries that look like this:

```
MIME Type                         Description              Suffixes    Enabled
application/x-shockwave-flash      Shockwave Flash          swf         Yes
application/futuresplash          FutureSplash Player      spl         Yes
```

These two lines indicate that the player is correctly installed. Now you can test the player by visiting a Flash-based web site, such as the "fantastic" *http://www.badgerbadgerbadger.com*.

Use Java in Firefox

Java is a popular cross-platform programming environment in which you can theoretically write a single program, and have it run on a number of different operating systems and web browsers. Although the Java language was developed by Sun Microsystems, it has been licensed openly enough to allow a number of Java software interpreters to be developed by various companies and organizations.

To run Java programs, you need a Java Runtime Environment (JRE). This software lets you run Java programs either in a web browser or as a normal application. By far one of the most popular JREs available is from Sun at *http://java.sun.com/j2se/*. Other Java environments are available that work well with Firefox and normal Java desktop environments, but this hack covers just the official Sun incarnation.

One issue to bear in mind in terms of getting the right JRE is finding one that is compatible with Firefox. The first place you should check for this information is *http://plugindoc.mozdev.org/*. Traditionally, in terms of using Java within Firefox, the main source of problems is that the browser should be compiled with the same major version of the GNU C Compiler as the versions of the JRE you will be using. At the time of this writing, Firefox requires version 1.4.2 or later of the Sun JRE, as this version and most distributed versions of Firefox were compiled with version 3 of the GNU C Compiler. You can check which version your Firefox was compiled with by typing this into the address bar:

```
about:buildconfig
```

It is likely that your version of the browser was compiled with GCC 3.x and should be compatible with the Sun JRE 1.4.2 or above.

When you have downloaded and installed the Sun JRE, you will have a directory with all the files that are part of the JRE distribution. Inside this is a *plugins* directory. To enable Java support in Firefox, you need to create a symbolic link inside your Mozilla plug-ins directory. The actual file in the JRE that you are linking to is *libjavaplugin_oji.so.* You can create this link by going to your Mozilla plug-ins directory in your home directory (this should be *.mozilla/plugins* or *.firefox/plugins*), and type in the following command:

```
foo@bar:~$ ln -s /sources/jre/plugin/i386/ns610-gcc32/libjavaplugin_oji.so
```

This command assumes your JRE is in */sources/jre*; you will need to adjust it for the actual directory on your machine. One point to note is that inside the */sources/jre/plugin/i386* directory are a number of subdirectories which correspond to different versions of Netscape. The *ns610-gcc32* directory contains the correct plug-in for recent versions of Mozilla-based browsers (such as Firefox). If you want to make Java support available to every user on the system, you will need to make the symlink available in the system Mozilla *plugins* directory (such as */usr/lib/mozilla-firefox/plugins*) as opposed to a particular user's plug-ins directory.

You can check that your installation works by typing this into the address bar:

```
about:plugins
```

You should see a number of lines showing that Java support is working. Then you can test the installation by accessing a web site that uses Java, such as *http://java.sun.com/*.

HACK #63 Create an Internet Phone

Talk to the world and save money while doing so.

As the number of broadband installs increases and the connections get faster and faster, the potential to use quality audio and video applications over the Internet has become more feasible. These kinds of heavy-bandwidth applications are no longer the domain of just large corporations with money to spend on expensive Internet access; cable modems and DSL lines bring the technology to the home.

This hack explores how to use two applications to make phone calls to others over the Internet. Although using these applications is fairly straightforward, the configuration of firewalls and security can be a barrier to getting started. In addition to exploring Internet-based calls, I also discuss what options are available to call regular phones from the Internet. A number of services offer PC-to-phone and vice-versa services, and the cost compared to regular phones is often minimal.

GnomeMeeting

GnomeMeeting is a fully open source audio and video conferencing tool. This hack focuses on audio; "Motion Capture and Video Conferencing Fun" [Hack #64] focuses on the use of GnomeMeeting as a video conferencing tool.

When you use GnomeMeeting, a gatekeeper manages your connection. This central server provides a directory of connected clients and their call status. The gatekeeper offers a telephone directory-type service for users, complete with a user profile. This hack doesn't cover how to set up a gatekeeper, but information on this is available at *http://opengatekeeper.sourceforge.net*.

Using GnomeMeeting is fairly simple if you have a working sound card— just connect to the default gatekeeper and go. Using GnomeMeeting gets more complex when you roll a firewall into the mix. GnomeMeeting requires a number of ports to be open on the firewall for the software to work. Opening these ports can be a concern for those who feel uncomfortable about providing additional access past the firewall. Unfortunately, to use GnomeMeeting, you must ensure these ports are forwarded to the machine running GnomeMeeting (or are opened entirely if more than one machine will run GnomeMeeting), or it won't work. One slight consolation is that you can change some of the ports for different numbers by adjusting some settings in *GConf* (the GNOME Configuration program that comes with most GNOME installs). The ports to be forwarded are as follows:

TCP port 1720

> You can change this port if you modify the /apps/gnomemeeting/ports/ listen_port key in *GConf*.

TCP port range 30000–30010

> If you and the remote connection are using H.245 Tunneling, you don't need to forward this range of ports. Microsoft Netmeeting does not support H.245 Tunneling, so you do need to allow and forward this range of ports if you need to connect to Netmeeting clients. You can adjust this range of ports if you modify the /apps/gnomemeeting/ports/tcp_ port_range key in *GConf*.

UDP port range 5000–5007

> This mandatory range of ports is used for audio and video transmission and reception.

UDP port range 5010–5013

> These ports are used when registering to a gatekeeper. You don't need to allow and forward these ports if you don't plan on using a gate-keeper. You can change this range of ports if you modify the /apps/ gnomemeeting/ports/udp_port_range key using GConf.

Once you have set up your firewall to forward these ports [Hack #81], you must also ensure that these ports are available to the outside world. Smoothwall includes an External Services Access screen where you can configure this. If you're accessing the Internet from a LAN, you should turn on "Enable IP translation" in the H.323 Advanced section of the GnomeMeeting preferences so that GnomeMeeting can apply some processing to work over Network Address Translation (NAT) routers. Previous versions of GnomeMeeting (0.94 and before) required that a special library called *RSIP* (*http://openresources. info.ucl.ac.be/rsip/*) be installed to achieve the same feature.

With the network settings complete, you can plug in your microphone. Make sure the mic volume is turned up; many people forget to do this. If you are using an ALSA-based setup, you can adjust the volume by using alsamixer or the volume controls on your desktop. With all of this complete, GnomeMeeting is ready to make calls.

Skype

The new kid on the block in the Voice over IP world is Skype (*http:// www.skype.com*). This multiplatform Internet phone uses proprietary peer-to-peer technology to provide an efficient way of connecting to another client. If you don't have a problem with the proprietary nature of Skype, it is a highly recommended tool. The sound quality and performance are simply incredible. One particularly interesting feature about Skype is that it requires no port-forwarding or adjustments to your firewall. This feature can be a saving grace for those who have battled to get GnomeMeeting working and have found the hill too steep to climb. Skype, by comparison, is a breeze to set up.

Calling Regular Phones

Both GnomeMeeting and Skype support PC-to-phone calls, but each has a different method of dealing with these types of calls. In Skype, you simply need to register a SkypeOut account, and then buy credits that allow you to call regular phones. No additional software or hardware is required.

If you want to call phones with GnomeMeeting, the process is more complicated. First, you need to purchase some Quicknet hardware at *http:// www.linuxjack.com*. Due to the patented nature of the G.723.1 audio codec that is required to make phone calls, the codec cannot be included in the GnomeMeeting code. But if you buy the Quicknet hardware, the codec is included in the hardware itself, along with features, such as a speaker phone, hardware support, and other niceties. Once you have installed the hardware and it is working, you need to install the latest version of the

Open H323 driver from *http://www.openh323.org*. It is required to make PC-to-phone calls. To actually make calls with GnomeMeeting you need to register a MicroTelco account on *http://www.linuxjack.com*. This gives you a login and PIN number that you can enter into the GnomeMeeting settings. Finally, plug your normal phone device (analog phone, cordless phone, etc.) into the Quicknet hardware, and dial the phone as normal.

Motion Capture and Video Conferencing Fun
#64   Keep an eye on the world with your webcam.

Some years back, it was the height of geek cred to have a webcam. At that point in history, the average webcam was a hulking device that looked more like a CCTV camera and cost an inordinate amount of money. Many of these bulky units also needed an expensive video card to squeeze the huge amounts of data through weedy '486 processors. Since those early days, the success of the webcam has catapulted and virtually everyone has picked one up for peanuts.

With this explosion of webcams and the rapid growth in broadband speed, videoconferencing has become something of a reality. "Create an Internet Phone" [Hack #63] covered how to use the GnomeMeeting application to make phone calls over the Internet. In this hack, I cover the video conferencing side of GnomeMeeting as well as explore how to enable motion capture so that you can use it to form a security system in your home/office.

Setting Up a Webcam

Before you get started using GnomeMeeting and motion capture, the first step is to ensure that you have a working webcam configured. With more and more people using Project Utopia [Hack #93], device configuration is becoming less of an issue, but it probably needs a brief discussion.

First, you should find out which driver your webcam needs. A number of online hardware databases and some sensible Google searching can help you with this. Then you can find out if that driver is included in your kernel version or if you need to upgrade to a later kernel [Hack #89] that does support your webcam. If the driver is not included in the latest kernel version or you need a newer version of the driver than the one that's included in the kernel tree, you will probably need to patch the kernel source to get the driver you need.

In addition to using a driver for your webcam, you should also ensure that you compile Video 4 Linux support into your kernel. Video 4 Linux provides a standardized method for the kernel to handle video devices. Support for this is in the main kernel tree. It is recommended that this be compiled as a module that can be loaded when you access your webcam.

Most webcams are USB-powered, so you need to ensure that your USB system is configured correctly [Hack #93]. When you plug in a camera, it should load the Video 4 Linux module. Check that it does with this command:

```
foo@Bar:~$ lsmod
```

In the output you should see videodev listed. If it is not listed, you should insert it with insmod:

```
foo@bar:~$ insmod videodev
```

Once Video 4 Linux is loaded, it creates one or more *video* entries in */dev*. Check this with:

```
foo@bar:~$ ls -al /dev/video*
```

When you run this command, you should see at least one entry appear. If this is not the case, your camera is not working with Linux. You should double-check your previous work to make sure you did everything necessary.

Using GnomeMeeting

When you first run GnomeMeeting, you are taken through a configuration druid that helps you set up and configure the program. Included in this setup routine are some features for ensuring your webcam is working properly. At the end of this process, you can click the webcam icon and see the video from your camera in the window.

If you see a corrupted picture when viewing video in GnomeMeeting, the webcam driver might have some bugs that might require an update to a newer driver version; this has been a problem with the OV511 chip-based range of devices. You should check your camera with a range of software such as *xawtv* or Camorama. If you can get video working in other tools, it might be a problem with how GnomeMeeting is accessing the device. If this is the case, you should contact the GnomeMeeting developers at *http://www.gnomemeeting.org*.

Creating a Motion Capture Camera

The concept of motion capture is fairly simple. You set up a camera in a particular location and the camera registers when a particular threshold of pixels changes. As an example, you could have a camera focused on a room, and if someone walks past the camera the recording software is triggered by the motion.

This hack covers a tool called *motion* that is incredibly flexible in dealing with a variety of motion capture needs. What is particularly interesting about *motion* is the range of responses that can be triggered when motion occurs. The software can send you an email, update a database, save a picture, record a video clip, play a sound, and more. *motion* is also flexible in how it is configured and used.

To get started, first you should install *motion* using your distribution package manager, or from the official web site at *http://www.lavrsen.dk/twiki/bin/view/Motion/DownloadFiles*. You also need to download the software dependencies if you want to save images and movies when movement occurs. Details about these requirements are on the *motion* web site.

Running *motion* is simple; just run it from the command line:

```
foo@bar:~$ motion
```

motion reads a central configuration file called *motion.conf*, which is normally stored in */etc*. This easy-to-configure file contains settings for all features within *motion*. The first section that you should concentrate on is called Capture Device Options. Here you should set videodevice to the device in */dev* that you are using (this is usually */dev/video0*). You should also adjust the frame rate, as this affects the accuracy of the webcam. The next important section to complete is Motion Detection Settings, where you should set the threshold setting to something that is suitable. This setting specifies how sensitive the motion capture is. To test this, run *motion*, move in front of the camera, and see how the software reacts. A good test is to look at the camera, stand still, and move your eyes, mouth, and other parts of your face to see if the movement triggers the camera.

The rest of the file contains settings that can be used to send you an email when motion occurs, store information in a database, and store images and video. If you want to store images and video, you should ensure that you set the target_dir setting to a directory where you want to store the images/video.

motion also includes a comprehensive set of command-line options that negate the need for a configuration file in some cases. These command-line options are useful if you want to use *motion* in a very specific way, possibly in a script or cronjob. In addition to this flexibility, *motion* includes a special execute option with which you can specify a script or command that can be executed when motion is detected.

Put Screenshots Automatically on the Web

#65 Show off to the world what you're up to.

This little hack is fun. It does not improve system performance in any way, but it allows you to share with the world what you're currently doing. This hack is a perfect way for you to demonstrate how cool your Linux desktop is by automatically taking screenshots of your desktop and uploading them to a web server.

The script this hack uses to upload the screenshot is written in Perl and requires Net::FTP, a web server, and a simple program called *scrot*; all of these are freely available online.

Installing scrot

You can find *scrot*, a command-line screen-capture tool (similar to import, which is included with ImageMagick), at *http://linuxbrit.co.uk/scrot/*. Extract, compile, and install the software with these few commands:

```
foo@bar:~$ wget http://linuxbrit.co.uk/downloads/scrot-0.8.tar.gz
foo@bar:~$ tar -zxvf scrot-0.8.tar.gz
foo@bar:~$ cd scrot-0.8
foo@bar:~$ ./configure
foo@bar:~$ make
foo@bar:~$ su -c "make install"
```

With *scrot* installed, you can use it to take screenshots anytime you want; just find the nearest terminal and type **scrot**. For more information on *scrot*, see the manpage.

Perl is likely to be installed already on your Linux system, but if it isn't, you should use your distribution's installation tool to install it. In addition to the stock Perl installation, you also need the Net::FTP module that you can install by using CPAN, Perl's module repository:

```
foo@bar:~# perl -e shell -MCPAN
foo@bar:~# install Net::FTP
```

The Code

This is where all the magic is. Just write each line into your favorite text editor, whether it is *emacs* or *vim* or something else, and save it as *autoscreenshot.pl* in *$localfolder*:

```
#!/usr/bin/perl -w
use Net::FTP; # Start FTP

## Define your variables
$delay = "60"; # Set the screen captures in seconds
$quality = "50"; # Set the quality of the screenshot
$thumb = "25"; # Set percentage of the thumbnail produced
$server = "your.server.com"; # Hostname of the server
$username = "username"; # Put your username for the server here
$password = "password"; # Put your password for the server here
$serverfolder = "/home/me/www"; # This is the folder that you want the
pictures to end up in
$localfolder = "/home/me/autoscreensnap"; # This is the folder in which you
are going to locally save the screenshots

while()
```

```
    {
      system("scrot $localfolder/currentscreen.jpg --thumb $thumb --quality
    $quality"); # Let's take the screenshot

      $ftp = Net::FTP->new($server, Debug => 0); # Connect to FTP server
      $ftp->login($username, $password); # Let's log in
      print "OK Connected \n";
      $ftp->cwd($serverfolder); # Change to the directory you want uploaded
    image to be in
      print "OK Changed directories \n";
      $ftp->binary(); # Set binary mode so the picture works
      $ftp->delete("$serverfolder/currentscreen.jpg"); # Delete old screenshot
      $ftp->delete("$serverfolder/currentscreen-thumb.jpg"); # Delete old
    thumbnail
      print "Deleted old screenshots\n";
      $ftp->put("$localfolder/currentscreen.jpg"); # Uploading...
      $ftp->put("$localfolder/currentscreen-thumb.jpg"); #Upload some more..
      print "OK Finished uploading files\n";
      $ftp->quit; # Close session
      print "Sleeping for $delay seconds\n\n";
      system("sleep $delay");
    }
```

The first half of the script is just to define all your variables. It is safe to
change these and it is recommended that you do change them to suit your
needs. These options include the following:

$delay

> Determines how long the script will wait, in seconds, until it repeats the
> loop.

$quality

> Controls the quality of the screenshot that will be taken. I suggest you
> use a low number so that it doesn't take long to upload or download the
> screenshot.

$thumbnail

> Defines what percentage of your resolution the thumbnail should be.

$server

> The host of your web server; hopefully it has FTP running on it.

$serverfolder

> The folder on your web server that will be accessible by the World Wide
> Web.

$localfolder

> Represents the folder where you are going to store the screenshots. I rec-
> ommend you put it in your home folder just to make everything easy.

The second half of the script uses a loop that repeats itself over and over
again. The first command tells the script to use *scrot* to take a screenshot

and create a thumbnail. Then it connects to the web server and changes to a directory visible on the Internet. Once the script has completed, it deletes any old screenshots and thumbnails and uploads the new ones. After it completes this job, it sleeps for 60 seconds by default (this is adjustable) and then continues the loop once again.

Running the Code

To run the script first change the directory to *$localfolder*. Your *autoscreenshot.pl* script should be sitting in this folder. Now you can run it in two different ways. You can run the script independently with the following commands:

```
foo@bar:~$ chmod 777 autoscreenshot.pl
foo@bar:~$ ./autoscreenshot.pl
```

An alternative is to run it with the Perl interpreter:

```
foo@bar:~$ perl autoscreenshot.pl
```

—John Cheng

Scan for Wireless Networks
Detect which networks are available in your area.

Wireless networks are rapidly gaining use in homes, businesses, schools, and other places. You can often access these networks for your personal use. As an example, if you are visiting a conference and a number of different wireless networks are available, you need to be able to distinguish one network from another and log on. To discover which networks are available to you, you need to use a network scanner.

Another reason to scan a network is to determine how wide-reaching and secure the network is. If you are running a wireless network that is not encrypted, a house down the street might be able to connect and gain free access to your LAN. In some cases, you might want to have an open network (some people leave their wireless networks open to create free Internet hotspots), but in other cases, this might be expressly what you don't want.

Although anyone can connect to a wireless network easily enough, scanning for networks is a different ballgame. First of all, you need to put your network card into a special mode called *monitor mode* that can scan for networks, and then you need to be able to control the card to determine when a network has been detected. You can achieve all of this with a suitable wireless card and a tool called Kismet (*http://www.kismetwireless.net*).

Although every wireless card allows you to connect to a network, not all cards support monitor mode. If you are unsure whether your card supports this mode, some sensible Google searching is likely to indicate if your hardware supports it. When you have determined monitor mode is available, you need to find which driver the card uses. If you are already using the card in Linux, you can probably see which driver is loaded by using this command:

```
foo@bar:~# lsmod
```

Take a look at the list of drivers supported by Kismet at *http://www. kismetwireless.net/documentation.shtml* and see if your driver is included in the list. The cards listed in the Kismet documentation are known to work, but drivers, patches, and third-party support might be available for your card elsewhere. Many of the members of the Kismet mailing lists and IRC channels have experience in a range of different cards, and they can help you determine if your card is supported. If your card isn't fully supported by Kismet, you need to peruse the mailing lists (available at *http://www. kismetwireless.net/forum.php*) and IRC channel (#kismet on *irc.freenode.net*) to see what level of support is available for your hardware.

Patching the Driver to Enable Monitor Mode

Though some wireless cards do support the use of monitor mode, the default Linux drivers aren't coded to support it. Many of these drivers have patches that can be applied to the kernel driver source code to enable monitor mode support. To use these patches, make sure the patch is suitable for the version of the driver included in the kernel. To find out the version of your driver, look in the *Documentation* directory inside the kernel source code and look through the files in the networking directory. You can also do a search to see which files contain the word *wireless*:

```
foo@bar:~$ grep -rli wireless networking/
```

When you are ready to patch the kernel device driver, download your driver patch to a directory on your hard disk. You can test that the patch will apply cleanly without actually patching the code by running the following command from inside your kernel source tree (usually */usr/src/linux-<version>*):

```
foo@bar:~# patch -p1 --dry-run < /path/to/patches/patch.diff
```

If you don't get any FAIL errors when you run this command, you are ready to patch the file with this command:

```
foo@bar:~# patch -p1 < /path/to/patches/patch.diff
```

Read the documentation files that come with the patch. These instructions might indicate it is necessary to patch the driver from a directory other than */usr/src/linux*, or that you can compile the driver separately from recompiling the kernel.

Now recompile the kernel to build the driver. Then ensure that you are loading the updated driver. This might require a reboot or manually removing the old module from memory and inserting the new one. You can do this with the *rmmod* and insmod commands:

```
foo@bar:~$ rmmod orinoco
foo~bar:~$ insmod orinoco
```

Running Kismet

Kismet is a special tool that can scan for wireless networks and indicate which ones are available for you to connect to. Kismet is packaged for many Linux distributions and the source code is available at *http://www.kismetwireless.net*. Detailed instructions on how to install and set up Kismet are included with the software, so I won't cover that here. The documentation will require you to make some adjustments to your */etc/kismet.conf* file, which controls Kismet's configuration. When you are reading the documentation, you should pay particular attention to the suiduser and PID parts, as these could cause problems with Kismet running.

To start Kismet, run the command-line program:

```
foo@bar:~$ kismet
```

When the program starts, you see an interface that displays a list of networks Kismet has detected. Each network is color-coded to indicate if it is open (red) or encrypted (green). If you have configured speech=true in */etc/kismet.conf* and you have the *festival* speech synthesis software available on your system, Kismet speaks to you and tells you when it detects a network.

Inside the Kismet interface, you can press h to display a help list, which tells you the commands for accessing the application's features. Once you have some sniffed networks displayed in the main window, you need to turn off the default Autofit mode so that you can get more information about the different networks. You can display information in Kismet in a variety of different ways, and you can't use all functions in all modes. To turn off the mode, press the s key, and select another way to sort the networks. Now you can select a network with the arrow keys.

If you press the i key with a network selected, you can find out general information about it. The r key gives you a detailed ASCII graph with the current packet rate—useful for determining how much traffic is available. Another useful mode is the statistics view (a key), which indicates channel usage and the total number of servers and networks.

You also can use Kismet in conjunction with a GPS unit to plot wireless networks on a map [Hack #67].

> Using Kismet might leave your network card in an unstable state. Reload your network card drivers if you experience problems after using Kismet.

Dumpster-Diving the Kismet Way

At this point in your use of Kismet, you have looked at the main methods of scanning for networks. Although the information inside the Kismet interface is useful, you also can use Kismet's other tools to find out even more information about the traffic on the network. The most common method of doing this is by capturing the raw data sent across the wireless network and then using some tools to crack open and sift through the captured information.

When you run Kismet, the raw data it collects is stored in your home directory in a series of *.dump files. These files contain data stored as pcap information (a common network packet format). You can use packet analysis tools to open these dumps and identify patterns in their contents. A number of packet analysis tools are available for Linux, but one of the most popular is Ethereal (http://www.ethereal.com). You can use Ethereal to open these dump files and look for plain-text data, as well as to capture live data. If you use Ethereal to capture live data while your network card is in monitor mode, you will see the low-level frame information about the wireless network, and this can be useful when diagnosing problems with wireless software.

Another useful function of Ethereal is for strengthening network security. If you run Ethereal while connected to a network, the packet data from normal communications is logged, and you can use it to see if plain-text passwords or other sensitive data is being transferred over the stream. A useful feature in Ethereal is the ability to follow a TCP stream conversation, and determine how data is sent back and forth between the client and the server. With this information, you can perform an autopsy on how the traffic is formed and how secure it is.

Map Your Meatspace

HACK #67

A bird's-eye view of the world on your Linux desktop.

When Global Positioning System (GPS) technology was launched, it was heralded as the next big thing. Although its usefulness has not been quite as explosive in the consumer market as many people predicted it would be, GPS has proved useful in areas, such as satellite navigation systems and mapping tools. Although many people think only ramblers and walkers use GPS, the technology actually is useful in numerous applications, many of which you can perform from your Linux desktop. This hack shows you how you can hook up a GPS unit to your Linux desktop and use some open source tools to help map out your area.

Connect the GPS to Linux

A number of GPS units are compatible with Linux, and all of them come with either serial or USB connections. Although two types of connections are available, the USB connector simply uses a special chip called the FTDI chip to convert a legacy serial connector to a USB connector. This chip requires a special driver to convert from a USB to a serial port. A Linux driver has been developed for this and it is available at *http://ftdi-usb-sio.sourceforge.net/*.

Each connector is compatible with Linux, and most of the USB GPS units include the FTDI driver in the kernel. If you are using one of these USB devices, you need to ensure that you have USB drivers compiled into the kernel. You should ensure you have the UHCI, UHCI Alternate Driver, or OHCI options from the USB Support page in the kernel configuration tool. Which option you choose depends on your motherboard; consult your motherboard's manual for information on this.

When you have installed the USB or serial drivers and you have plugged in the device, the GPS unit should be available on the system in */dev/ttyS[n]* for a serial GPS or */dev/ttyUSB[n]* for the USB equivalent. Now you can look in */dev* to see the name of the port from which you can access the GPS:

```
foo@bar:~$ ls -al /dev/ttyS*
```

Or, if you have a USB device:

```
foo@bar:~$ ls -al /dev/ttyUSB*
```

At this point your GPS is recognized by the system, and you can configure your GPS applications to look at this port for your GPS unit. If you are thinking of purchasing a GPS unit, it is recommended that you get one with full NMEA compatibility. This will ensure that the unit will work with most of the common GPS software tools.

Use Mapping Software

You probably want to use GPS so that you can view a map of your area as you travel through it. Some GPSes display a general map with streets and street names, and other maps go one step further to provide instructions on where to go (such as "at the end of the road, turn left" instructions). The former system uses general mapping information and the latter is a vector-based satellite navigation system.

For general mapping information, a useful tool is GpsDrive (*http://gpsdrive. kraftvoll.at/*). You can use this application to indicate your current location, to plot waypoints (locations in latitude and longitude), and to interact with other GPS users over a wireless network.

Although GpsDrive is a useful tool, one of its problems is that free maps of Europe and many other parts of the world are not available for use with it. The lack of free maps is a big problem with GPS software in general. GpsDrive does spider some online mapping web sites to download maps for the areas you are in, but that is useful only when a map is available, and only if you have wireless connectivity when you enter a new area. To solve this problem, you need to use a script that can download maps of entire areas in advance of your visit (this script is covered later in this hack).

Another option, particularly if you just want to see where your location is in the world, is to use the free NASA maps to plot your position inside GpsDrive. Before you do this, you should ensure you have at least 3GB of disk space available, as the NASA maps are huge. You need to download two maps from *ftp:// mitch.gsfc.nasa.gov/pub/stockli/bluemarble/* called *MOD09A1.W.interpol.cyl. retouched.topo.3x21600x21600.gz* and *MOD09A1.E.interpol.cyl.retouched.topo. 3x21600x21600.gz*. When you have downloaded the files, create a *nasamaps* directory inside your *~/.gpsdrive* configuration folder:

```
foo@bar:~$ mkdir ~/.gpsdrive/nasamaps
```

Now copy the files into this directory, and rename them to *top_nasamap_ east.raw* and *top_nasamap_west.raw*, respectively:

```
foo@bar:~$ mv MOD09A1.E* top_nasamap_east.raw
foo@bar:~$ mv MOD09A1.W* top_nasamap_west.raw
```

Now when you run GpsDrive, the smaller maps for the different parts of the world will be created on-the-fly from these larger maps. To see these maps, you need to select "Topo map" in the "Show map type" field.

Spidering Mapping Information

Although GpsDrive allows you to download maps displaying the area you are in, it is likely that you will want to download a number of maps displaying different parts of your area or country. You can do this with a small shell script called *gpsfetchmap.pl*, which is included with GpsDrive. You can use this script to spider a number of maps between two sets of longitude and latitude points and download all the content for use with GpsDrive. All these maps will be downloaded from the Expedia Germany web site (*http://www.expedia.de/*).

To use the script, you need to pass it the latitude and longitude of the top left corner and bottom right corner of the region you want maps for. The top left corner is referred to as the starting latitude/longitude, and the bottom right corner is the ending latitude/longitude. You should also pass the script the scale of the map. For street-level detail, a scale of 1500 is recommended. Here is an example of the command in use:

```
foo@bar:~$ gpsfetchmap107.pl --start-lat 52.2401 --end-lat 52.3096 --start-
lon 13.2265 --end-lon 13.3203 -sc 1500 -a 4 -p
```

Connect to a Microsoft PPTP VPN

When your place of business has chosen to protect access to its network with a Microsoft VPN, you need a Linux way to make a secure connection.

At home you are running the "One True" operating system, but at work you are languishing in a solid Microsoft shop. Your business is so far into the Microsoft camp that, horror of horrors, it has chosen to protect network access using a Microsoft VPN server. It won't even allow an SSH connection, which means you can't use port forwarding in SSH to access internal resources [Hack #75]. As a Linux user, you can use the plentiful open source tools to access your work email and files, and even remotely control your desktop PC. All that is stopping you from this computing-at-home nirvana is being able to connect to the existing Microsoft VPN server.

To connect and make your work machine available at home, you need to install some software known as PPTP Client. This package allows a Linux system to connect to a Microsoft PPTP VPN. The project is hosted at *http://pptpclient.sourceforge.net/*, but you might find the software is already available in your current distribution. The project web site has details on how to install the software if your distribution does not include it.

Configuration

Before you can start using PPTP Client, you need some information from you network administrator, namely:

- The IP address or hostname of the PPTP server (server)
- The authentication domain name (domain)
- The username you are to use (username)

- The password you are to use (password)
- Whether encryption is required

Using this information, you can start editing the configuration files. Fire up your favorite text editor, create a file called */etc/ppp/peers/office*, and insert the *username* and the options file that contains your PPP configuration to use (*options.pptp*). As an example, you could have a file with the following settings:

```
# PPTP Tunnel configuration for tunnel office
#
# Specify our login username (may need to be domain\\username)
#
name username
#
# get all other options from the file /etc/ppp/options.pptp
#
file /etc/ppp/options.pptp
```

Depending on the VPN server you are connecting to, you might have to change *username* to *domain\\username*, where both values are replaced with the information your network administrator gives you. Next, edit the */etc/ppp/options.pptp* file, which should contain the following:

```
#
# Lock the port
#
lock

#
# We don't need the tunnel server to authenticate itself
#
noauth

#
# Turn off transmission protocols we know won't be used
#
nobsdcomp
nodeflate

#
# We want MPPE
#
require-mppe
```

If your kernel does not already support it, you also need MPPE support to be built-in. Run this command as root:

```
foo@bar:~# modprobe ppp-compress-18
```

If the module loads without error, everything is well; otherwise, you need to obtain or build the *ppp_mppe* kernel module. If you are using a stock distribution kernel, this could be as simple as installing the required package. If a package isn't available, you need to build a custom kernel. The required kernel option (using menuconfig) is Network Device Support → PPP (point-to-point protocol) Support → PPP MPPE Compression (encryption).

You also need to use Version 2.4.2 or above of the *ppp* package. Now you need to edit the */etc/ppp/chap-secrets* file to contain the following:

```
## OUTBOUND CONNECTIONS
username  "*"  password
```

Again, you should replace both **username** and **password** with the values your network administrator gives you. If you are running a firewall at your end (you should be!), you need to configure the firewall to allow all packets out on TCP port 1723 to the VPN server. This is used to negotiate the connection and to pass link control traffic. The only other change that is required is to allow all GRE protocol packets (protocol number 47) between the client system and the VPN server. You should do this for both inbound and outbound traffic.

Starting the VPN

Now everything should be ready to go. To make a connection, log in as root and run the following command:

```
foo@bar:~# pptp-command start office
Using interface ppp0
Connect: ppp0 <--> /dev/pts/1
MPPE 128-bit stateless compression enabled
Cannot determine ethernet address for proxy ARP
local  IP address www.vvv.xxx.yyy
remote IP address www.vvv.xxx.zzz
pptp-command: added route add default dev ppp0
Tunnel office is active on ppp0. Local IP Address: www.vvv.xxx.yyy
```

Now try pinging a server on the remote end, which should give a result similar to the following:

```
foo@bar:~# ping -c 1 www.vvv.xxx.aaa
PING www.vvv.xxx.aaa (www.vvv.xxx.aaa) 56(84) bytes of data.
64 bytes from www.vvv.xxx.aaa: icmp_seq=1 ttl=126 time=45.8 ms

--- www.vvv.xxx.aaa ping statistics ---
4 packets transmitted, 4 received, 0% packet loss, time 3002ms
rtt min/avg/max/mdev = 42.745/45.541/48.479/2.052 ms
```

Applications

OK, so now you should have a working connection to the office VPN server (and the office LAN), so what are you going to do with it? Perhaps the simplest thing to do now is to launch your favorite web browser, and point it at the company's intranet server. If you have a Microsoft Exchange server, try pointing your web browser at *http://mailserver/exchange*, where *mailserver* is the actual name of your Exchange server. Then you should be able to log in with your username and password and access your email. Alternatively, you can set up the email client on your Linux machine to pull mail from your corporate mail server, or you can access your work machine via RDP if it is a Windows XP desktop, or VNC if it is anything else **[Hack #30]**. Basically, once you have a VPN connection to your corporate network, you can do anything you would do at work, just a little more slowly.

It is important to remember that all packets passing over the VPN are encrypted, which introduces a bit of latency. This does not normally present a problem with most applications—e.g., web, email, file transfers. Some applications, such as Voice over IP, will be affected by this latency and will require careful tuning to operate successfully.

—Ron Wellsted

Play Restricted Media Formats

HACK #69

For licensing reasons, not all distributions come preconfigured to play several popular media formats.

Out of the box, many Linux distributions do not include support to play a few restricted media formats, such as DivX, Windows Media (WMV), Quicktime, and DVDs. The distros don't include the codecs to play these formats due to licensing restrictions. However, you can download the codecs yourself, and use them with media player backends, such as mplayer and xine. Getting DVDs to play is a bit trickier.

Playing non-DVD Media Formats

Mplayer is a cross-platform multimedia player that is quite popular on Linux. The makers of mplayer host the sites where you can obtain the codecs for media formats that aren't normally supported on Linux. These codecs are usually the *Win32.dll* files that are used on Windows systems, and mplayer is programmed to let you use these codecs on Linux. You can obtain the most commonly used media codecs by downloading the essentials package from *http://www.mplayerhq.hu/homepage/dload.html*. These codecs can be used with the other popular media player on Linux, xine.

Uncompress the download and put the contents in */usr/lib/win32*, which is where mplayer and xine will look for codecs by default:

```
dbrick@rivendell:$ tar -jxvf essential-20050216.tar.bz2
dbrick@rivendell:$ sudo cp essential-20050216/* /usr/lib/win32/
```

Restart your media player, and you should now be able to play most restricted formats. For a full list of formats that are supported, visit: *http://www.mplayerhq.hu/homepage/design7/info.html*.

> Mplayer and xine each have several frontend GUIs, such as kmplayer, kaffeine, namp, Totem, and oxine. So, regardless of the media player your distribution is configured to use, you can probably drop the codecs into the */usr/lib/win32* directory and have it just work.

Playing DVDs

Getting DVDs to play on your Linux box is usually a bit trickier. Distributions, such as Suse, Mandrake, Fedora, and Debian, do not provide support for DVD playback compiled into the binaries of their media players (mplayer and xine usually). Your options are either to compile the support into the players yourself or to find a binary that already has it for you.

The best place I've found for instruction on DVD playback is at *http://www. geniusweb.com/LDP/HOWTO/html_single/DVD-Playback-HOWTO/*. By using the instructions on this website, you should be able to get DVD playback working for most distributions. For each distribution, there are usually several links that take you to download sites where you can get the latest packages of the media players or required libraries. Read each section carefully, and make sure you are installing only what is necessary to enable a particular media player backend; there is no need to perform the instructions for both mplayer and xine if you are only using one. The instructions also push the *ogle* frontend. You should feel free to use your preferred frontend it its place.

You'll notice that each distribution's instructions have you install the *libdvdcss* library. This library is used to playback encrypted DVDs (which is nearly all of them), so it is a requirement regardless of the backend you choose. In some countries, it may be illegal to use this library.

DVD playback requires quite a bit of processing power. Depending upon your setup, you may be able to get by with a processor as slow as Pentium II 500Mhz, but you probably can't go any slower than that. As mentioned on the website, you should also be sure to enable DMA on your DVD drive **[Hack #55]**. If you don't, you'll experience jerkiness in your video playback regardless of processor speed.

—David Brickner

## CHAPTER 9

Administration and Automation

Hacks #70–87

Administering and automating maintenance tasks isn't important just for server users. It's extremely important for desktop users, too, especially for those who want to get the most out of their Linux desktop. This chapter is a treasure house of information on administering and automating Linux tasks.

These hacks make mundane tasks easy or automatic (such as keeping your clock synchronized), and they make seemingly impossible tasks possible (such as restoring a Debian system that appears damaged beyond hope).

Regardless of your specific desires or needs, this is one chapter you do not want to gloss over. One or more of these hacks will prove useful to you, even if you're a casual desktop user. Or you can find a way to adapt the hack to be even more useful for your specific needs. Count on it.

HACK #70 Automate Your Life with cron

Computers love boring work, so why not use cron to work them harder?

One of the great benefits of using computers is that they are ideal candidates for performing the uninteresting jobs humans get tired of doing. Most of us would be bored senseless making database backups everyday, cleaning out disks, updating report files, and managing system logs. These activities are typically linear, mundane processes that are straightforward enough to require little intervention, which makes them ideal candidates for automation.

One of the most fundamental pieces of the toolbox within all Unix-type operating systems is called *cron*. This small utility is like an alarm clock. When the alarm goes off, it tells the computer to do whatever you have configured it to do. As an example, if you perform a backup every day, you can get *cron* to perform this for you at a specific time. Another example is if you need to generate a weekly report about a project—*cron* can generate this report automatically.

An important point to note is that *cron* does not actually perform these activities itself. *cron*'s only function is to trigger a specific process or series of commands at a certain time. When the specified time occurs, the commands and tools that are needed to complete the activity are run. As such, to automate a process on your computer, you need to determine how you can complete your task with a series of command-line tools. This usually means you need to create a script with the commands for *cron* to run at specified intervals.

Create a Cronjob

The *cron* program reads in a special file called a crontab. This file specifies jobs to be run and their times. You can access this file by running:

```
foo@bar:~$ crontab -e
```

This command uses the system's default command-line editor so that you can edit the crontab. If you want to set this editor to a different one (such as *jed*), set the $EDITOR environment variable prior to editing crontab:

```
foo@bar:~$ export EDITOR=jed
```

If this is your first use of *cron*, it is likely that your crontab is empty; unless some special system cronjobs were added (these automatically added crontabs are quite common in a number of Linux tools and utilities). Each cronjob consists of a single line containing the time of the cronjob, as well as the command to run.

A simple example of a crontab entry is:

```
30 3 1 * * /home/foo/createreport.sh
```

This example runs a script called *createreport.sh* at 3:30 a.m. on the first day of each month. The numbers on the left side of the line identify the time at which the script should be run, and the */home/foo/createreport.sh* part shows the location and name of the script. It is always important that you use full and absolute paths when referring to scripts and files, as *cron* does not understand relative paths.

The numbers and stars on the left side of the line are entries in five different columns. Here are the columns, from left to right.

Minutes
> This column indicates the minute part of the time in which the cronjob is to be run.

Hours
> This column indicates the hour of the job and is given in 23-hour time (0_23). The time between midnight and 1:00 a.m. is the 0 hour.

Day

This is the number of the day in the month when the job is to be run.

Month

This is the month number between 1 and 12.

Day of the week

This is the day of the week, between 0 and 6, where 0 is Sunday.

In this example, you indicated the time as 3:30 a.m., and the day as the first day of the month. The two asterisks (*) show you want to run the script for each time increment in that column—i.e., every day or month. As per the example, the * in the month and day-of-the-week columns means the cronjob will run every month and every day.

When you have finished editing the crontab, saved the file, and exited, the changes are automatically enabled. You can view the entries in the crontab file by running:

```
foo@bar:~$ crontab -l
```

You can also remove the entire crontab by using the -r option:

```
foo@bar:~$ crontab -r
```

More Advanced Crontabs

Although creating a crontab is fairly simple, if you need to have cronjobs running at specific intervals during a day, month, or year, this can result in a number of duplicated crontab entries with different times. To solve this problem, *cron* has a number of special symbols you can use to configure more elaborate times.

The first symbol is a comma (,), and you can use this to add multiple entries to a column. As an example, you can run the cronjob on the 5th, 10th, and 15th of each month with this line:

```
30 3 5,10,15 * * /home/foo/createreport.sh
```

Another useful symbol is the dash (-). You can use this to set a range for a particular column. For example, you can run the cronjob every day for the first week of a month with this line:

```
30 3 1-7 * * /home/foo/createreport.sh
```

A final symbol that is useful is the slash (/). You can use this to divide a column into regular intervals. In the following example, the */6 option means the cronjob will be run every six minutes:

```
*/6 * * * * /home/foo/createreport.sh
```

Make cron Email You

To cement your knowledge of *cron* let's try creating a cronjob that does something dynamic. The following cronjob emails you a daily report showing the current disk usage on your computer:

```
0 0 * * * echo -e "This is a summary of disk usage on your
server:\n\n `df -h`" | mail -s 'Disk report for `hostname`
on `date`' foo@bar.org
```

In this example, use the echo command to create the text of the email; then embed the df (disk free) command in backticks and pipe the output to the mail command. Then the command creates the subject line of the email dynamically by calling the date and hostname commands.

This example illustrates that you can perform quite complex tasks as cronjobs, but that the crontab file itself can start to look very confusing. If you intend to do more complex tasks, such as the one in the previous example, it's probably better to put the code that does the actual work into a separate script file, and then just call it from the crontab. For safety it's also considered good practice to have your *cron* entry test that the script it is trying to call actually exists and can be executed. For the previous example, you can create a script called */home/foo/diskreport.sh* like this:

```
#!/bin/sh
echo -e "This is a summary of disk usage on your
server:\n\n `df -h`" | mail -s 'Disk report for `hostname`
on `date`' foo@bar.org
```

Then in your crontab, you can place an entry to call the script like this:

```
0 0 * * * test -x /home/foo/diskreport.sh || exit 0; /home/foo/diskreport.sh
```

The test -x checks whether the file exists and is executable, and it lets *cron* exit cleanly without an error instead of generating an error message if it can't run the script.

 H A C K
#71

Update Your Clock via the Internet

Staying in time is easier when you let someone else set your clocks.

There is little doubt that time is an important part of your daily life. Everything from watching the latest episode of your favorite TV program to having a meeting with your boss is based around time, and your computer is no different. Inside your computer, hardware and software rely on time to help keep you up-to-date. If our computers didn't know the time, our calendar, email, and personal-information management would be a mess. Each of these tools relies heavily on having an accurate clock, and the challenge is keeping this clock accurate.

This hack explores a little tool called the Network Time Protocol (NTP) that can solve your inaccurate-clock problems. The NTP software synchronizes your computer's clock with a central server on the Internet with impressive accuracy, and if you set this synchronization to occur when your system boots (or at regular intervals), your clock will never be inaccurate again.

Getting NTP

The NTP software is available for download from *http://www.ntp.org*, but it is probably best to use your distributions package-management program to obtain the software.

With the software installed, you need to find a server with which to synchronize your clock. Many ISPs provide NTP services to their subscribers; contact your ISP to see if it has a server to synchronize with. If your ISP does not provide a server, a number of public NTP servers are available for different regions of the world. The easiest way to find these servers is to search on Google for your location/country and the words *public NTP server*. For quick synchronizations which lead to a more accurate clock, choose a server as physically close to your geographic location as possible. Also, because you are an end user, you should not synchronize to a stratum 1 server. These servers are reserved for use only when you are setting up your own NTP server that will service thousands of clients.

Synchronizing Your Clock

Within the NTP software is a tool called *ntpdate* that is used to synchronize your clock with an NTP server. With the server address you just obtained and *ntpdate*, you can easily synchronize your clock with this command:

```
foo@bar:~$ ntpdate ntp.yourserver.com
```

When you run this command, *ntpdate* will connect to the server and perform the synchronization. For an even easier method of running NTP, create a configuration file, */etc/ntp.conf*, with your servers included. Use this format to add your server:

```
server ntp.yourserver.com
```

With the file created, you need to use the *ntpd* daemon to read the file and synchronize your clock. You can start it manually with this command:

```
foo@bar:~$ ntpd
```

You should use your distribution's startup services software manager to load *ntpd* when the system boots.

Automate NTP Synchronization

Apart from setting your clock, one of the best uses of NTP is to synchronize your clock regularly to compensate for the natural drift that occurs with a hardware clock. This drift is caused by various issues such as power fluctuations and hardware problems, but if you synchronize with NTP as often as possible, you can reduce this drift.

To schedule synchronization at regular intervals, use a cronjob to automate these NTP updates. "Automate Your Life with cron" **[Hack #70]** fully explains the uses of *cron*. You can create your cronjob by opening the cron file with:

```
foo@bar:~$ crontab -e
```

Then add a line to define the cronjob. As an example, to synchronize your clock once a day at 3:00 a.m., use this line:

```
00 03 * * * ntpdate ntp.yourserver.com > /dev/null
```

When you save and quit the editor, your cronjob will be enabled and your clock will be updated regularly.

HACK #72 Start Desktop Applications Automatically

Start tools, utilities, and applications automatically as soon as you start your favorite desktop or window manager.

You might want to start a number of programs automatically as soon as you launch your window manager or desktop environment. For example, assume you set up your LinEAK keyboard utility so that you can use all the special keys on your Internet and multimedia keyboard **[Hack #29]**. Naturally, you want to run this utility every time you start your window manager, but you don't want to have to start it manually. What you need is a way to have LinEAK and any other program you want running launch automatically as you start up your graphical desktop.

Some of the solutions that follow are features of the X Window System, so they will work regardless of the window manager or desktop you use. But many window managers and desktops also have their own special and interesting ways to start up programs automatically, so this hack covers those as well.

Back to Basics

One of the most basic ways of starting a window manager is to create a file called ~/.xinitrc, and set it up so that it runs your favorite window manager whenever you issue the command startx. Assuming you use this approach, here's the simplest form of the .xinitrc file using Fluxbox as an example window manager to launch:

```
exec /usr/bin/fluxbox
```

All this does is start up the Fluxbox window manager. To start LinEAK, the custom keyboard utility, add the following line to the *.xinitrc* file before you start Fluxbox:

```
lineakd &
exec /usr/bin/fluxbox
```

Notice the ampersand (&) following `lineakd`, which tells *lineakd* to start in the background. Unless a program places itself automatically in the background without a trailing ampersand, you need to make sure you add the ampersand. Without the ampersand, the `lineakd` command will not release control back to the ~/*.xinitrc* script, and Fluxbox will never start.

You can launch many additional commands via ~/*.xinitrc*, including commands that control how your X11 graphical system behaves. For example, the `xset -b` command turns off beeps in terminal windows. You can also use `xset` to set the volume and duration of beeps, control the lights (LEDs) on your keyboard, and much more. In this case, you don't need an ampersand after the `xset` commands, because `xset` returns control to the script on its own. Here is a slightly more advanced *.xinitrc* file:

```
xset -b
xcompmgr -cCfF -l 0 -t 0 -r 5 -o .6 &
lineakd &
exec /usr/bin/fluxbox
```

This script also includes the `xcompmgr` command **[Hack #33]** (which works only with Xorg-X11 6.8 or better). This command sets window drop shadows and fade effects. Unlike *xset*, the *xcompmgr* program needs an ampersand to be told to run in the background.

Using the Window Manager and Desktop Features

Window managers and desktop environments often provide their own means of starting programs automatically. The rest of this hack covers specific window managers and how they automatically run programs.

WindowMaker. WindowMaker uses a script file to start programs automatically. The script file is ~/*GNUstep/Library/WindowMaker/autostart*. You can edit the ~/*GNUstep/Library/WindowMaker/autostart* file to include commands much like the ones you would place in your *.xinitrc* file. For example, put this commented command in the *autostart* file to launch the utility that enables your Internet/multimedia keyboard:

```
# XOSD-enabled internet/multimedia keyboard utility
lineakd &
```

XFce 4. When XFce 4 is started with the command `startxfce4`, it will automatically start anything you place in the *~/Desktop/Autostart/* directory. You can place scripts, programs, or symbolic links to scripts and programs in this directory, but you must have permission to execute the scripts and programs for this to work. For example, the following script will find the location of `lineakd` and start it:

```
#!/bin/bash
LINEAKD=`which lineakd`
$LINEAKD &
```

You can create the script with your favorite editor, save it as *startlineakd*, make it executable (**chmod +x startlineakd**), and place it in the *~/Desktop/Autostart* directory.

KDE. KDE is a good example of a desktop environment that offers more power than you can configure out of the commands available to a startup file such as *~/.xinitrc*.

Many desktop environments consist of much more than a window manager. They include panels, launchers, and more. When you start a desktop environment, such as KDE, it automatically starts these extra features. All of these features running together are considered a *session*. You can configure KDE to remember what applications you are running when you log out, and KDE will consider those programs as part of the next session and start them automatically the next time you start KDE. So, one of the simplest ways to start programs automatically in KDE is to save your current session when you exit KDE. In fact, most distributions preconfigure KDE to behave this way automatically, so most of you won't have to turn on this feature. Those of you who don't want KDE to restart the programs you have running when you log out will have to turn off this feature.

Some Linux distributions customize the KDE Control Center, but the typical KDE control panel lets you control session management this way. Start up the Control Center from the main menu, and select KDE Components → Session Manager to see the options for how you want KDE to handle sessions. You can have KDE start a new session each time, restore the last session, or start a manually configured session.

Alternatively, you can start up programs or open files simply by placing them in the *~/.kde/Autostart* directory. There are actually two *Autostart* directories. One is used by KDE to start up applications for every user. The other, the *~/.kde/Autostart* directory, is for personal use. If you want to start programs, you can place a symbolic link to the program in this directory.

You can do this for scripts as well, or even place the script itself in this directory. In all cases, however, you must have permission to execute any scripts or links you place in this directory.

You can also place KDE application launcher files in the *~/.kde/Autostart* directory. You can create a launcher file by right-clicking the desktop, and then selecting Create New → File → Link to Application. The dialog that appears is self-explanatory. You specify the name for the launcher icon in the first tab, and click the icon to select a new icon if you want. Click the third tab labeled Application to specify a command to run. For example, if you specified Firefox as the name of the launcher in the first tab, you would enter **firefox** as the command in the Application tab. This creates a new icon on your desktop with the name Firefox. Drag this icon into your *~/.kde/Autostart* directory to start Firefox every time you start KDE.

The KDE *~/.kde/Autostart* directory also boasts another significant capability that is worth special notice. You don't have to limit what you place in this directory to scripts, programs, or *.desktop* files. You can also place normal files, such as OpenOffice.org documents, pictures, spreadsheets, or whatever you want in the *~/.kde/Autostart* directory. KDE will automatically open these documents as though you clicked their icons in a folder. KDE opens these files by performing the default action for that file type, the same way it has a default action for launching a file when you click it.

GNOME. As with KDE, one simple way to make sure certain programs start automatically when you start GNOME is to set GNOME to save the current session when you exit GNOME. GNOME automatically restores the session the next time you log in to GNOME.

If you want to customize which applications you want started automatically, you need to do it through the sessions manager. The menu item for this program appears in the GNOME menu in various places, depending on the Linux distribution, but the menu selection itself is usually called Sessions. Click the third tab of the Sessions dialog and enter a command you want to execute automatically every session (Figure 9-1).

Figure 9-1. The Gnome Sessions settings dialog

Don't Let Elvis Leave the Building

#73

Keep a program running in the background by automatically restarting it whenever it exits.

Some programs behave contrary to our wishes and exit prematurely, either because they are designed to do so, or because they are flaky and prone to crashing. This hack provides a neat trick to restart such programs automatically every time they exit.

The *xcompmgr* program that provides drop shadows and other special effects for Xorg is still a work in progress, and it often exits unexpectedly. With a simple script, you can automatically restart it every time it exits. First, log in as root, fire up your favorite editor, and create the following script, naming it */usr/local/bin/keep-xcompmgr-running*:

Don't Let Elvis Leave the Building

```
#!/bin/bash
# start up xcompmanager with drop shadows and fade effects
instances=`ps ax | grep "xcompmgr -cCfF" | grep -v grep | wc -1`
if [ $instances == 0 ]; then
while true; do xcompmgr -cCfF -l 0 -t 0 -r 5 -o .6 ; done
else
exit 1
fi
```

The first thing the script does is check to see if the command is already running. If so, the script exits. Perhaps you forgot you already started this script, or perhaps you started the command manually. In either case, you don't want to start two instances, and this portion of the script prevents that.

Notice that the xcompmgr command is not followed with an ampersand. That would launch *xcompmgr* in the background and return control to the script. Then the script would proceed to try to launch more instances of *xcompmgr* over and over again. Trust me. That's a bad thing.

Now save your work and make this script executable with this command:

```
# chmod +x /usr/local/bin/keep-xcompmgr-running
```

The script is a simple infinite loop. But it doesn't just start new instances of *xcompmgr* over and over again. The *xcompmgr* program does not return control to the script unless it fails, so this script will get to the point where it launches the xcompmgr command and its arguments, and then stop running. If *xcompmgr* encounters a bug that causes it to exit unexpectedly, control returns automatically to the script, and the loop continues by starting *xcompmgr* all over again. Then the script stops running until *xcompmgr* fails again. (See the sidebar, "How to Ignore grep.")

Putting the Respawn Trick to Work

One great place to use this trick is in a *.xinitrc* startup script (or any other method of starting up an application automatically when you run a window manager or graphical desktop). The following *.xinitrc* script will work, but if xcompmgr crashes, it will stay crashed:

```
xcompmgr -cCfF -l 0 -t 0 -r 5 -o .6 &
exec /usr/bin/fluxbox
```

If you instead start up the script that keeps *xcompmgr* running, it will restart every time it crashes:

```
/usr/local/bin/keep-xcompmgr-running &
exec /usr/bin/fluxbox
```

How to Ignore grep

Many people use the expression ps ax to see which processes are running, and then pipe the command through a grep command (a search utility) to see if a certain program is in the list. A common problem often occurs when you use a command such as the following in a script to see if *xcompmgr* is already running:

```
ps ax | grep xcompmgr
```

The problem is that even if *xcompmgr* is not running, the command might return a result—the grep command itself. The grep command finds the word "xcompmgr" in the process list, because it put the word there:

```
22833 pts/1    R+     0:00 grep xcompmgr
```

One way to prevent this is to pipe the results through a second grep command. This time, you pipe it through the command grep -v grep. The -v switch tells grep to ignore lines that include the word "grep."

This is how the following line uses the technique to make sure *xcompmgr* is not running:

```
instances=`ps ax | grep "xcompmgr -cCfF" | grep -v grep | wc -1`
```

First, it generates a process list and pipes it through grep to find lines that contain the string xcompmgr -cCfF. If xcompmgr -cCfF is running, this command might return two lines. One line will show the *xcompmgr* process running, and the second line will show the grep command that is looking for this program. Then those lines are piped through *grep* again, this time eliminating lines that contain the word "grep." Finally, it pipes the results through wc -1, which is a command that counts lines of text. If one line is left over after grep removes itself from the list, xcompmgr -cCfF must be running. If no lines are left over after the grep command is removed from the list, you know xcompmgr -cCfF is not running.

You might also be wondering why the script looks for xcompmgr -cCfF rather than something simpler such as xcompmgr. I confess that it's force of habit. Suppose you were looking to see if the *xset* program is running. If we look for the word "xset" it might find the *xsetpointer* program, because the xset string appears in that program, too. The script would get the mistaken idea that *xset* is running, because it found a program with a name that contains the xset string. To avoid this, I have developed the habit of finding ways to make the search string as unique as possible.

Clone Your Linux Install

#74   Deploy a single installation of Linux across many computers.

Cloning is simply a method by which some data is copied exactly, from one medium to another. This can be a physical CD being copied into a CD image (such as an ISO image) or, in the case of this hack, copying a hard-disk partition into a file that can be stored for archival purposes or deployed to several machines. The use of cloning is very widespread on the Internet, with CDs and floppies being distributed as images that are just a bit-for-bit copy of the original medium. Cloning can also be used to move your Linux system to a larger hard drive.

Create an Image

Linux systems generally have a utility installed called *dd* (data dump) that can accept an input from a device and pipe the output as an exact copy of the original to another device or a file. This is the tool you should use when creating a cloned image of an installation.

First, you need to find out which partition on the hard disk contains the root filesystem. You can do this using the mount command:

```
foo@bar:~# mount
```

It should give some output similar to the following:

```
/dev/hda1 on / type ext3 (rw,noatime)
none on /proc type proc (rw)
none on /sys type sysfs (rw)
```

The entry you're looking for is the one mounted on the root filesystem, /. In this case, it is */dev/hda1*. Now that you know the device for the root partition, you can use *dd* to clone the partition. However, it is very unwise to start trying to clone a partition while it is still mounted, because processes that are currently running on the box constantly change the data and the image produced will be inconsistent. The best method is to enter single-user mode when you boot your system, then run a command to remount the root filesystem as read-only. (Other methods are available for doing this; you could use a Knoppix boot CD and log in via a virtual terminal to run your commands, for example.)

To boot into single-user mode, you need to add the kernel argument single on startup. You can find details on how to add kernel arguments to your bootloader in "Give Your Computer the Boot" **[Hack #1]**. If you use this method, you cannot simply unmount the root partition, as it contains the binary for *dd*, which you need to perform the hack. Also while a partition is being cloned, you cannot write the resulting image to anywhere on that partition, because the write process will change the partition while you are copying it. So, you need to find another partition to which you can write the image (it doesn't have to be a Linux partition, but it must have more free space than the size of the partition you are cloning). As such, create a mount point for the partition to which you are going to write the image (*/mnt/foo* in this example):

```
foo@bar:~# mkdir /mnt/foo
```

Then mount your destination partition on that mount point so that you can write the image to it. Another option is to use an external USB hard-disk drive and load the usb_storage module to read it. Most systems have the usb_storage module already compiled, but if yours doesn't, you need to compile it [Hack #88]. You need to have the option under Device Drivers → USB support → USB Mass Storage support set to "Compile as a module." If you have the module loaded, it appears as a SCSI device which can be mounted:

```
foo@bar:~# modprobe usb_storage
foo@bar:~# mount /dev/sda1 /mnt/foo
```

Finally, you need to sync and remount the root partition as read-only so that things cannot change when you are creating the image:

```
foo@bar:~# sync
foo@bar:~# mount -o remount,ro /
```

Now you are ready to create the image. The following command copies the contents of */dev/hda1* and places it as an image file called *image.bin* on the filesystem mounted on */mnt/foo*:

```
foo@bar:~# dd if=/dev/hda1 of=/mnt/foo/image.bin
```

The dd command takes two arguments: if= and of=. The if= argument points to the device or file from which it is to take its input (i.e., the device you are cloning), and of= points to the device or file where you want to dump the clone. Depending on the size of your root partition, this could take a very long time, indeed. Go have a cup of coffee or tea, or watch television. When it's finished, it should tell you how many in and out records it has read and written. If it says "Input/Output error," something's gone wrong (such as a bad block on the hard disk), but all is not lost. A tool called *dd_rescue* will skip over the bad blocks and clone as much of the filesystem as possible. You can read more about this tool at *http://www.oreillynet.com/pub/wlg/5205*.

Restore the Image

Now you should have a large file called *image.bin* in the root directory of */dev/sda1* (or whichever partition you mounted on */mnt/foo*). At this point, you should unmount the disk to which you wrote the image. If you used an external USB drive, you can plug it into any computer onto which you want to clone this Linux install.

To restore the image, you literally do the commands in reverse. You need a Linux boot CD of some sort (such as Knoppix, SUSE, Ubuntu, or Red Hat) and boot into a recovery mode, or gain access to a shell (Ctrl-Alt-F2 when you are in the installation portion of a distribution). Then you can load the usb_storage module again, and mount the external hard disk:

```
foo@bar:~# mkdir /foo
foo@bar:~# modprobe usb_storage
foo@bar:~# mount /dev/sda1 /foo
```

Now you need to partition the disk on the new machine using *fdisk* or a similar partitioning tool. A root partition and a swap partition are required. Assuming that the root partition is the first partition on the disk and the swap is the second, you need to format the swap partition using the following command:

```
foo@bar:~# mkswap /dev/hda2
```

It isn't necessary to write a filesystem to the root partition, because the image is providing a filesystem. At this point you can load the image file onto the hard disk using the dd command again:

```
foo@bar:~# dd if=/foo/image.bin of=/dev/hda1
```

As you can see, the command just reverses the source and destination of the input and output. When this is finished, you need to mount the partition and *chroot* into it so that you are "inside" the Linux installation:

```
foo@bar:~# mkdir /install
foo@bar:~# mount /dev/hda1 /install
foo@bar:~# chroot /install /bin/bash
```

The last line tells the system to pretend the root directory is */install*, and run the bash shell upon entering it. Now you need to sort out the bootloader for the system. Most systems use either LILO or GRUB. In the case of LILO, you need to run lilo in the *chroot*ed environment. This will write the necessary code to the master boot record:

```
foo@bar:~# lilo
```

With GRUB you need to run grub-install:

```
foo@bar:~# grub-install /dev/hda
```

If all has gone well, you can exit the *chroot* environment and reboot the system. It should boot up as normal.

—George Wright

Forward Ports over SSH

Keep network traffic to arbitrary ports secure with SSH port forwarding.

In addition to providing remote shell access and command execution, OpenSSH can forward arbitrary TCP ports to the other end of your connection. This can be very handy for protecting email, web, or any other traffic you need to keep private (at least, all the way to the other end of the tunnel).

Ssh accomplishes local forwarding by binding to a local port, performing encryption, sending the encrypted data to the remote end of the *ssh* connection, then decrypting it and sending it to the remote host and port you specify. Start an *ssh* tunnel with the -L switch (short for Local):

```
root@laptop:~# ssh -f -N -L110:mailhost:110 -l user mailhost
```

Naturally, substitute *user* with your username, and *mailhost* with your mail server's name or IP address. Note that you will have to be root on laptop for this example, since you'll be binding to a privileged port (110, the POP port). You should also disable any locally running POP daemon (look in */etc/inetd.conf*) or it will get in the way.

Now to encrypt all of your POP traffic, configure your mail client to connect to localhost port 110. It will happily talk to mailhost as if it were connected directly, except that the entire conversation will be encrypted.

The -f forks *ssh* into the background, and -N tells it not to actually run a command on the remote end (just do the forwarding). If your *ssh* server supports it, try the -C switch to turn on compression—this can significantly improve the time it takes to download your email.

You can specify as many -L lines as you like when establishing the connection. To also forward outbound email traffic, try this:

```
root@laptop:~# ssh -f -N -L110:mailhost:110 -L25:mailhost:25
-l user mailhost
```

Set your outbound email host to localhost, and your email traffic will be encrypted as far as mailhost. This generally is only useful if the email is bound for an internal host, or if you can't trust your local network connection (as is the case with most wireless networks). Obviously, once your email leaves mailhost, it will be transmitted in the clear, unless you've encrypted the message with a tool such as *pgp* or *gpg*.

If you're already logged into a remote host and need to forward a port quickly, try this:

- Hit Enter
- Type ~C
- You should be at an ssh> prompt; enter the -L line as you would from the command line.

For example:

```
rob@catlin:~$
rob@catlin:~$ ~, then C (it doesn't echo)
ssh> -L8080:localhost:80
Forwarding port.
```

Your current shell will then forward local port 8000 to catlin's port 80, as if you had entered it in the first place.

You can also allow other (remote) clients to connect to your forwarded port, with the -g switch. If you're logged in to a remote gateway that serves as a NAT for a private network, then a command like this:

```
rob@gateway:~$ ssh -f -g -N -L8000:localhost:80 10.42.4.6
```

will forward all connections from gateway's port 8000 to internal host 10.42.4.6's port 80. If the gateway has a live Internet address, this will allow anyone from the Net to connect to the web server on 10.42.4.6 as if it were running on port 8000 of the gateway.

One last point worth mentioning: the forwarded host doesn't have to be localhost; it can be any host that the machine you're connecting to can access directly. For example, to forward local port 5150 to a web server somewhere on an internal network, try this:

```
rob@remote:~$ ssh -f -N -L5150:intranet.insider.nocat:80 gateway.nocat.net
```

Assuming that you're running a TLD of *.nocat*, and that *gateway.nocat.net* also has a connection to the private *.nocat* network, all traffic to 5150 of *remote* will be obligingly forwarded to *intranet.insider.nocat:80*. The address *intranet.insider.nocat* doesn't have to resolve in DNS to *remote*; it isn't looked up until the connection is made to *gateway.nocat.net*, then it's gateway that does the lookup. To securely browse that site from *remote*, try connecting to *http://localhost:5150/*.

Although *ssh* also has functionality for acting as a Socks 4 proxy (with the -D switch), it just isn't well suited for routing all network traffic to the other end of a tunnel. See the documentation for the -D switch; it's a pretty neat feature. (What, did you think we'd do *all* of the work for you? ;)

Ssh is an incredibly flexible tool, with much more functionality than I can cover here. See the references below for more fun things you can do with *ssh*.

See also:

- *Ssh* manpage
- *SSH, The Secure Shell: The Definitive Guide* (O'Reilly)

—Rob Flickenger

Take Control of New User Setups

Customize how each new user account is configured by default.

Whenever you create a new user for your system, Linux sets up the home directory with a slim pack of default files. These files are usually located in */etc/skel*, the skeleton directory for all new user homes. This hack explains what you can and cannot do (easily, anyway) to customize */etc/skel* to fine-tune how a new user home directory will look and behave.

Wouldn't it be nice if you could create a default configuration for GNOME or KDE, then place all the default configuration files in */etc/skel* so that they are copied into each new user's directory? Everyone would start out with the same menus, same wallpaper, etc. Well, dream on, because although it might not be impossible, it's nothing close to easy. KDE and GNOME have their own methods for setting up new users, and neither is careful to make one user's configuration portable to another. Usernames and full paths to home directories are littered throughout the configuration files. So, when you copy them from one home directory to another, the target user gets a slew of files pointing to configurations in someone else's inaccessible home directory. It's a mess.

That's why the */etc/skel* directory has so little inside. If you visit the */etc/skel* directory and look at the hidden files, you'll probably see something such as the following (if you're lucky, you might find one or two more files than those listed here):

```
# ls -a /etc/skel
.alias
.bash_logout
.bash_profile
.bashrc
.cshrc
```

Improve What Is Already There

If you have fine-tuned your personal settings in one or more of these files and believe others would benefit from changes you make for your own personal preferences, edit the existing /etc/skel to use default settings taken from your personal settings. Take a look at "Colorize Files in Your Pager" [Hack #15]. This particular hack redefines some command aliases so that you can see a color listing of files in your pager. All it takes is to replace the existing alias definitions (usually found in .bashrc) to read something more like this:

```
alias ls="ls --color"
alias less="less -R"
```

Make those changes in the /etc/skel/.bashrc file, and all new users will benefit from the hack, assuming your users are as pleased with the idea as you are.

Create Application Defaults

The /etc/skel directory is also an ideal place to put customizations for individual programs, as long as those configuration files do not include usernames or paths to user directories. It's quite easy to find out if a file or directory has hardcoded references to a username or user directory. For example, assuming your username is carlotta, try this command in your home directory:

```
$ grep -r carlotta .kde
```

You might be shocked at how many configuration files, among other things, show up with the username hardcoded. You can't transfer these files to /etc/skel and expect them to work for a new user, because they're filled with references to you and your home directory.

But if you run the same test on another configuration file or directory and your username never shows up, there's hope that you can use the configuration in the /etc/skel directory.

One good candidate for placement in /etc/skel is the .Xdefaults file ("Stop Using Terminal Command-Line Switches" [Hack #50] gives examples of the benefits you can reap by customizing this file). You can set up an improved look and feel for a number of X terminals once, place it in /etc/skel, and every new user will automatically benefit from those customizations.

You might also want to customize the command-line prompt in the /etc/skel directory, assuming you think everyone will like a custom prompt [Hack #13].

Be Selfish

Not all the changes you make will be for the benefit of new users. For example, I use a character-mode editor called *joe* in part because I have made major modifications to the key assignments so that the editor behaves exactly the way I like it. All the settings are in the file *~/.joerc*.

When I create a new user, I log in as the new user and run joe to make some final adjustments to the files. Naturally, nothing works in the editor the way I expect it to work. because this new user's home directory does not have my *.joerc* configuration file. It's possible to make a copy, but that involves logging back in as root and changing ownership—which involves more work than it should. So, for my benefit as an administrator, I have placed a copy of my *.joerc* file in the */etc/skel* directory so that *joe* works the way I expect it to work every time I create a new user account and log in as that user.

Default Desktop Environments

I have had some limited success at setting up a very basic user configuration from scratch, and then copying the user's *.kde* directory into */etc/skel* so that it becomes the default for new users. The one catch is that KDE usually puts the username in the *~/.kde/share/config/ksmserverrc* file. You can delete the line containing the username, which might or might not make it possible to use */etc/skel/.kde* as a default configuration. Sometimes it works, sometimes it doesn't. If you can't blame it on different Linux distributions, maybe it's sunspots.

Another thing you can do is create a default *Desktop* directory, with various desktop icons. But even in this case you have to be cautious. because some desktop environments might still detect that the new users are starting GNOME, KDE, or whatever for the first time, and override your desktop configuration by creating their own idea of what a default desktop should look like.

One sure bet is not to bother trying to create a default configuration in */etc/skel* with GNOME. GNOME sets up a number of default directories, and launches a settings daemon called *gconfd*, which remembers settings and even rewrites them to your home directory if you delete them manually. If there's a way to set up a skeleton version of GNOME in */etc/skel* that can be copied to new user home directories, either a lot of hard work or a lot of magic must be involved.

Send Email Alerts for System Events

#77

Track log entries and send an email to yourself when something looks
suspicious.

In "Make Applications Trigger On-Screen Alerts" **[Hack #27]** you used X11 On-
Screen Display (XOSD) to make system alerts (such as possible attempts to
break into the system) as visible as possible. As effective as that approach
can be, it doesn't work very well if you're not looking at your monitor when
the alert appears.

The next best thing is to have a program send you an email alert. This
"hack" is simply an explanation of how you can configure two different log
monitor programs, *swatch* and *logsentry*, to send you email alerts.

Fortunately, if you use *swatch* to monitor one of your logs for keywords, you
don't have to settle for one method of notification. You can list several ways
to have *swatch* notify you of an alert. For example, you can have *swatch*
check to see if the word "failure" appears in your authentication log (that
might indicate someone is trying to guess a password). Normally, it echoes
the log entry to the screen where you started *swatch*. "Make Applications
Trigger On-Screen Alerts" **[Hack #27]** explained how to make the log entry
appear on-screen. The following entry in the *.swatchrc* file does both of
these things and also sends you an email alert:

```
watchfor /failure/
        echo bold
        pipe "osd_cat -c magenta -p middle -f -*-helvetica-*-*-*-*-20-*-*-*-
*-*-*-* -d 60 "
        mail person-to-alert@yourdomain.com, subject="Alert from swatch"
```

Assuming you are running *swatch* as root, all you have to do is edit your */root/*
.swatchrc file to include the previous lines, and then start *swatch* with this
command:

```
# swatch -t /var/log/auth.log
```

The logsentry Difference

The *logsentry* program is similar to *swatch* in that it monitors logs for keywords and sends alerts. The difference is that *swatch* does it all in real time,
but *logsentry* is usually set up to run as a cronjob every hour or so. Most
packaged versions of *logsentry* place a file, such as *logsentry.cron* in */etc/cron.*
hourly, where programs are run every hour. Here is the simple *logsentry.cron*
file:

```
#!/bin/sh

/bin/sh /etc/logcheck/logcheck.sh
```

The *logsentry.cron* file simply runs the */etc/logcheck/logcheck.sh* program.

The */etc/logcheck* directory contains more than the *logcheck.sh* program. It also includes these files:

- *logcheck.sh*
- *logcheck.hacking*
- *logcheck.ignore*
- *logcheck.violations*
- *logcheck.violations.ignore*

The *logcheck.sh* file checks your logs according to the keywords and key phrases in the other files. The *logcheck.hacking* and *logcheck.violations* files contain many keywords and key phrases that might indicate trouble. The *logcheck.ignore* and *logcheck.violations.ignore* files include keywords and key phrases that either are false alarms or aren't useful. The default values in these lists are quite reliable, but you are free to modify the lists to trigger more alerts and/or ignore more events.

You need to configure the *logcheck.sh* file to have it send alerts by mail. The SYSADMIN entry should point to the email address where you want alerts sent:

```
SYSADMIN=person-to-alert@yourdomain.com

$LOGTAIL /var/log/messages > $TMPDIR/check.$$
$LOGTAIL /var/log/auth.log >> $TMPDIR/check.$$
$LOGTAIL /var/log/syslog >> $TMPDIR/check.$$
```

The rest of the variables you want to customize for your system are the lines that point to the logs you want to monitor. Each Linux distribution uses different log names for different purposes. Make sure you're monitoring the right logs, or *logsentry* will be useless to you.

The only other entry you might need to change is the definition of the mail program on your system. *logsentry* assumes you have the *mail* program installed, and that your mail program accepts the -s argument for the Subject line. If you don't have *mail* installed, or your version of mail does not support the -s switch, you need to find a substitute that does and redefine the program name in your *logsentry.sh* file. The *mailx* program is a likely candidate:

```
# Linux, FreeBSD, BSDI, Sun, etc.
MAIL=mail
```

Create a Passwordless Login

#78   Forget about those passwords and make administering a remote server easier.

By far, the most common method of remotely logging in to Linux machines is by using the Secure SHell (SSH). This encrypted method of accessing far-flung computers is a popular choice for system administrators, but despite its popularity, repeatedly logging in and out of computers and entering passwords over and over again can be a chore. This chore is significantly increased when you manage a number of different computers, all with different passwords.

This hack explores how to create a passwordless login. Although this sounds like security suicide, it isn't because it uses special encrypted keys to allow access to the remote computer. You do this by generating both a public and a private key. The public key (a key that you can give to people) is uploaded to the remote server as an authorized key, and when you connect to the remote server, the private key on your local machine is compared to the public key. If they work together, access is granted.

The other benefit of the passwordless login is that you can tie it into your desktop environment and manage files on the remote machine graphically. I discuss this later in this hack.

Generate Public and Private Keys

To create a passwordless login, you need to generate your public and private keys. First, create a new directory called *sshkey* in your home directory in which to store the keys:

```
foo@local:~$ mkdir sshkey
foo@local:~$ cd sshkey
```

When you generate the keys, you have a choice of either the DSA or RSA encryption algorithms, with RSA being the newer version in Version 2 of the SSH protocol. You can generate the keys with:

```
foo@local:~$ ssh-keygen -f id_rsa -t rsa
```

When you run this command, you are asked for a password; press Enter when prompted for the password. This creates two keys with a blank password. One is called *id_rsa* (your private key) and the other is *id_rsa.pub* (your public key).

Create the Login

With the keys generated, the next step is to upload the public key to the remote server. If you have never dealt with SSH keys before, you probably do not have a *.ssh/authorized_keys* file on the remote server. If this is the case, you can simply copy the *id_rsa.pub* to the remote server and call it *.ssh/authorized_keys*:

```
foo@local:~$ scp id_rsa.pub foo@remote:/home/foo/.ssh/authorized_keys
```

If you have already created an *authorized_keys* file on the remote server, you can simply log in to the remote server, open *authorized_keys* in a text editor, and paste the contents of *id_rsa.pub* on the local machine into the file on a new line. This is how you add multiple keys on the remote server.

Whichever method you use to get your public key on the remote server, you must set the permissions on the files and directory correctly. Simply issue the following commands:

```
foo@remote:~$ cd ~/.ssh
foo@remote:~$ chmod 700 ./
foo@remote:~$ chmod 600 *
```

These commands ensure that your *.ssh* directory and files are secured. Finally, on the local machine, copy the generated *id_rsa* file to the *.ssh* in your home directory to make it the default key for SSH:

```
foo@local:~$ cp id_rsa ~/.ssh
```

Now you can test to see that the connection works:

```
foo@local:~$ ssh foo@remote
```

You should be able to log in automatically with no password prompt.

Graphically Manage Remote Files

One of the benefits of creating a passwordless login is that it makes graphical administration of a remote server much easier. Not only does this give you the ability to connect to a remote resource in your favorite file manager, but also you can put an icon on your desktop that opens the specified directories and files of the remote server when you click it. This gives you the ability to transfer files by dragging and dropping.

You can display a remote file structure by clicking an icon on your desktop in a number of ways, but this hack covers how to do it for the two major desktop environments, KDE and GNOME.

To access a networked resource in KDE, add a new icon to the desktop by right-clicking the desktop and selecting Create New → Link to Application. Inside the dialog box that pops up, click the Application tab, and you'll see a Command box that you can use to indicate the location of the remote server. This is done with the format:

fish://*user@server/path*

When you click the icon, Konqueror loads, and you can use it to deal with the remote server graphically.

To connect to a networked resource in GNOME, click the main Computer menu in the top panel, and then select Disks from the menu. When the window appears that displays your disks and drives, click File → Connect to Server. Inside this dialog box you can select an SSH connection from the Service Type combo box, and then add the server name, port, folder, and username details. Finally, you can name the icon by adding a label to the "Name to use for connection" box. Now the icon will be added to your desktop and will appear in the Network Servers window.

Magically Empower Your Network Cable

H A C K
#79

Configure your Ethernet devices simply by plugging in or unplugging the cable.

This hack is actually a utility called *ifplugd*, a daemon that watches your Ethernet connection to see if it is live or disconnected. Plug the wire into the network, and *ifplugd* configures the interface. Unplug the wire, and *ifplugd* disables the interface. Plug the wire back in, and it reconfigures the interface, even if it needs to use DHCP to get an IP address. It's a perfect utility for laptops that frequently change their network connections, but it can come in handy for workstations, too.

The *ifplugd* utility simply checks your network interface(s) to see if they have a link beat, which indicates a live connection to a network. When a link beat appears, *ifplugd* configures the interface (eth0, for example) as being up and ready to use. When the link beat disappears (you disconnect the cable), *ifplugd* brings the interface down.

Most distributions package *ifplugd* in such a way that it uses the default method for bringing down the interface if there is no connection, and then it uses the default method for bringing up the interface when *ifplugd* detects a connection. In other words, on a Debian system with the interface eth0, it uses the default methods of ifdown eth0 and ifup eth0 for disconnect and reconnect, respectively. It simply obeys how you originally configured eth0 to work.

You don't usually need to use *ifplugd* if you are using a laptop with a PC Card/PCMCIA network adapter and static IP address, for two reasons. The PCMCIA driver generally configures the device automatically anyway, and *ifplugd* is rarely able to detect a link beat through a PCMCIA device.

> *ifplugd* is known to have problems with some USB network adapters (wireless or otherwise), especially when the driver is available only from a third party and is not part of the default Linux kernel. This is a driver issue related to the kernel's ability to activate and deactivate the USB device. This cannot be fixed by new versions of *ifplugd*; it is something the kernel driver must handle. If you have not yet purchased a USB network adapter, research the latest kernel versions to find out which ones are best supported. If you already have your USB network adapter, report problems to the manufacturer. Some companies are surprisingly accommodating and eager to fix problems such as these.

Protect Yourself from Windows Applications
Minimize the risk of viral infection in Windows emulators and Windows documents.

CodeWeavers's *(http://www.codeweavers.com)* CrossOver Office and Wine enable you to run many Windows applications under Linux. In fact, they do such a good job of providing a Windows-like environment that they can be susceptible to some of the same security issues as Windows. Use this hack to protect the rest of your computer from the havoc an emulated Windows environment gone wild can cause.

This hack uses *sudo* to open Windows documents in a restricted area. Some people use *chroot* for this purpose, but the *sudo* approach accepts a certain level of risk in exchange for being much easier to set up than *chroot* for the same purpose. (A utility currently in development called *chroot_safe* looks like it will be a more promising alternative in the long run.)

If you're a Linux user who must use some Microsoft applications (through CrossOver Office or Wine), this hack lets you do things such as open non-trusted Microsoft Word files that you get as email attachments with Microsoft Word itself, yet without risking the integrity of your other Word documents. For example, you can set up your Mozilla Mail client to open Word files in this restricted environment where an infected document can do little or no damage. Once you understand the methodology you use for Word, you can apply the same techniques to view any kind of file in a safe, restricted environment.

This hack requires several steps:

1. Install *sudo*, if you don't already have it installed.

2. Create a user and a group named `jail`.

3. Install Wine or CrossOver Office as the user `jail` in the */home/jail* directory.

4. Create the */home/jail/Documents* directory, and give everyone read/write access to the directory.

5. Set up the *sudoers* file to enable you to run certain applications as the `jail` user.

6. Install a special script in */usr/local/bin* that automatically uses Microsoft Word, running in the jailed environment, to open any Word document in read-only mode.

Get Your Safe Environment Set Up

Create both a user and a group named `jail`. Make the `jail` user a member of the `jail` group, but do not add this user to any other groups. You want the `jail` user to have as few privileges as possible. Your Linux distribution probably includes a graphical application to manage users and groups. If you prefer to use the command line, one way to create this user is to log in as root and issue the following commands:

```
# groupadd jail
# useradd jail -d /home/jail -m -g jail -s /bin/bash
# passwd jail
New UNIX password: <password>
Retype new UNIX password: <password>
passwd: password updated successfully
```

 Though you are providing a password, you will configure *sudo* such that users do not need to enter the password to use the `jail` account to do things such as view Word documents.

Now log in as the `jail` user, and install CrossOver Office or Wine in the */home/jail* directory. Then install Microsoft Word or Microsoft Office via your choice of Windows emulator in the */home/jail* directory. Make sure that you can launch Microsoft Word and that everything works before you continue.

> Once you are completely done installing everything you need in the */home/jail* directory, you can log out of the `jail` account and then add another level of safety by editing the `jail` user entry in */etc/passwd* to change the shell from */bin/ bash* to */bin/false*. Using a nonexistent shell makes it impossible for anyone to log in to the `jail` account to get to a command-line shell.

Now install *sudo* if it is not already installed for your distribution. Some distributions package it under the name *sudosh*. Log in as root, and run the visudo command to edit the *sudoers* file that controls the behavior of *sudo*. Edit the *sudoers* file to include these lines:

```
# Runas alias specification

Cmnd_Alias VIEWERS = /bin/rm, /home/jail/cxoffice/bin/winword

Defaults:ALL    env_reset
Defaults:ALL    env_keep=DISPLAY
Defaults:ALL    always_set_home

ALL ALL = (jail) NOPASSWD: VIEWERS
```

In case you're not familiar with *sudo*, the Cmnd_Alias VIEWERS line defines a list of programs to make available to the `jail` user. You can add other viewers to the VIEWERS alias list later if you want, but until you are certain everything works, keep it simple. The last line of the example file says that ALL users on ALL hosts can run as the `jail` user without having to enter a password. Save your changes and exit *visudo*.

Incidentally, the *env_reset* setting tells *sudo* to eliminate all but the most basic environment variables. This way, your personal environment variables will not "leak" into the `jail` account while you're using it. env_keep=DISPLAY simply retains the DISPLAY environment variable so that the program will show up on the current display. The always_set_home variable makes sure that when you use *sudo* to run a program as the user called `jail`, it will set the HOME variable to be */home/jail* instead of retaining the HOME variable of your user account.

While you are still logged in as root, create the following */usr/local/bin/ wordview* script:

```
#!/bin/bash

if [ -r "$*" ]; then
    chmod 444 "$*"
    cp "$*" /home/jail/Documents
    filename=$(basename "$*")
```

```
    cd /home/jail/cxoffice/bin
    sudo -u jail /home/jail/cxoffice/bin/winword f:"$filename"
    sudo -u jail rm -f /home/jail/Documents/"$filename"
else
    echo "No such file, or file is not readable"
fi
```

Save your work, and make the file executable:

```
# chmod +x /usr/local/bin/wordview
```

You have to take care of two obscure details to make this work. First, you must configure CrossOver Office (or Wine) to equate DOS drive f: with the */home/jail/Documents* directory. Here's how to do that with CrossOver Office:

```
# su - jail
$ cd /home/jail/.cxoffice/dotwine/dosdevices
$ ln -sf /home/jail/Documents "f:"
$ exit
```

If the DOS drive f: is already defined by CrossOver Office, choose another driver letter, but make sure it matches the drive letter in the */usr/local/bin/ wordview* script that looks like this:

```
sudo -u jail /home/jail/cxoffice/bin/winword f:"$filename"
```

If you are using something other than CrossOver Office, you also have to adjust one other line in the */usr/local/bin/wordview* script. This line points to the executables directory for CrossOver Office:

```
cd /home/jail/cxoffice/bin
```

It needs to be changed to point to the location of the executable files you are using:

```
cd /home/jail/<route to your winword executable file>
```

Give Your Creation a Try

Now you're ready to try it out. Log in as a normal user and find a Microsoft Word document to which you have legitimate access (such as a Word document in your home directory). For this example, assume the file is named *dangerous.doc* and is located in your home directory, */home/carlotta*. Log in as carlotta, start up your favorite desktop environment or window manager, open a terminal, and issue this command to open the document using the script you just created:

```
$ wordview dangerous.doc
```

The script makes a copy of *dangerous.doc* in */home/jail/Documents*, and then, running as the jail user, it opens the document as read-only in Microsoft Word. When you are done viewing the document and you exit

Microsoft Word, the script will delete the temporary copy of *dangerous.doc* from */home/jail/Documents*. (This is why you made the /bin/rm command available to the jail user. It's not a necessary step, so you can modify *sudoers* and the script accordingly, but it does keep the */home/jail/ Documents* directory uncluttered.)

> This is definitely not a good technique for viewing personal or company documents. Even though the script deletes the document after you are done viewing it, the document remains in the *Jail* directory as long as you have it open. During this time, anyone has the capability to read the document you have open, and they can even save a private copy for themselves. So, reserve the use of this for documents that are coming from an unknown or untrusted source.

Automating Wordview in Mozilla

Not every application makes it possible to customize what action it will take when it opens a Microsoft Word document. Some applications that do make it possible don't make it easy.

But it should be easy for Mozilla users. The next time you come across a Word document while browsing a web page, you can adjust what Mozilla does when you click Word document links. When you click a link to a Word document, you should get a dialog box that asks you what to do (Figure 9-2). Tell Mozilla to open the document with */usr/local/bin/ wordview*.

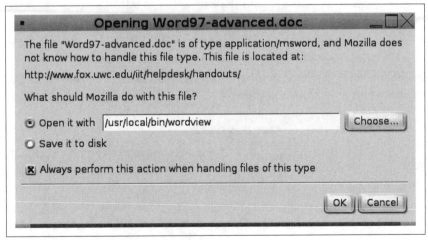

Figure 9-2. Dialog for setting document handling

You should see the same dialog if you try to open a Microsoft Word attachment using Mozilla Mail. Then you can set up Mozilla Mail to run */usr/local/bin/wordview* automatically when opening attached Word documents.

The technique for setting up the Mozilla Thunderbird email client is a bit different. When you receive a Word document, right-click it and choose Open. This brings up a dialog that gives you the choice of saving the file or specifying a program with which to open the file. In addition, a checkbox (similar to the one in Figure 9-2 for Mozilla) tells Thunderbird to treat this type of file the same way by default.

Unfortunately, it isn't quite as easy to make the Mozilla Firefox browser behave this way. I expect this limitation will disappear as the application matures. Fortunately, it looks like Firefox inherits the setting from Thunderbird. After setting up Thunderbird to view Word documents with *wordview*, that setting seems to have magically appeared in the preferences dialog for Firefox.

Preparing for Unlikely Damage

With everything protected in a *sudo* jail, the worst possible damage a virus could do is to infect your copy of CrossOver Office. Even though I am not aware of any virus that can attack CrossOver or Wine, it is theoretically possible, because both mimic Windows very closely. If you're worried this might happen, make a backup copy of CrossOver Office and your installation of Microsoft Word as soon as you're done installing these packages. If anything damages either CrossOver Office or Microsoft Word, you can overwrite the damaged files with the backup copy. Make sure you back up both the hidden and unhidden CrossOver Office directories:

```
# cd <backup directory>
# tar cjvf crossover.tar.bz2 /home/jail/.cxoffice /home/jail/cxoffice
```

In the unlikely event that you have to restore a damaged CrossOver Office environment, here's how to restore it:

```
# cd <backup directory>
# tar jxvf crossover.tar.bz2 /home/jail/
```

Obviously, if you are using Wine or some other means of running Microsoft Word, back up those directories instead of */home/jail/.cxoffice* and */home/jail/cxoffice*.

Build a Custom Firewall Computer

#81 Turn an old, underpowered computer into a lean, mean, firewall machine.

As more and more computers are getting plugged into the Internet, the risk factor associated with an online presence has also risen. The increase in hours online combined with the propagation of always-on broadband and high-speed cable/DSL Internet access has resulted in the need to secure even simple, one-computer home networks. As a result, the humble firewall has become a must-have item as opposed to a could-have item in a network.

The basic aim of a firewall is to keep unwanted people off of your network. The virtual wall of fire is essential in keeping out crackers who want to invade your security, as well as blocking the growing armies of worms, viruses, and other Internet nasties that crawl the Web looking for computers to exploit. The situation is very bad; an unprotected Windows machine can become infected in as little as four minutes after it is put on the Internet. If you are considering a firewall but are uncertain you want to put the effort into it, ask a friend who has one for a list of attempted intrusions on his network. You will probably be surprised by the frequency of attacks. My own firewall logged more than 100 attempted intrusions in the first few hours after I put it up.

Both software and hardware firewalls are available. Software firewalls are installed on each desktop on the network, and they protect that single machine. The hardware approach is to use a dedicated machine to protect the entire network from malicious traffic. This hack explores a dedicated firewall Linux distribution called SmoothWall, which you can install on an aging computer to provide a dedicated firewall appliance to protect your entire network. After the initial setup, you will find your SmoothWall box to be invaluable.

Gather the Ingredients

To create a SmoothWall firewall appliance, you need a computer to use. Anything from a '486 with 16MB of RAM on up is fine, but if you want to keep several days' worth of log files, I recommend you use at least a 4GB disk. You also need at least two Linux-supported network cards in the computer. Here is how you will use your network cards:

- If you have a cable/DSL modem that plugs into a network card, you need a card for this. This card is referred to as the *RED interface*.

- You need a network card to connect to the internal network. If you have more than one computer on your internal network, this interface is usually plugged into a hub, switch, or wireless access point. This card is referred to as the *GREEN interface*.

- If you have any computers that need to be accessed publicly, you need another network card for these. This card is referred to as the *ORANGE interface* and also is known as the snazzily titled *De-Militarized Zone* (DMZ), because it exists in a sort of no man's land between the public Internet and your private network.

You should install the cards you need in the computer, download the Smooth-Wall ISO from *http://www.smoothwall.org*, and then burn the ISO to CD.

The next step is to boot from the CD and install the SmoothWall software. If you cannot boot from the CD, try using the Smart Boot Manager discussed in "Give Your Computer the Boot" [Hack #1]. If this does not work, you can create a series of boot floppies from the files found in the *images* directory on the SmoothWall CD. There you'll find two boot floppy images called *bootdiskone-x.x.img* and *bootdisktwo-x.x.img*. Use *dd* to create the floppies (unmounting and changing the floppy between images, of course):

```
foo@bar:~$ dd if=bootdiskone-x.x.img of=/dev/fd0 bs=1024 conv=sync ; sync
foo@bar:~$ dd if=bootdisktwo-x.x.img of=/dev/fd0 bs=1024 conv=sync ; sync
```

If you need to create the floppies on a Windows system, you can use the *rawrite* program (*http://uranus.it.swin.edu.au/~jn/linux/rawrite.htm*) to create the disks.

Installing SmoothWall is a fairly simple process, but you need to know how you want your network to be set up in terms of IP addresses. Within the setup routine are a Networking section and an Addresses subsection. You set the IP addresses for each interface here. For example, a common setting for the GREEN interface is the IP address 192.168.0.1 and the network mask 255.255.255.0. The RED interface is typically set to DHCP to grab your Internet IP address from the cable modem, but you should check with your ISP to see how the cable modem gets its IP address. The other setting to configure is in the "DNS and Gateway settings" section. Set this to 192.168.0.1. Now you have your firewall set up as your Internet gateway that other machines can refer to when requiring Internet access.

Configure the Firewall

Once the SmoothWall firewall is installed, you can access it in two main ways. The most common and popular way is to access its special web-based interface, which is available on port 81. So, if your firewall's IP address is 192.168.0.1, you can access the web interface at *http://192.168.0.1:81*. SmoothWall's default configuration does not allow access from outside your internal network, so you cannot make changes to it from work or while traveling.

When you access the web interface, you are asked for the administrator password for the machine (which you created when you installed Smooth-Wall) and then you can configure it. Within the web panel is a huge range of options and features that you can configure. These options are grouped into categories which are visible at the top of the page.

If you need to do something that is not accessible in the web interface, you can use the included Java SSH applet to log in to the machine and type in commands to an SSH shell.

Enable Port Forwarding

A common requirement when running a network of machines is the need to have a connection from outside the firewall serviced by a machine inside the firewall (usually in the DMZ). This is the scenario for those who run a web or email server and need to have the relevant ports accessible to the outside world. When a computer connects to your IP address/domain, the first computer that receives the connection is the firewall. Because it is unlikely you are running a web or email server on the firewall itself (if you are, you really shouldn't be because bugs in these programs can compromise the security of the firewall) you need a method to get that request to the computer that can handle it. This is where port forwarding comes in. Its purpose is to take the request for a service and forward it to the specific machine on the network that can service the request.

To do this with SmoothWall, access the web interface and select Networking → Port Forwarding. You can leave the external source IP box blank if you want to accept all connection requests for the port in question (this is commonly the case for a public service such as web serving). In the Source Port box, specify the port you want to forward (such as port 80 for a web server). Finally, you can enter the destination computer IP address and its port number in the other two boxes. This is quite useful if you want to forward a normal port 80 connection to a machine with a different port number, such as port 8080; a common request with Apache virtual hosts. Once you have forwarded your ports, you need to select the External Services Access page and add the ports you have forwarded to that page. This enables access to the ports from outside the network.

SmoothWall is proven to be an incredibly capable and flexible firewall. Because of this a lot of organizations and homes use it to protect their networks. Although the GPL version of the firewall is very capable, the commercial version and its included support can be really useful for commercial organizations. Both versions give you the flexibility of a powerful and supported firewall that can protect a network of Linux, Windows, or Mac OS X machines.

Link Monitoring in Linux with Wavemon

HACK #82

Monitor radio parameters in real time using Wavemon, a curses-based tool for Linux.

When using Linux, the standard wireless tools provide a wealth of status information. These tools get their information from the standard kernel interface */proc/net/wireless*. While ideal for providing pinpoint accuracy in measuring signal strength and noise data, these tools are not designed to give an indication of performance over time.

Wavemon (*http://www.wavemage.com/projects.html*) is a terrific little tool that does precisely this. It polls */proc/net/wireless* many times each second to give you a rolling report of how your wireless connection is performing. Its simple curses interface keeps the code quite small and is ideal for including in embedded distributions to get real-time link data from remote access points.

The main interface provides a nice graphical representation of the current link state (Figure 9-3).

```
┌─Interface───────────────────────────────────────────────────────────┐
│ eth1 (IEEE 802.11-DS),  ESSID: "SWN-BelmontEast",  nick: "HERMES I"   │
├─Levels──────────────────────────────────────────────────────────────┤
│ link quality: 37/92                                                   │
│                                                                       │
│ signal level: -55 dBm (0.00 uW)                                       │
│                                                                       │
│ noise level: -92 dBm (0.00 uW)                                        │
│                                                                       │
│ signal-to-noise ratio: +37 dB                                         │
│                                                                       │
├─Statistics──────────────────────────────────────────────────────────┤
│ RX: 9805 (7184949),  TX: 6822 (1236654),  inv: 0 nwid, 0 key, 2 misc  │
├─Info────────────────────────────────────────────────────────────────┤
│ frequency: 2.4220 GHz,  sensitivity: 1/3,  TX power: 15 dBm (31.62 mW)│
│ mode: managed,  access point: 00:02:6F:01:85:74                       │
│ bitrate: 11 Mbit/s,  RTS thr: off,  frag thr: off                     │
│ encryption: off                                                       │
│ power management: off                                                 │
├─Network─────────────────────────────────────────────────────────────┤
│ if: eth1,  hwaddr: 00:30:65:03:E7:8A                                  │
│ addr: 10.15.6.33,  netmask: 255.255.255.0,  bcast: 10.15.6.255        │
├───────────────────────────────────────────────────────────────────┤
│ F1     F2lhist F3aplst F4     F5     F6     F7prefs F8help F9about F10quit│
└───────────────────────────────────────────────────────────────────┘
```

Figure 9-3. Wavemon in action.

All of the statistics are updated in real time, making it ideal for monitoring point-to-point links and fine-tuning antennas on long distance shots. For an even easier to read display, hit F2 to bring up the Level Histogram (Figure 9-4).

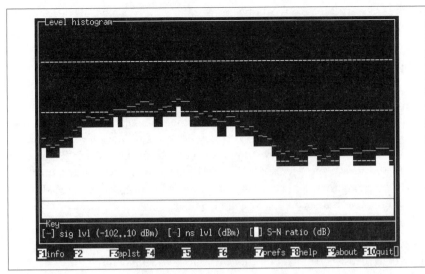

Figure 9-4. Pretty little scrolling waves of data.

This display is easy to read on a laptop even in bright sunshine, making it an ideal tool for outdoor work. The histogram slowly sweeps to the left, giving you a history of the last few moments of wireless connectivity. Wavemon runs in a terminal, so you can easily run more than one instance to monitor multiple radio links simultaneously.

When you need a high performance signal and noise meter for Linux, Wavemon is hard to beat. The current version is available from Freshmeat at *http://freshmeat.net/projects/wavemon/*.

—Rob Flickenger

Make Network Backups
#83

No need for cumbersome tapes and disks; save your precious data across a network.

The cost of computing is so low that it is not uncommon to have more than one computer in a house. Increasingly, people are buying many computers, networking them together, and using them for different purposes. For example, in my home are two Linux boxes, one Linux server, one Linux firewall, two Windows machines, and a Mac. With a large number of computers, each with important data on it, backups of that data become a very real and important issue to consider.

The natural assumption when faced with a need to perform backups is to use a medium such as tape or a CD/DVD. But in this hack you are going to perform a series of network backups that simply copy files from one machine on the network to another.

Simple Single-Shot Backup

If you want to do a simple full backup of a directory, you can do it with a single command by using secure copy (*scp*). This little tool lets you copy a number of files from one computer to another in a secure encrypted form. One of the major benefits of *scp* is that you can copy files across the Internet; you are not limited just to computers on your local network. To use *scp*, you need to have the Secure SHell (SSH) daemon running on the machine you are copying to and have the *scp* program (which is part of the SSH package) on the computer you are copying from.

To get started, you can copy a directory full of work from your machine martin to a machine called simon (if your hostnames are not resolvable, use their IP addresses). You can do this with the following command:

```
foo@martin:~$ scp -r importantwork simon:/home/alan
```

This command uses *scp* to recursively (-r) copy the files within the *importantwork* directory to the host simon and into the */home/alan* directory. Once you have entered the command, you see a status bar for each file as it is transferred. This gives you a visual indication of the copy's progress.

Elaborate Backups Using rsync

Using scp for backing up a configuration has a few inherent problems. The first issue is that each time you need to make a backup, the contents of your entire directory, *importantwork*, are copied over again, which can consume a lot of bandwidth and time. The other problem is that scp is rather inelegant in that it copies only specific files, and cannot easily distinguish between the files on the backed-up computer and the source files.

A better solution for managing backups of large groups of files and directories is *rsync*. This tool is easy to set up (you only need to install the *rsync* program on the remote and local computers), and it has the ability to intelligently copy files and directories over and during later syncs to copy only the specific files and directories that have changed. To use *rsync* you basically need to specify the machine and directory you are copying from and where you are copying the files to on the local computer. For example, you can copy some files from a remote machine called martin to your current machine:

```
foo@bar:~$ rsync -avz martin:/home/martin/importantwork /home/foo
```

In this example, you use two command-line switches that adjust how *rsync* works. The -v switch puts *rsync* in verbose mode and outputs what it is doing at all times, and the -z switch compresses the files to lower the bandwidth required to make the transfer. This compression is less important when copying files between computers on a local network than it is when copying files over the Internet, but using compression is not a bad habit to get into. The *rsync* program is very flexible, and a few other options are worth exploring when making backups such as this. First, you should be aware that *rsync*'s default behavior is to add files only when making a backup. This means that if you've backed up a file and you delete the local copy, the backed-up copy remains on the remote machine even during later syncs. In some cases this might be unsuitable, such as when you want to mirror a directory full of files and you want the backed-up files removed when they are removed from the main directory. To do this you can add --delete to the line:

```
foo@bar:~$ rsync -avz --delete martin:/home/martin/importantwork /home/alan
```

A particularly useful feature within *rsync* is the ability to exclude specific files from the backup. You can do this with the --exclude switch. For example, if you want to keep your *importantwork/passwords/importantpasswords.txt* file out of the backup, you can use this command:

```
foo@bar:~$ rsync -avz --delete --exclude=passwords/importantpasswords.txt
martin:/home/martin/importantwork /home/foo
```

If you need to exclude a number of files, include a number of --exclude flags for different files or directories, one after the other.

One final point to note about *rsync* is that as with many other network tools, all traffic is unencrypted and potentially subject to malicious people sniffing your traffic and discovering sensitive information. If you are concerned about your security, it is advisable to use the -e switch built into *rsync* to use an SSH shell to encrypt all traffic. Simply add the e to the collection of switches and specify ssh as the shell to use:

```
foo@bar:~$ rsync -avze ssh --delete --exclude=passwords/importantpasswords.
txt martin:/home/martin/importantwork /home/foo
```

Although the most common use of *rsync* is between a local and a remote machine, it really doesn't matter where the two machines are. As far as *rsync* is concerned, one is just a source and the other is just a destination. Both the source and destination could be on the local machine, or one could be local and one could be remote, or both could be on different remote machines.

Recover from Debian Disaster

Restore your Debian system from even the most seemingly unrecoverable disaster.

We all make mistakes, but the worst accident on a Debian system (or any Debian-based system, such as Knoppix) is one that causes you to lose the contents of your */var/lib/dpkg* directory. Once that directory is gone, you can no longer update or install software. These things happen even to the best of us, so here's a procedure to get your Debian system back where it was (or close), without losing any of your data or having to reinstall all of Debian from scratch.

OK, so you lost the */var/lib/dpkg* directory. Heck, if you had */var* on its own partition, you might have lost everything under the */var* directory. If that's the case, you'll have a lot more work to do than restoring your Debian package database. Unfortunately, because every system differs, it's up to you to figure out what you need to restore directories other than those required by Debian. At minimum, you'll need to create the following directories to start your recovery process. Log in as root, and run these commands:

```
# mkdir -p /var/cache/apt/archives
# mkdir -p /var/cache/debconf
# mkdir -p /var/log
# mkdir -p /var/lib/dpkg/info
# mkdir -p /var/lib/dpkg/parts
# mkdir -p /var/lib/dpkg/alternatives
# mkdir -p /var/lib/dpkg/methods
# mkdir -p /var/lib/dpkg/updates
```

The next thing you need to do is find out what version of *libc6* you have installed. Check the documentation for this information. For example, the first line of the *README* file in the documentation directory for *libc6* often tells you the version:

```
# less /usr/share/doc/libc6/README
This directory contains the version 2.3.2 release of the GNU C Library.
```

Now fire up your favorite editor to create the */var/lib/dpkg/status* file. Enter the following text in this file (substitute the version of your particular *libc6* for the version in our example):

```
Package: libc6
Status: install ok installed
Version: 2.3.2
```

Save this file and exit the editor.

Be sure to press Enter after you enter the version number in
this file. A new line must appear after the version number for
this recovery method to work.

Now you need to run the following commands. You *will* get error messages
and warnings, and the apt-get dist-upgrade command will not actually
install any files, as it should. It will simply download packages. Don't worry.
Just plow through these commands, ignoring the warnings and errors:

```
# dpkg --clear-avail
# apt-get update
# apt-get dist-upgrade
```

These commands cause your Debian system to download some critical
packages. Change to the directory where these packages are installed and
install them manually with the dpkg command. (Ironically, Debian might
complain that dpkg isn't installed, but it works anyway.) Note the * at the
end of the package names in the following commands. This is just a wild-
card that saves you the trouble of specifying the full package filenames. Here
are the commands to manually install the minimum required packages
you'll need for installing packages in a more automated fashion:

```
# cd /var/cache/apt/archives
# dpkg -i libncurses*
# dpkg -i perl-base*
# dpkg -i libstdc++*
# dpkg -i dselect*
# dpkg -i dpkg*
```

Read the error messages you encounter and be prepared to
be flexible if one or more steps give you trouble. I can almost
guarantee there's a solution to every glitch, so keep at it.
Remember that not all the error messages you see are important. Ignore the complaints about insufficient information
regarding *libc6*. These error messages go away by the end of
the procedure.

Now you're ready to get rid of that annoying message about insufficient
information regarding *libc6*. Type in the following command:

```
# apt-get install -reinstall libc6
```

Finally, you can run the dist-upgrade command once again. This causes
Debian to install all the base packages required for a bare-bones Debian distribution, because Debian doesn't know they already exist:

```
# apt-get dist-upgrade
```

At this point, you have only rebuilt the Debian database such that it "knows" about only the most fundamental packages you have installed. It doesn't know you have things such as KDE installed, or various productivity applications. These programs are on your system and they will work, but Debian doesn't know to upgrade them as new versions appear. The only way to get Debian to know about the packages you have installed is to install them again.

Don't worry. You won't have to reconfigure the packages you reinstall. But if you want your Debian package database to know they exist, you have to install them again. You can install your favorite programs any way you want, but this suggestion should make the process easier. Install the *synaptic* program:

```
# apt-get install synaptic
```

Then start up a graphical desktop, and run *synaptic* from a run dialog or terminal window. *synaptic* is a graphical, friendly package installer for Debian that sorts the available packages by category. You can browse through the various categories and checkmark all the programs you want on your system. Then have synaptic (re)install all of them in one big batch. *Voilà*. You have just recovered from one of the most disastrous types of damage one can inflict upon a Debian system.

 ## Prelink for Performance
HACK #85
Increase your application's performance by up to 50%.

One of the problems with software applications is that they depend on other software to run. In some cases, this dependency can be built into the application statically, but in most cases, the application accesses a range of special libraries for the dependent functionality. Even the simplest of applications can rely on a huge range of libraries, and every KDE and GNOME tool needs a number of dependent programs to run. When an application accesses a library, special symbols are transferred from the library to the memory that the application is running in. Unfortunately, this copying process (called *linking*) can take quite some time, particularly with C++-based software.

On the majority of systems, libraries are rarely changed and, consequently, when a program is run, the process of transferring these symbols is the same every time. A special tool called *prelink* uses this repetition to link once and store the result of the process in a file that can be executed. This method, called *prelinking*, can greatly improve performance, particularly in C++ software. Many users have experienced performance improvements of up to 50% in some KDE software. You'll see less impressive results in programs that aren't so heavily linked or are written in a language other than C++.

Run prelink

To use *prelink*, you need to ensure that you are running a compiler and libraries that support this feature. You should aim for a *gcc* newer than Version 3.1 and a *glibc* newer than 2.3. You also need to obtain the *prelink* tool from *ftp://people.redhat.com/jakub/prelink/*. The *prelink* tool is also available in the Debian archive, and RPMs are available at *http://www.rpmfind.net/linux/rpm2html/search.php?query=prelink*.

Once you have installed *prelink*, you need to run the tool on the binaries and libraries that are present on your system. To do this, you need to add a list of the directories containing binaries to */etc/prelink.conf*. Here is an example listing of directories to add:

```
-l /usr/local/sbin
-l /sbin
-l /usr/sbin
-l /usr/local/bin
-l /bin
-l /usr/bin
-l /usr/X11R6/bin
-l /usr/games
-l /usr/local/lib
-l /lib
-l /usr/lib
-l /usr/X11R6/lib
```

The -l option included at the beginning of each line ensures that *prelink* descends recursively into directories and works on dependent binaries and libraries. This works under the condition that the directory does not span across different filesystems or mount points.

To actually perform the prelinking, you need to run the following command as root whenever you add new software to the system:

```
foo@bar:~# prelink -afmR
```

This command prelinks all (-a) binaries and libraries in the paths within the configuration file. The other options are explained in man prelink. When you run the command, it is likely you will see some warnings about the linking. You can safely ignore these. Some distributions require a special environment variable to be set to indicate that the prelinking has been done. You can set this for the current session with this command:

```
foo@bar:~$ export KDE_IS_PRELINKED=1
```

For a more permanent solution, add this to */etc/environment* or to a file appropriate to your distribution for setting a system-wide variable.

Grab the Latest Source Code

Grab the source code for your favorite project, and compile or hack it.

Source code is the lifeblood behind any open source project, and its welfare is critical in pushing the code forward and improving it. To the nonhacker, this random collection of phrases and letters appears to be gibberish, but to the hacker, this code makes perfect sense. To remain productive, it is essential that hackers maintain their code in a clean and useful state. Although many hackers worry about keeping the source code usable, this is difficult when you consider that multiple developers from around the world working on a project hack a single set of source code files. These projects rarely have a single lead developer who decides what goes in and out of the source code tree, so how is this development managed?

The solution to this problem is a source control system. These systems essentially provide a metaphorical railway signal box to manage the different needs of the different hackers. The system stores the code in a *repository* on the server and allows access to only those users who have an authorized login account. With an account, users can copy a snapshot of the code to their computers (this is called *making a working copy*), hack the code, and then submit the changes to the main server. The source control system ensures that users cannot commit changes at the same time, and it only commits the differences made to the code back into the system. This ensures that bandwidth is not bogged down by the same content flying back and forth between the hackers and the source control server.

In this hack, you are going to get started with a popular source control system called CVS. This tool is in use by most of the large software projects, and you can use it to get read-only access to the developers' source code servers. This code can be useful if you want to explore the possibility of hacking on some code yourself, but it is also handy for those of us who like to compile unstable development code to see just what the hackers are putting in the software. For example, using the methods described here, you can compile the development branches of KDE or GNOME for a bleeding-edge desktop [Hacks #44 and #48].

Connect to a CVS Repository

To use CVS first you need to specify where the CVS source code server is located. You do this by setting an environment variable called $CVSROOT. This variable is often set in your shell's startup file (such as .bash_profile for the bash shell), but if you are unsure of which shell you are running, type the following command to see which one it is:

```
foo@bar:~$ echo $SHELL
```

You need to specify a $CVSROOT that indicates the location of the CVS server, the username to connect with, and where the code is stored on the server. The $CVSROOT is set as an environment variable with three distinctive parts:

```
[authentication type]:[user@location.domain]:[location of the code on
server]
```

If you want to connect to the KDE CVS server, for example, you can get read-only access in which you can just download the code by using the anonymous username. Many CVS services offer an anonymous user in which onlookers can download the code but not make changes to it.

If, for example, you are using the bash shell, add this line to your *.bash_profile* to add a connection to the KDE CVS server:

```
export CVSROOT=:pserver:anonymous@kde.org:/home/kde
```

If you want to set this value from the command line in a bash shell, you can use this command (good only for your current session):

```
foo@bar:~$ export CVSROOT=:pserver:anonymous@kde.org:/home/kde
```

When you have set the variable with one of these methods, you can check that it is working by typing:

```
foo@bar:~$ echo $CVSROOT
:pserver:anonymous@kde.org:/home/kde
```

With this complete, now you can log in to the CVS server. To do this, type:

```
foo@bar:~$ cvs login
```

You are prompted for a password. Just press Enter to use a blank password. Now you are returned to the prompt.

> Considering the vast amount of different open source projects and the huge amount of code sitting on the Internet in CVS servers, you might want to use different CVS servers. To do this, you need to set your $CVSROOT to the new server and log in again.

On a CVS server, code is grouped into modules that contain code for related projects and tools. For example, the KDevelop project is contained within the kdevelop module on the KDE CVS server. You can see a list of these modules by typing:

```
foo@bar:~$ cvs co -c
```

To get a module from the server, you need to check it out using the CVS co option. For example, you can check out the kdevelop module with:

```
foo@bar:~$ cvs co kdevelop
```

Then you'll see the code checked out to your computer, one file at a time. To update your local copy with the latest changes from the CVS server, you need to go into a checked-out directory (such as the *kdevelop* directory in our example), and type:

```
foo@bar:~$ cvs update -PAd
```

When you run this command, only the files that were changed since your initial checkout will be copied to your computer. This ensures that a minimal amount of bandwidth is used for keeping your code current.

CVS is a powerful and competent source control system, but it is also one of the most confounding pieces of software to use, particularly when adding files to a server. For more information, I recommended you read the free book *Open Source Development with CVS* at *http://cvsbook.red-bean.com/*.

New Kid on the Block: Subversion

Although CVS has been around for a long time and a lot of open source projects use it, it has some limitations which some developers find frustrating, including not being able to store metadata (properties) associated with files and not being able to properly version directories. An alternative system called Subversion, which overcomes these limitations, is rapidly taking over as a replacement for CVS, and many projects now provide access to their source code using Subversion.

The command for accessing a Subversion repository is very simple:

```
foo@bar:~$ svn checkout http://repo.example.com/project project
```

This will check out the latest copy of the project tree into a local working copy named *project*.

Then you can keep your local source tree up-to-date by entering it and typing svn up, which will fetch any files that have changed since your last update and will merge the changes into your local tree.

The Subversion project is very active and has a very helpful mailing list. You can find the main project page at *http://subversion.tigris.org*, and you can also access the free book *Version Control with Subversion* at *http://svnbook.red-bean.com*.

HACK
#87

Speed Up Compiles

While compiling, make full use of all of your computers with a distributed compiling daemon

Many other distribution users make fun of the Gentoo fanboys, because Gentoo users have to spend a lot of time compiling all of their code. And even though these compiles can take hours or days to complete, Gentooists still tout their distribution as being one of the fastest available. Because of their constant need to compile, Gentoo users have picked up a few tricks on making the process go faster, including using *distcc* to create a cluster of computers for compiling. *Distcc* is a distributed compiling daemon that allows you to combine the processing power of other Linux computers on your network to compile code. It is very simple to set up and use, and it should produce identical results to a completely local compile. Having three machines with similar speeds should make compiling 2.6 times faster. The *distcc* home page at *http://distcc.samaba.org* has testimonials concerning real user's experiences using the program. Using this hack, you can get *distcc* to work with any Linux distribution, which will make compiling KDE and GNOME from scratch quick and easy.

> *Distcc* does not require the machines in your compile farm to have shared filesystems, synchronized clocks, or even the same libraries and headers. However, it is a good idea to make sure you are on the same major version number of the compiler itself.

Before getting started with *distcc*, first you must know how to perform a parallel make when building code. To perform a parallel make, use the -j option in your make command:

```
dbrick@rivendell:$ make -j3; make -j3 modules
```

This will spawn three child processes that will make maximum use of your processor power by ensuring that there is always something in the queue to be compiled. A general rule of thumb for how many parallel makes to perform is to double the number of processors and then add one. So a single processor system will have -j3 and a dual processor system -j5. When you start using *distcc*, you should base the -j value on the total number of processors in your compiling farm. If you have eight processors available, then use -j17.

Using distcc

You can obtain the latest version of *distcc* from *http://distcc.samba.org/download.html*. Just download the archive, uncompress it, and run the standard build commands:

```
dbrick@rivendell:$ tar -jxvf distcc-2.18.3.tar.bz2
dbrick@rivendell:$ cd distcc-2.18.3
dbrick@rivendell:$ ./configure && make && sudo make install
```

Speed Up Compiles

You must install the program on each machine you want included in your compile farm. On each of the compiling machines, you need to start the *distccd* daemon:

```
root@bree:# distccd –daemon –N15
root@moria:# distccd –daemon –N15
```

These daemons will listen on TCP port 3632 for instructions and code from the local machine (the one which you are actually compiling software for). The -N value sets a niceness level so the distributed compiles won't interfere too much with local operations. Read the *distccd* manpage for further options.

On the client side, you need to tell *distcc* which computers to use for distributed compiles. You can do this by creating an environment variable:

```
dbrick@rivendell:$ export DISTCC_HOSTS='localhost bree moria'
```

Specify localhost to make sure your local machine is included in the compiles. If your local machine is exceptionally slow, or if you have a lot of processors to distribute the load to, you should consider not including it at all. You can use machine IP addresses in place of names. If you don't want to set an environment variable, then create a *distcc* hosts file in your home directory to contain the values:

```
dbrick@rivendell:$ mkdir ~/.distcc
dbrick@rivendell:$ echo "localhost bree moria" > ~/.distcc/hosts
```

To run a distributed compile, simply pass a CC=distcc option to the make command:

```
dbrick@rivendell:$ make –j7 CC=distcc
```

It's that simple to distribute your compiles. Read the manpages for *distcc* and *distccd* to learn more about the program, including how to limit the number of parallel makes a particular computer in your farm will perform.

Distribute Compiles to Windows Machines

Though some clever people have come up with very interesting ways to distribute compiles to a Windows machine using Cygwin, there is an easier way to perform the same task using a live CD distribution known as distccKnoppix, which you can download from *http://opendoorsoftware.com/cgi/http.pl?p=distccKNOPPIX*. Be sure to download the version that has the same major version number of gcc as your local machine.

To use distccKnoppix, simply boot the computer using the CD, note it's IP address, and then enter that in your *distcc* hosts file or environment variable as instructed earlier. Happy compiling!

—*David Brickner*

Kernel

Hacks #88–91

When people speak of Linux, they are usually referring to an operating system, but most Linux users know Linux is just a kernel and not a complete OS. Of course, the kernel is the most critical piece of software on a Linux system. Luckily for us Linux users, the open source ethos that is ingrained in kernel development, and the hundreds of developers who peer over the code and improve it, ensure that we have an incredibly stable and secure kernel that forms the backbone of our operating system.

Unlike closed source operating systems in which you are given a one-size-fits-all kernel that needs to account for a variety of hardware, the Linux kernel can be customized to fit your system. This approach has both pluses and minuses. One the one hand, this ability gives you an efficient kernel that can perform well on a resource-poor system, or give you increased stability by not running software that isn't needed. On the other hand, it means you are often faced with the task of compiling a kernel to add support for specific hardware or to gain additional functionality.

Compiling kernels is not a difficult or scary process, but the thought of doing so can be a bit nerve-wracking. With the range of hacks included in this section, you will have no problem compiling the ideal kernel for your computer.

Compile a Kernel

HACK #88

Compiling a Linux kernel isn't so much a necessity as it is a rite of passage.

Linux device support is largely a double-edged sword. On the one hand, an up-to-date distribution with a recent kernel is likely to configure all your hardware automatically, and you won't need to lift a finger. On the other hand, if you have some hardware that is not supported within the kernel itself, life suddenly becomes a lot more difficult; manuals need to be read,

Google needs to be searched, and your head needs to be scratched. Lack of universal device support is why Linux users need to research their peripheral purchases before they buy.

When your Linux kernel doesn't already support a particular device, you often need to compile in support yourself. If the code for your device is experimental, you might need to patch the kernel before you compile it. Many users are nervous about compiling any program, and recompiling the kernel makes them even more so. The "archaic" process of compiling the kernel is often avoided by many users who live in hope that the kernel that ships with the next version of their distribution will provide the hardware support they need.

Although daunting at first, compiling a kernel can provide a number of benefits, both for yourself and for your humble computer. The first boon is that you are able to tweak your kernel so that it is custom-built for your specific hardware configuration. This can potentially increase your computer's performance. Another benefit is that you can patch the kernel with the latest "experimental" drivers, which might not be present in the official source code or in your vendor-provided kernel. Although patching code can seem a little nerve-wracking, it can greatly extend your system's flexibility—the bar for getting drivers in the official kernel release is quite high, and sometimes patching is the only way you can use a specific feature or driver.

The process described here is a generic approach that should work on any Linux system. However, many Linux distributions provide certain tools for compiling and packaging a kernel specifically to work with that distribution. If you use a distribution such as Debian, which provides kernel packaging tools, you should probably use them if possible for maximum convenience.

Get the Code

First, you need to download the source code for the tree from one of the mirrors at *http://www.kernel.org/mirrors/*. Once you have downloaded the tree, copy it to */usr/src*, and unzip and extract it. If you are downloading a . *bz2*-compressed tree, extract it with this:

```
foo@bar:~$ bunzip2 -d linux-x.x.x.tar.bz2
```

where x.x.x represents the kernel version number you downloaded. Then you can extract the tar file with this:

```
foo@bar:~$ tar xvf linux-x.x.x.tar
```

Now you have a new directory called *linux-x.x.x*. For simplicity in managing your kernel, you should rename this to *linux*:

```
foo@bar:~$ mv linux-x.x.x linux
```

An alternative is to keep the *linux-x.x.x* directory and instead create a symlink called *linux* to point to it:

```
foo@bar:~$ ln -s linux-x.x.x linux
```

This enables you to keep multiple source trees on your machine and just change the symlink to point to whichever is your current tree. It also helps you remember which version of the source you are working with.

> A number of different kernel source code trees (in addition to the official one) are available. Each contains official kernel source code that has been tweaked and modified by someone to achieve a specific goal, such as increased hardware support or system performance improvements. "Use CKO to Make Your Desktop Go to 11" **[Hack #90]** has more information about these alternate kernel sources. The steps in this hack are directly applicable to alternate kernel sources.

Configure the Code

Before you begin to configure your kernel, first you should ensure that you have all the software necessary to compile it. This list of requirements is shown in the *README* file in */usr/src/linux*. If you are satisfied that everything required is installed, you can launch the configuration tool by running one of the following commands.

make menuconfig
> This is for text-based color menus, radio button lists, and dialogs.

make xconfig
> This X Windows (Qt)-based configuration tool is available only in the 2.6 kernel series and higher.

make gconfig
> This X Windows (Gtk)-based configuration tool is available only in the 2.6 kernel series and higher.

make oldconfig
> This option gives you the opportunity to take a *.config* file from an older kernel (such as a 2.4 series kernel), compare it to the options available in a new kernel, and then answer some configuration questions about the new options. This is a convenient way to upgrade a kernel, because it allows you to transfer your old settings to the new configuration file.

If you are running a graphical interface (such as KDE or GNOME), I recommend you use either *xconfig* or *gconfig*. If you need to configure the code in a console terminal, use *menuconfig*. I don't suggest you use *oldconfig* unless absolutely necessary; it can be a long and drawn-out process.

Each configuration program (apart from *oldconfig*) organizes options into a series of categories. If you start at the first category and go through each section, you can turn an option on, turn it off, or mark it to compile as a loadable module. I recommend you turn on essential features that you will use all the time and configure less essential features as loadable modules. For example, you should compile support for your filesystems into the kernel, but you might want to configure support for your webcam as a module. If you are going to be dealing with USB devices, you should read "Perfect USB Devices with Project Utopia" **[Hack #93]**.

Each configuration option has some help associated with it. This is particularly useful in the graphical configuration tools, where you can read the help while configuring your kernel.

Compile the Code

Once you have configured the kernel, save your changes and quit. Now you need to enter a series of commands to compile the code. The first command creates of list of dependencies. This list is a preconfiguration step that sets up various kernel configuration files based on your kernel configuration settings. To create the dependency list, run this command:

```
foo@bar:~$ make dep
```

The next command cleans out any unwanted junk, such as temporary compilation files that were collected from previous compiles or when you created your dependencies:

```
foo@bar:~$ make clean
```

Now you can actually compile the kernel. This process can take quite some time depending on which features you selected and how fast your computer is. Start the build with this:

```
foo@bar:~$ make bzImage
```

The next step is to compile the modules you selected in the configuration tool. Compile these with this:

```
foo@bar:~$ make modules
```

Finally, you must install the modules into the correct part of your system as root. This ensures that your modules are accessible when you boot the system:

```
foo@bar:~# make modules_install
```

Though you can run these steps one by one, most people combine them into a single command, such as this:

```
foo@bar:~# make dep && make clean bzImage modules modules_install
```

Joining the commands using && allows your system to proceed with each step automatically if no errors occur in the previous step. This is a very useful trick to remember for other situations in which you want to string a series of commands.

A few distributions might have specific methods you can follow to compile a kernel. For instance, Debian provides a method for compiling a kernel and creating a Debian package out of it. This makes it easy to install on your machine, and it makes a convenient package to transfer to other machines that need the same kernel. Debian Universe (*http://www.debianuniverse.com/ readonline/chapter/21*), a web site created by Jonathan Oxer, has details on this method.

Install the Kernel

The compiled kernel is placed in */usr/src/linux/arch/<platform>/boot* and is called *bzImage*, where *<platform>* is a placeholder for the type of computer on which you are performing the compile. For example, if you compiled your kernel on an x86 machine, such as a Pentium, Athlon, Celeron, etc., you will find the kernel image in */usr/src/linux/arch/i386/boot*. You must copy this image over to */boot*. You also should rename it to include the version of the kernel in the filename so that when you have multiple kernels you can easily tell which is which. Also, the Linux kernel image has traditionally been referred to as *vmlinuz*, and many users continue to call it this. So, if you have a 2.6.5 kernel, you could copy the file with this command as root:

```
foo@bar:~# cp /usr/src/linux/arch/i386/boot/bzImage /boot/vmlinuz-2.6.5
```

You should also copy the *System.map* file (this file has a map of the positions of symbols in the kernel and is used by programs such as *depmod*) to the */boot* directory using a similar naming scheme:

```
foo@bar:~# cp /usr/src/linux/arch/i386/boot/System.map
/boot/System.map-2.6.5
```

To complete the process, just adjust your bootloader to load the new kernel [Hack #1].

> Another useful command-line option is make install. This option will copy the kernel to */boot* for you, copy associated files, and run LILO for you.

Upgrade Your Kernel to 2.6
HACK #89
Hot rod your computer with a new kernel.

Upgrading your kernel from one minor version to another quickly becomes old hat. But when a new major series of kernels comes out, such as the recently released 2.6 kernel series, many people are left scratching their heads not knowing exactly how they should move to this new version.

In this hack, you will migrate from a 2.4 series kernel to a 2.6 series. This hack assumes you know how to compile a kernel and that you have compiled the 2.4 series before [Hack #88]. Starting in mid-2004, most distributions released 2.6 series kernels. If you don't want to compile your own 2.6 kernel but you do want to take advantage of its new features, check your distributions package manager to see if there is already a 2.6 kernel for you to use.

Get the Source

The first step is to grab the latest version of the 2.6 kernel from *http://www. kernel.org/*, and save it to */usr/src*. Then you should extract it and rename the resulting directory to *linux*. If you have compiled 2.4 before you should rename that source code to something unique such as *linux2.4*.

With the source code installed, you should read the *Changes* file in */usr/src/ linux/Documentation*. This file gives you a list of points and some notes about the changes you will find in the new kernel. More importantly, this file contains a list of software requirements and their minimum version numbers. The file also includes a command that shows you how to find out what version of the software is on your system. You should ensure that you check every piece of software listed, and upgrade your software if necessary. Do not feel tempted to skip something just because the version number is similar; the kernel hackers indicate these version numbers for a reason.

Configure the Code

Although a barrage of new features is included in each new release of the kernel source, the configuration process has remained largely the same; you select options from a menu, and decide if they should be compiled into the kernel or available as loadable modules. What *has* changed within the configuration process are the configuration programs and how they can work for you. The 2.6 kernel experienced an evolution in this area and saw the birth of two new additions for configuring your kernel. One of these tools is based on the GTK widget set (used by GNOME), and you can run this version with the following:

```
foo@bar:~$ make gconfig
```

Another available configuration tool uses the Qt widget set (used by KDE), and you can run this with the following:

```
foo@bar:~$ make qconfig
```

Although these two new graphical configuration tools are part of the 2.6 kernel, you can still use `make menuconfig` for a console-based menu tool.

Users who are migrating from the 2.4 series kernel to 2.6 can use their old *.config* file. To do this simply copy the *.config* file from your original 2.4 source code directory to your new 2.6 directory and run `make oldconfig`. This converts the *.config* file to one that can be used with the 2.6 kernel. You'll be asked a lot of questions concerning the new features in the 2.6 kernel, but most should be fairly simple to answer.

New Features in 2.6

Version 2.6 has a number of new features and improvements that can be useful in the context of desktop Linux. A huge number of new options are available, and you should explore them fully and choose the ones most pertinent to your needs. Here is a summary of some of the most interesting features.

Kernel preemption
> The use of kernel preemption produces a lower delay in general applications and, more specifically, multimedia applications. This is particularly useful if you want to use your desktop as a sound recording or video editing workstation.

ALSA
> One of the most substantial additions to the 2.6 series is the Advanced Linux Sound Architecture (ALSA), and it is now the default sound system for Linux. Although ALSA is within the source tree, you will need to run through a few additional steps to get it working. First, you should ensure that you include all the options necessary for your sound card. To find out what options are necessary, look at the excellent ALSA web site at *http://www.alsa-project.org/alsa-doc*, and select your card from the combo box. Documentation is available for many of the cards ALSA supports, and this documentation can help you get the most out of your card.

New filesystems
> A number of additional filesystems have made their way into 2.6, and they include support for *ext2, ext3, reiserfs, jfs, xfs, minix, romfs, iso9660, udf, msdos, vfat, ntfs* (read-only), *adfs, amiga ffs,* Apple Macintosh *hfs,* BeOS *befs* (read-only), *bfs, efs* (read-only), *cramfs,* free *vxfs,* OS/2 *hpfs, qnx4fs, sysvfs,* and *ufs.* Although the kernel is a stable version, you should check that any new filesystems in 2.6 are fully tested before you store important data on them.

Compiling the Kernel

When you have configured the kernel, you can compile it with this:

```
foo@bar:~$ make
foo@bar:~$ make modules_install
```

You no longer need to run make dep, make modules, and make clean.

Install the Kernel

The compiled kernel is placed in */usr/src/linux/arch/<platform>/boot* and is called *bzImage*, where *<platform>* is a placeholder for the type of computer on which you are performing the compile. For example, if you compiled your kernel on an x86 machine, such as a Pentium, Athlon, Celeron, etc., you will find the kernel image in */usr/src/linux/arch/i386/boot*. You must copy this image over to */boot*. You also should rename it to include the version of the kernel in the filename so that when you have multiple kernels you can easily tell which is which. Also, the Linux kernel image has traditionally been referred to as *vmlinuz*, and many users continue to call it this. So, if you have a 2.6.5 kernel, you could copy the file with this command as root:

```
foo@bar:~# cp /usr/src/linux/arch/i386/boot/bzImage /boot/vmlinuz-2.6.5
```

You should also copy the *System.map* file (this file has a map of the positions of symbols in the kernel and is used by programs such as depmod) to the */boot* directory using a similar naming scheme:

```
foo@bar:~# cp /usr/src/linux/arch/i386/boot/System.map
/boot/System.map-2.6.5
```

To complete the process, just adjust your bootloader to load the new kernel [Hack #1].

HACK #90   Use CKO to Make Your Desktop Go to 11

Make your desktop quick and responsive, without making your music player skip, or your videos drop frames.

A number of custom kernels are designed to increase performance in one area or another. The Con Kolivas Overloaded (CKO) kernel is probably the most famous for improving desktop performance (Con Kolivas has branched out into improving server performance, too). I also recommend the CKO kernel, because it has the frame-buffer splash patch built-in (unfortunately, it is not the type of frame-buffer splash patch needed by the Debian system boot in "Jazz Up Your Debian System Boot" [Hack #8], although I expect Debian to eventually switch to the CKO boot splash patch). It also includes a more modern VESA frame-buffer driver for more recent cards. This can be useful for getting set up for the fancy login consoles [Hack #20], which uses the Qingy frame-buffer login manager. If you intend to implement any hacks that require frame-buffer support, using the CKO kernel is an easy way to prepare.

This pack of hacks shows you the advantages of using the CKO kernel, and one way to tweak CKO performance in real time as you need it.

Before getting started, you should be forewarned. Only one hard and fast rule applies when it comes to tweaking the performance of any kernel, whether it's a standard or a custom kernel: the rules will eventually change. The Linux standard plain-vanilla kernel has been changing rapidly in terms of the way it handles memory and swapping, for example, so what you might have learned months ago about tweaking memory swap performance in the standard kernel might be useless knowledge today. The same is also true for custom kernels, such as the CKO kernel. The best way to find out if or when the following advice becomes obsolete is to visit the Con Kolivas kernel patch home page at *http://members.optusnet.com.au/ckolivas/kernel/*.

You can usually find the latest CKO patch set at *http://kem.p.lodz.pl/~peter/cko/*. The page also includes a link for patch sets for older kernels, too. Download the patch for the kernel you are using (or want to use). Apply it to your kernel this way (assuming you are using kernel Version 2.6.9, which would require the *patch-2.6.9-cko3.bz2* patch):

```
# cd /usr/src/linux-2.6.9
# bzcat /<path to>/patch-2.6.9-cko3.bz2 | patch -p1
```

Compile CKO with Optimizations

A number of CKO kernel configuration optimizations are available for you to try, but the following should suffice for starters. The latest 2.6 kernels already include the option to make the kernel *preemptible* (i.e., the kernel can be interrupted by other tasks), but the CKO kernel adds the option to preempt the "Big Kernel Lock." Unfortunately, Con Kolivas doesn't explain what the "Big Kernel Lock" is or what advantage there is to making it preemptible, but it sure sounds impressive, and the menu configurator comments recommend selecting "Yes" for this option if you're building for a desktop. Enable this option by selecting Processor Type and Features → Preemptible Kernel → Preempt The Big Kernel Lock.

You can also play with the kernel's internal timer frequency by selecting Processor Type and Features → Kernel Internal Timer Frequency (1000).

The internal timer frequency determines how long a process will run until the kernel interrupts it to see what else needs to be done. In this case, there will be 1,000 interrupts per second. This means the timer will trigger an interrupt every millisecond. You can set the number lower, but you shouldn't set it higher. A higher number (more interrupts per second) can improve or degrade performance depending on your machine's speed. If you're running anything better than a '486 on your desktop, you should be happy with the default setting of 1,000. But by all means, feel free to drop it down to 500, and see how that affects the kind of desktop computing that suits your style. You never know, the less overhead of having to interrupt the CPU so often might actually improve performance, depending on what kind of work or play you are doing.

The rest of the special configuration optimizations are riskier, so stop here for now. Finish configuring the kernel for your machine's specifications, build it, and add it to your bootloader to try it out.

Tweaking CKO in Real Time

Memory and disk swapping are two of the most critical factors in desktop performance. A system that is heavily swapping to disk is stealing time from the tasks you want to perform without interruption, such as playing music or videos. The CKO kernel addresses this by setting a "watermark" threshold for the amount of memory applications can use before the kernel starts to do what could be intrusive swapping. The default watermark is 66% of available memory.

This means Linux will allocate up to 66% of available memory to applications, and only 33% of memory for data caching. This often improves desktop performance, because Linux normally tends to use memory to cache datafiles. This makes Linux somewhat aggressive about swapping an application out to disk in favor of swapping data out to disk. If, for example, it swaps your browser to disk, you will notice a delay the next time you use your browser. The fact that CKO reserves 66% of memory for applications makes it less likely that your application will be swapped out to disk, so switching between running applications should be snappy.

Sometimes, however, you will want Linux to use more memory for data than for applications. Fortunately, you can change this watermark in real time, while your system is running the CKO kernel (a roughly equivalent setting is also available in a plain-vanilla Linux kernel; see "Tweak Your Kernel Without Recompiling" [Hack #91]). Indeed, I often change the watermark as my work needs change throughout the day. The default of 66% is great for doing a bit of word processing while listening to music. If I build a large application, however, the compiler will run faster if it has access to a lot of memory with which to store compiled code for linking and reuse. A database also runs faster when you give it more memory to cache indexes and data. So, when I am running an intense database program or happen to be building a large program in the background, I reset the watermark to 33%, which allows the data cache-intensive applications to run at a decent pace without having one or more desktop applications become totally unusable. Here is how to change this watermark in a running CKO kernel:

```
# echo "33" > /proc/sys/vm/mapped
# echo "66" > /proc/sys/vm/mapped
```

schedtool and Isochronous Scheduling

The CKO kernel also allows you to launch applications with isochronous scheduling. Not all applications respond correctly to this technique, but those that do start at a high priority and then drop priority faster than normal. This guarantees that when they "wake up," they'll do so quickly, but they won't retain such a high priority that they starve the rest of the system and bring all other tasks to a crawl.

You need a special tool to use this feature. If your Linux distribution doesn't provide the *schedtool* package or something with a similar name, you can get the source code from *http://freequaos.host.sk/schedtool/* and compile it yourself. Unless you have multiple CPUs in your machine, compile it this way (actually, I recommend this even if you do have multiple CPUs):

```
# make no_affinity
# make install
```

Affinity is a multi-CPU concept. It gets Linux to more likely assign a certain task to a particular CPU. Most of the time, the only people who should work with processor affinity are high-level programmers, such as SQL database programmers. Unless you really know what you're doing, it's better to let Linux decide what tasks to assign to any given processor on a multiprocessor machine.

Here's how to launch an application with isochronous scheduling:

```
$ schedtool -I -e <application name>
```

This will start your application at a high priority, which means it should start up more quickly than usual.

Tweak Your Kernel Without Recompiling
#91
You can tune even a plain-vanilla kernel at boot time and during runtime.

You don't need to compile a hot rod version of a Linux kernel or even recompile your existing kernel to improve Linux performance on the desktop. If you're running one of the later 2.6 kernels, this pack of hacks includes a few tricks you can use to modify the performance of the kernel you already have installed and running.

One of the most hotly debated performance topics is how Linux should determine what memory to swap to disk, how much it should swap, and when to do it. The answer is simple. Use one or more of the following tweaks to control this process yourself.

Setting Swappiness via /proc

A kernel parameter is available that is represented as a pseudofile called */proc/ sys/vm/swappiness*. The default value for the parameter is 70. You can log in and view the default value with this command:

```
# cat /proc/sys/vm/swappiness
70
```

The number is a rough gauge for how likely it is that Linux will swap to disk whatever it considers to be swappable. If you set it to 100, it will swap most aggressively. If you set it to 20, it will tend to swap a lot less. Here is how you can set it to either value (logged in as root):

```
# echo "100" > /proc/sys/vm/swappiness
# cat /proc/sys/vm/swappiness
100
# echo "20" > /proc/sys/vm/swappiness
# cat /proc/sys/vm/swappiness
20
```

The argument for either side goes like this. Set the swappiness value to a high number, even to 100, if you run several bloated applications and do not often switch between them. The end result will be that when you do switch to an application you left unused for a while, it might take several seconds to respond, because it must be swapped back into memory from disk. However, any application you use at any given time should run faster, because it is not competing with seldom-used applications for memory, as those applications are likely to be swapped out to disk.

On the other hand, if you set the swappiness value to a low number, your applications are likely to respond instantly when you switch between them, even if you leave one or more of them unused for long periods of time. The possible downside to this approach is that if one or more of your applications needs a lot of memory to store data (such as a database application), it will run slower than if you set the swappiness value higher.

So, here's what you should do. Set the value to a high number, use your computer for desktop operation as you normally would, and see how things behave for a few hours. Then set it to a low number, continue to use your computer for desktop operation as you normally would, and see for yourself what the difference feels like. Then pick the performance characteristics you like best. Perhaps you'll even be happiest with a default value of 70.

Tuning Network Performance via /proc

Here are a couple more parameters you might want to tweak, especially if you are using a home computer hooked directly to a DSL or cable router:

```
# echo "0" > /proc/sys/net/ipv4/tcp_sack
# echo "0" > /proc/sys/net/ipv4/tcp_timestamps
```

These settings turn off some unnecessary network activity. You might not perceive any change in performance, but it's worth a try.

Tuning Disk Access via Your Bootloader

Each program you run under Linux will want to access the disk at some point or another. The Linux kernel determines how to prioritize how each program gets access to the disk, using three methods: Anticipatory Scheduling, Complete Fairness Queuing, and Deadline Queuing. (Actually, the kernel uses a fourth method, called *noop*, but *noop* is not likely to be applicable as a default method for a desktop user.)

Each method has its advantages and disadvantages. Only two of them are likely to be appropriate for desktop performance: Anticipatory Scheduling and Complete Fairness Queuing. Most people seem to favor Complete Fairness Queuing for best desktop performance, but some argue that Anticipatory Scheduling is actually superior for desktop performance. Here's how the three methods work.

Anticipatory Scheduling
> The kernel tries to anticipate how the disk will be accessed. If a program is reading data, the anticipatory scheduler assumes it's likely that it will want to continue reading data. So, while it pauses according to a schedule, it anticipates picking up where it left off. If it guesses correctly, the disk heads don't have to jump around much and you get better performance.

Complete Fairness Queuing
> The kernel queues the disk to be used equally by every running program. No single program can hog disk access. If several programs are using the disk at the same time, each one will be responsive. On the other hand, this can also cause the disk head to jump around a lot more than it has to, thus slowing the entire system's overall responsiveness.

Deadline Queuing

This type of queuing allows an application to dominate disk access. Other applications that want to use the disk are put on the queue and must wait. If the application hogging the disk exceeds a certain deadline, the kernel passes disk access to the next requesting application on the queue. This is a good queuing system for a database server, but it is least likely to be best for a desktop system.

The choice really comes down to Anticipatory Scheduling and Complete Fairness Queuing. There are advocates for both when it comes to desktop performance, so you should try both and decide for yourself how they suit your desktop use.

You can specify your choice of scheduler by passing parameters to the kernel in your bootloader.

LILO lets you append instructions to the boot process by adding a line such as the following for each boot entry in the */etc/lilo.conf* file:

```
append="<added instructions>"
```

If you want to use the Anticipatory Scheduler, use this:

```
append="elevator=as <possibly more added instructions>"
```

If you want to use Complete Fairness Queuing, use this instead:

```
append="elevator=cfq <possibly more added instructions>"
```

A complete example might look like this:

```
image=/boot/vmlinuz-2.6.9
    label=Linux
    root=/dev/hda1
    append="elevator=as video=vesafb:ywrap,mtrr,1024x768-16@60"
```

Run the lilo command after you make your changes to *lilo.conf*, and then reboot for the changes to take effect.

With the GRUB bootloader, you simply append the instructions to the kernel line yourself. For example, if you want to use Anticipatory Scheduling, your boot entry might look like this:

```
title My Default Linux
root (hd1,0)
kernel /boot/vmlinuz-2.6.9 ro root=/dev/hda1 elevator=as
```

If you want to try Complete Fairness Queuing, make your boot entry look more like this:

```
title My Default Linux
root (hd1,0)
kernel /boot/vmlinuz-2.6.9 ro root=/dev/hda1 elevator=cfq
```

You do not need to set up GRUB again. Simply reboot for the change to take effect.

> If you are using the Con Kolivas Overloaded kernel **[Hack #90]**, it defaults to Complete Fairness Queuing. If you are using a plain-vanilla kernel, it defaults to Anticipatory Scheduling. These default settings have changed over time, and they might change again in the future, so it is best to specify the queuing method you want.

Hardware
Hacks #92–100

We're always told Linux can't be a viable desktop operating system unless it has certain pieces of software, but mentioned less frequently is that Linux won't be adopted on the desktop unless it can use a broad range of hardware. A high-end sound or video card isn't of any use if you don't have the drivers to run it. Hardware vendors seldom write drivers for Linux—they prefer to spend their time writing drivers for Windows, because that is what runs on 95% of all computers sold.

This means Linux hackers have to pick up the slack and write drivers for various pieces of hardware. As a result, it can be weeks or months before certain pieces of hardware are well supported under Linux. Even when drivers are available, they might not be integrated into the distributions, because they are too new, they are unstable, or they were written by a hardware vendor under a license which prevents the driver from being distributed with a free Linux distribution.

This chapter has a broad range of hacks that show you how to use various pieces of hardware under Linux. It starts with Bluetooth and USB connectivity, moves on to optimal monitor setups and a clever method of using Windows to print to a printer that doesn't have a Linux driver, then covers power management on a laptop, and finishes up with a couple of hacks on using portable music players under Linux.

HACK #92 Make an Internet Connection Using Bluetooth and a Mobile Phone

Use the power of Bluetooth to connect to your devices wirelessly.

Linux now has good support for Bluetooth networking with mobile embedded devices. This is useful for laptop and desktop users who want to use a mobile phone for quick dialup access. But configuring the multitude of

Bluetooth options is still fairly cumbersome and unwieldy. This quick and dirty hack uses simple shell scripts to establish a dialup Internet connection, using Bluetooth as the link between a laptop and mobile phone. Once it is set up, you can use the Bluetooth tools to easily interface with a mobile phone's phone book and provide SMS capability using a third-party utility, such as gnokii (*http://www.gnokii.org*). It is also trivial to replace the laptop used in this hack with a desktop PC equipped with a low-cost USB Bluetooth dongle adapter device.

Bluetooth support in Linux is provided through the BlueZ software stack (*http://www.bluez.org*). This is a collection of utilities and drivers that configure the underlying hardware, as well as provide the interface seen by software applications. Each Bluetooth device contains a unique identifier—much like a network MAC address—that is used in communications to determine the source and destination of the data being transmitted. Certain operations cannot be performed unless the two communicating devices have been *paired* or logically bound together using a password. In this way it is possible to provide some level of safeguard against unauthorized use of a mobile phone, while allowing those who have paired with it free reign to make any calls they want. The script in this hack relies on such a pairing to reduce the hassle of calling an ISP to a single click of a desktop icon.

To begin, you must install the BlueZ protocol stack. The good news is that BlueZ support is standard in most recent Linux distributions, including those based on kernels 2.4 and 2.6. Linux supports most of the inexpensive Bluetooth devices on the market (especially those using the popular CSR chipset) because they are usually based on the same generic parts, but with a different badge and label on the box. Most distribution kernels are built with support for all the currently supported Bluetooth hardware devices, but some older systems must be updated for Bluetooth support. If the tools mentioned here are not available on your system, first check to see if they are included on the distribution installation discs or as downloads on the BlueZ web site. Red Hat, SUSE, Mandrake, and Debian all ship with Bluetooth support, but the Bluetooth tools might not have been installed when you installed your distribution.

As a minimum, you should ensure that the *bluez-utils*, *bluez-pin*, and *bluez-sdp* packages are installed on your system. These provide the tools and utilities required by Bluetooth, a GUI application for pin entry, and a server program that can advertise the system to other compatible Bluetooth devices. The *bluez-utils* package also contains a range of useful utilities, including *hcitool* and *rfcomm*. You can use the former to enumerate available Bluetooth devices, and the latter to establish a connection. With the necessary packages installed, the following command should tell you the Bluetooth address of the host Linux laptop:

```
foo@bar:~$ hcitool dev
Devices:
        hci0    00:09:DD:10:3F:8B
```

To communicate with a Bluetooth-enabled mobile phone, switch on its Bluetooth function and ensure that it is set up to advertise its presence to other devices (it needn't advertise itself once the following steps have been completed, however). Look for Bluetooth devices using the hcitool command (this will take some time to complete):

```
foo@bar:~$ hcitool scan
Scanning ...
        00:E0:03:3D:58:2E        bob
```

This shows that the Nokia 6230 mobile phone used in this example has a hardware address of 00:E0:03:3D:58:2E and is called bob. It is now possible to communicate with that device and establish a connection to the modem device within it. This will show up as an extra serial port (called */dev/rfcomm0*) that you can use to dial connections to an ISP. Connect to the phone using a command similar to the following:

```
foo@bar:~$ rfcomm bind 0 00:E0:03:3D:58:2E 1
```

You should ensure that you replace the hardware address 00:E0:03:3D:58:2E with the appropriate address discovered previously on your own device, but leave the rest of the command intact. Now you can use the phone's internal modem via the */dev/rfcomm0* serial device. You also can script these actions and store them in a file. This example uses a file called */usr/local/bin/bluetooth_call.sh* with the following contents:

```
#!/bin/sh
echo Configuring bluetooth...
rfcomm release 0
rfcomm bind 0 00:E0:03:3D:58:2E 1
```

Most Linux distributions provide an easy-to-use GUI tool for dialup configuration. Locate the appropriate tool for your system and configure a new connection using */dev/rfcomm0* in place of */dev/modem*, or whichever modem device is selected by default on your system. In the case of *pppd* running on Debian, it is possible to call an ISP through a single command appended to the previous script:

```
pppd call my_isp
```

You can reduce this entire process to a single desktop icon click by adding a new desktop launcher icon and configuring it to execute the appropriate script. Note that it will be necessary to run any such script using a wrapper such as gnome-sudo to run with root privileges. On a GNOME desktop, you can configure a launcher icon to run the previous script:

```
foo@bar:~$ gnome-sudo /usr/local/bin/bluetooth_call.sh
```

—Jon Masters

Perfect USB Devices with Project Utopia
Kick your desktop into the Plug and Play world with your USB devices.

Few would argue that USB has not had a tremendous impact on the computer world. Everything from sound cards to network cards to lamps and beyond is available with a USB connector hanging off the side.

Linux support for devices has traditionally been a slightly crufty area. Devices that are plugged in usually require several manual steps before the OS recognizes them, and they are accessible to the user. But in the last two years the ease of hardware handling has improved dramatically. One of the major projects to work on this problem is Project Utopia. This collection of developers has worked to create a software stack that enables you to plug a device into your USB port and have it just work. This stack includes the following tools:

udev
>   This tool replaces the kernel-managed */dev* with an equivalent user-space that makes it easier for devices to be handled.

dbus
>   This allows programs to communicate with each other and respond to specific events.

Hardware Abstraction Layer (HAL)
>   This component ties together the other technologies to provide information about system events, as well as an abstracted layer in which to interact with hardware. Traditionally, most programs that deal with hardware have done it in their own way, but HAL provides a consistent way of dealing with hardware while getting the benefits of device detection and other features.

In addition to these tools, you need to be running a 2.6 series kernel [Hack #89] and a recent version of *linux-hotplug*. Project Utopia is a fairly complex system to build, so I recommend you install the binary packages that are available for your distribution. If you are intent on compiling the source code, however, you should look at the documentation available at *http://hal.freedesktop.org*.

Install the Packages

You need to install the packages in the right order. If you are using a system that figures out the dependencies and installs them in the correct order (such as APT or *portage*), this should be easy for you. If you are installing the packages individually, here is the required order:

- Kernel 2.6
- *linux-hotplug*
- *udev*
- *dbus*
- HAL

In addition, if you are using the GNOME desktop, you should install the GNOME Volume Manager. This package (often named *gnome-volume-manager*) requires the following packages to be installed:

- *python-gnome2*
- *libgnomeui*
- *gnome-common*
- *libglade2*

You probably have some of these packages available already.

Configure the Automounter

When you plug a device into the system, you want to be able to automatically access the device. For units such as digital cameras and other USB mass storage devices, you ideally want to plug in the device and be able to use it right away—no more manual mounting of disks. On a Linux system, mounted disks are typically managed by */etc/fstab*. One option for automatically mounting inserted media uses this file. This program, called *fstab-sync*, is part of the HAL package and it modifies */etc/fstab* each time a device is plugged in and used. When you install the HAL package, *fstab-sync* is installed automatically for you.

Another option is to use *pmount*, written by Martin Pitt. This handy little tool replaces the mount command with a version that can be used in userspace so that nonroot programs can access devices. The Ubuntu distribution uses this method with a good degree of success, but it requires a little more work to get going. To use *pmount* you need to use a special patched GNOME Volume Manager. At the time of this writing the GNOME Volume Manager does not include built-in support for *pmount*, but you should check to see if a newer version with *pmount* support has been released by having a look on Google.

If the versions of GNOME Volume Manager available to you don't contain *pmount*, you will need to patch the GNOME Volume Manager source yourself and compile it. Before you do this, be certain you have the following programs installed:

- *pmount*
- *python-gnome2-dev*
- *libgnomeui-dev*
- *libglade2-dev*

You can download the source code to the GNOME Volume Manager from *http://ftp.gnome.org/pub/GNOME/sources/gnome-volume-manager*, and you can get the *pmount* patch from *http://people.debian.org/~mpitt/gnome-volume-manager.pmount.patch*. Extract the Gnome Volume Manager code to a work directory, copy the patch to that directory, and cd to the work directory. Then patch the code using this command:

```
foo@bar:~$ patch -p1 < ubuntu-pmount.diff
```

You might see some patch errors referring to a Debian control file. You can safely ignore these errors when you're not running on a Debian system. Finally, you can compile the code with this:

```
foo@bar:~$ ./autogen.sh
foo@bar:~$ make
foo@bar:~$ make install (you may need to be root to do this)
```

Now you have a patched GNOME Volume Manager that can use *pmount*.

Configure Your System

With the GNOME Volume Manager installed you can configure your system to respond intelligently when devices are plugged in. You configure this with the *gnome-volume-properties* tool. You should run this tool from the command line, and then check the "Mount removable drives when hotplugged," "Mount removable media when inserted," and "Browse removable media when inserted" checkboxes. For the other options in the properties box, try the following commands:

Audio CDs
```
gnome-cd --unique --play --device %d
```
Blank CDs
```
nautilus --no-desktop burn:
```
DVD videos
```
totem dvd://
```
Digital cameras
```
/usr/share/gnome-volume-manager/gnome-volume-manager-gthumb.sh %h
```

These options enable the most common actions you will want when you insert new media into your computer.

Optimize Your Refresh Rates

#94

Reduce eyestrain by fine-tuning your monitor's refresh rates.

Many of you reading this book spend a lot of time in front of a computer at work, at school, or in your home. As you rack up hours in front of the whirring machine, your eyes take the brunt of the physical effects of your computer use. Most people see flicker on their monitors when the monitor refresh rate is lower than 72MHz. This flicker causes eyestrain, headaches, and general fatigue. This hack explores how you can tune your X configuration to optimize your picture's quality and its refresh rates. But beware, using excessive refresh rates that your monitor does not support can potentially cause physical damage to the monitor in the same way revving an engine too high can destroy your engine. Although this is less common with modern monitors, you should be cautious when experimenting with this hack.

Find Out More About Your Monitor

To get the best use from your monitor, you need to determine its optimum refresh rate. You can do this by gathering some information about your monitor, running that information through a web-based tool that can determine your optimal settings, and then entering those settings in your X configuration file (usually */etc/X11/XF86Config-4* or *xorg.conf*).

The web-based tool requires a couple of pieces of information: your monitor's resolution and the dot clock frequency (also known as the pixel clock). But to complete this hack, you also need to know the horizontal and vertical sync (refresh) ranges.

You can gather some of the information you need from the label on the back of your monitor, your monitor's built-in menu system, your monitor's manual, and by Googling for your monitor specifications on the Web. I've always found a Google search to be a particularly effective way to get the horizontal and vertical sync ranges. You can also use the *xvidtune* utility:

```
foo@bar:~$ xvidtune
```

In the bottom right of the xvidtune window, you should see the "Vertical sync rate in Hz" box. If the setting in that box is lower than 72Hz, you likely can optimize your X configuration. The exception is if you are using an LCD monitor, which refreshes differently than a CRT and normally has a value of around 60Hz. The other values you need that this tool provides are the pixel clock rate and the HDisplay and VDisplay values, which combined make up your current monitor resolution.

To determine your optimal refresh rate, visit *http://xtiming.sourceforge.net/cgi-bin/xtiming.pl*, and enter your monitor specifications in the Basic Configuration section. Do not enter a value for Refresh Rate; that is what you are seeking to calculate. Unless you have a widescreen display, your Aspect Ratio is 4:3. Most modern monitors are noninterlaced, but if your monitor is more than four years old, you should double-check whether it is noninterlaced by Googling for specifications. There is seldom a reason to check Doublescan. Once you have filled out the information, click the Calculate Modeline button at the bottom.

When the web page refreshes, a new section at the top will provide you with a modeline to use in your *XF86Config-4* file. Copy this so that you can use it later.

Configure Your Monitor

To optimize your monitor settings, you need to adjust your X configuration file (usually *XF86Config-4*, but if you are using Xorg, the file is *xorg.conf*). Before you change anything in your X configuration, though, you should back up your X configuration file with this, or a similar command:

```
foo@bar:~$ cp /etc/X11/XF86Config-4 /etc/X11/XF86Config-4.backup
```

Now you need to modify the configuration file. Within the *XF86Config-4* is a section called Monitor where you can configure general monitor settings. Adjust the section using the information you have from the X timing web site and the information you received from your monitor and *xvidtune*:

```
Section "Monitor"
        Identifier      "Whizzbang MonitorMan"
        HorizSync       28-64
        VertRefresh     43-60
        Option          "DPMS"
        Modeline        "1152x864@88" 83.91 1280 1312 1624 1656 800 816 824
841"
EndSection
```

One intriguing option within this block is the DPMS setting. This highly recommended, power-saving feature puts your monitor into standby mode if you have not used it for a while. HorizSync and VertRefresh are the ranges you found earlier from your monitor's documentation or from searching the Web. Modeline, which describes to X your monitor's frequencies, timings, and resolution, comes from the X timing web site.

The name of the mode defined in the example is 1152x864@88. It is a unique identifier describing the preferred resolution at 88Hz (this is a crisp resolution).

Configure the Resolution and Refresh Rate

To change the resolution and refresh rate inside X, you need to adjust the Screen part of the configuration file. This section contains some important settings which, if configured incorrectly, could stop X from working properly.

The first part of the block contains information about your monitor. Some of the details you added to the Monitor block earlier should be copied over to this block. For the main part of this block, you need to set two things: the resolution and the color depth. You use the DefaultDepth option to set the color depth, and you use the Modes section to specify the first part of the custom mode you obtained from the X timing web site (1152x864@88 for this example). You should ensure that modes you don't use are removed from the Modes line. Here is an example block:

```
Section "Screen"
        Identifier  "Screen 1"
        Device      "Acme VideoKing"
        Monitor     "Whizzbang MonitorMan"
        DefaultDepth 16
        Subsection "Display"
                Depth      16
                Modes      "1152x864@88"
                ViewPort   0 0
        EndSubsection
EndSection
```

Now restart X. If you are starting X with *startx*, simply log out and restart the server. For example, if you are using a display manager such as GDM, you will need to restart it with this:

```
foo@bar:~$ /etc/init.d/gdm restart
```

HACK #95 Print to Unsupported Printers

Use a Windows machine as a print server, when you can't print from Linux.

Linux's support for printers increases with every passing day; the team at *http://linuxprinting.org* and the army of software developers building free drivers for new printers do a sterling job. However, printers are still on the market (and new ones are being released each day) that Linux does not support; no driver is available, so Linux users cannot print to these unfortunate devices. This problem has no direct solution, but if you find yourself in this situation and you can attach your printer to a Windows machine, you can hack a solution.

Under normal circumstances a printer connected to a Windows machine can be used by Linux (via Samba). But this doesn't work when a Linux printer driver is not available. This hack delivers an interesting solution to this problem. It uses a generic printer driver on Linux to send a PostScript print job to a Windows machine sharing the printer. The Windows machine interprets the PostScript using a local copy of Ghostscript, which then sends the information to the Windows printer driver and on to the printer.

How Printing Works

The normal process of printing from Linux to a supported shared Windows printer is as follows:

1. You print from the application (say, a word processor) on the Linux box.

2. The print job goes to the print server on the Linux box, which is likely to be CUPS. CUPS has a printer driver for this model of printer, and it converts the print job into a set of instructions telling the printer how to print the job. (These instructions are, to some extent, printer-specific, which is why a specific driver is required for each printer.)

3. The stream of instructions flows across the network to the print server on the Windows machine.

4. The instructions are fed by the Windows print server to the printer.

5. The printer prints the job.

This hack changes this process a little by adding a couple of extra steps. After it has been set up, the process works like this:

1. You print from the application (say, a word processor) on the Linux box.

2. The print job goes to the print server on the Linux box. CUPS processes the print job using a generic printer driver that can output PostScript. PostScript is a generic way of describing print jobs; if the "set of instructions" that describe how to print a job are in PostScript, any printer that understands PostScript can understand them.

3. The stream of PostScript instructions flows across the network to the print server on the Windows machine. At this point, they are unusable by the Windows printer driver.

4. The instructions are fed by the Windows print server to a "redirected printer," which is actually a connection to Ghostscript, a free software PostScript interpreter.

5. Ghostscript, which is running as an application on the Windows machine, sends the job to the *real* printer (it can print to the real printer because it is running on Windows and can therefore use the Windows printer driver).

6. The printer prints the job.

Because steps 4 and 5 are where the magic happens, the rest of this hack covers setting up Ghostscript as a pseudoprinter.

Creating a Redirected Printer

The first step in getting the redirected printer working is to install Ghost-Script and some supported programs on Windows. Download and install the following programs:

- Ghostscript (*http://www.cs.wisc.edu/~ghost/doc/AFPL/get814.htm*)
- RedMon (*http://www.cs.wisc.edu/~ghost/redmon/*)
- GSview (*http://www.cs.wisc.edu/~ghost/gsview/index.htm*)

GSview is sometimes packaged with Ghostscript, so you might not need to install it separately.

Within the directory containing *gsprint.exe* (*C:\GS\GSVIEW*, by default), create the file *gsprint.cfg* with the following content:

```
-noquery
-color
-printer
windows_printer_name
-ghostscript
"C:\GS\GS8.14\BIN\GSWIN32C.EXE"
```

You can remove the -color line if you are using a black-and-white printer. The path in the last line should be the actual path to *gswin32c.exe*. The line windows_printer_name must *exactly* match the name the real Windows printer has in the control panel. Be careful about spaces; there must not be any trailing or leading spaces on any of the lines, and there must not be any blank lines in the file (including at the end).

Next, create a new printer in the control panel that uses the Apple Laser-Writer II driver (this driver is for a PostScript printer). This PostScript printer is necessary, because your Linux box knows how to print to Post-Script printers, but not to your Windows printer; next, you'll set up the PostScript printer so that it passes documents sent from your Linux box on to Ghostscript. View the properties of the just-created PostScript printer, click Add Port on the Ports tab, and select "Redirected port" (this option appears only once you install the RedMon utility). Call the port **RDR1:** and click OK. Click Configure Port and enter the following settings:

Field	Value
Redirect to program	*C:\GS\GSVIEW\GSPRINT.EXE*
Arguments for program	- (a single dash, no spaces)
Output	Program handles output
Run as user	Select this option

After saving the details, go back to the Ports tab of the PostScript printer's properties and set the Port to be RDR1:. Now print a test page to the Post-Script printer; it should print out of the real printer. The print job that is sent to the PostScript printer is being sent on to Ghostscript (the printer is "redirected to a program," as noted in the previous table), and then Ghost-script prints the job to your Windows printer, because it was configured to do so (when you put the name of the Windows printer in *gsprint.cfg*).

The printer should be available to all users; to do this, you need to copy the settings in the registry that define the printer from your user account to the default user account. Export the registry key HKEY_CURRENT_USER\Software\ Microsoft\Windows NT\CurrentVersion\Devices from RegEdit to a file. Edit the exported file, and change the line [HKEY_CURRENT_USER\Software\ Microsoft\Windows NT\CurrentVersion\Devices] to [HKEY_USERS\.DEFAULT\ Software\Microsoft\Windows NT\CurrentVersion\Devices]. Save the changed file, and double-click it to load it into the registry.

Finally, go back to the PostScript printer's properties, choose Ports, select RDR1: and Configure Port, and uncheck Run as User. Now share the Post-Script printer with a short share name (less than eight characters). Remember this name: you'll need it shortly.

Printing to the New Printer

On the Linux machine, set up the printer as you would normally set up a Windows printer. For example, under GNOME, in the Printers window, click Add Printer → Network Printer → Windows Printer (SMB), and enter the NetBIOS name of the Windows box under Host. Put the share name you created earlier in the Printer field. You might also need to add a username and password to access the printer; consult the Samba documentation for details. Select the printer type as an Apple LaserWriter II or a generic Post-Script printer.

Under KDE, select "SMB shared printer (Windows)" from the KDEPrint Add Printer wizard, and enter the details as for GNOME. Again, select the printer type as an Apple LaserWriter II or a generic PostScript printer. Now your Linux applications should be able to print to the printer successfully!

For more information and details, take a look at *http://mywebpages.comcast. net/heretrythis/hp3100/psemunt.html*.

—*Stuart Langridge*

Control Your Power with ACPI

#96 Extend the life of your laptop battery by limiting your computer's appetite for power.

The Advanced Configuration and Power Interface (ACPI) is an open industry specification that allows for power management on laptops, desktops, and servers. Compaq/Hewlett-Packard, Intel, Microsoft, Phoenix, and Toshiba first released it in 1996. These developers aimed to replace Advanced Power Management (APM), the previous industry standard for power management.

You can configure ACPI and control it from within the operating system. This is a step forward from APM, which was affected only by system idle time and could be configured only from within the BIOS screens during startup. ACPI can be used by most new laptops, although some brands have specific configuration issues. Be sure to do a web search for your specific machine to see what limitations your system has.

ACPI has several different software components:

- A subsystem, which monitors and affects hardware, including thermal control, motherboard configuration, and power states
- A policy manager, which allows the user to modify system states
- Drivers to control and monitor devices, such as laptop batteries, SMBus (communications/transmission path), and EC (embedded controller)

Installing ACPI

A number of things must be in place to use ACPI successfully. Your kernel must have the correct configuration, you must have the relevant modules loaded, and you should be running an application to monitor the status of your system.

To confirm that the kernel is properly configured, launch a kernel configuration tool and go to the General Setup section. Inside this section, confirm that Power Management Support is enabled. Also, make sure APM is disabled. Select all options to do with ACPI that are relevant to your hardware. You can choose either M for modules or * to compile directly into the kernel. Save the new configuration and exit. Then compile your kernel and modules, as discussed in "Compile a Kernel" [Hack #88].

ACPI is always under revision. It is available in later versions of the 2.4.x series kernel (2.4.22 and higher) and all 2.6.x series kernels. You should always use the latest stable version of the kernel that your system can support. Even the most recent kernel can have minor bug fixes available as a patch, so be sure to check for one at *http://acpi.sourceforge.net.* If your distribution has already patched your kernel, you might have difficulty applying a second patch for ACPI. Read */usr/src/kernel-source-<version>/README* to see if your kernel has already been patched.

If you are already running a kernel with ACPI support, you can check the ACPI revision date with the following command:

```
foo@bar:~$ cat /proc/acpi/info
```

This might give you detailed list or only a version number. You are looking for the line that starts with version:.

Load Related Modules

The next step is to check to see that each ACPI module is loaded after your machine boots. You can do this with the lsmod command. You are looking for the following options: button, battery, fan, ac, thermal, and processor. If you chose Y instead of M (modules) when you compiled your kernel, you will not see this list, because the components were compiled into the kernel itself. Otherwise, the output should look similar to this:

```
Module          Size  Used by
button          2420  0 (unused)
battery         5960  0 (unused)
ac              1832  0 (unused)
fan             1608  0 (unused)
thermal         6664  0 (unused)
processor       8664  0 [thermal]
```

If you compiled ACPI support as modules and you do not see the ACPI modules listed, you need to load the modules by hand. The modules should be in */lib/modules/<kernel-version>/kernel/drivers/acpi/.*

To prevent having to load the modules each time you reboot, you can do one of two things: compile them directly into the kernel (a bit late for that, though, eh?) or add them to your */etc/modules* file. If you do not already have a copy of the file, just create a new one and add each module name (remember, no *.o*) on a separate line. You can also try running update-modules which should automatically update your */etc/modules.conf* configuration file.

Use ACPI

You can install a few different applications/daemons on your system: *acpid* (the daemon that controls your hardware states), and a monitoring program. Be sure to remove the APM daemon (*apmd*) if you are running ACPI. In addition to using an application to monitor your system, you can also check the ACPI files individually. Look in the */proc/acpi* directory for various things of importance. For example, if you want to look at your battery status you need to read the battery state file:

```
foo@bar:~$ cat /proc/acpi/battery/BAT0/state
present:                yes
capacity state:         ok
charging state:         charging
present rate:           37 mW
remaining capacity:     44400 mWh
present voltage:        12456 mV
```

More information on ACPI in Linux, including information on power management (sleep and suspend), is available at *http://acpi.sourceforge.net.*

—*Emma Jane Hogbin*

HACK #97   Use an iPod with Linux

You don't need a Windows PC or Mac to use an iPod.

This hack shows how to use an iPod with Linux. It's aimed at Linux purists—that is, people who don't want to have to use a Mac or Windows–based PC, nor Wine nor Windows software—to get going. (I fall into this category, not because of any religious convictions, but merely because Linux is all I have. For updates, visit *http://pag.csail.mit.edu/~adonovan/hacks/ipod.html*)

> This hack assumes that you have reasonable level of Linux competence. You should be comfortable with downloading, compiling, and installing software, as well as general system administration tasks.

Here's what you'll need if you want to use an iPod with your Linux box:

A Mac or Windows iPod (obviously)

The iPod is basically just a FireWire hard disk, with its own operating software stored in one partition. The two variants of the iPod are formatted with different filesystems: HFS+ in the case of the Mac, and FAT32 in the case of Windows. Indeed, this is the only difference.

Ideally, you want to start with a Windows iPod. Linux has extremely limited support for the Apple HFS+ filesystem, and thus it is necessary to convert HFS+ iPods to FAT32, erasing the disk in the process. The iPod firmware is identical, though, so you must save this before you begin.

To do the conversion, don't mess around with Wine, or with Winnie-Pod Updater, the Apple-sanctioned tool for HFS-to-FAT32 conversion. The GNU instructions for how to convert are sufficient and require only fdisk, dd, and mkfs.vfat, which are standard Unix tools.

The latest breed of iPod appears to come in a single flavor called "for Windows and Mac." They are actually HFS-formatted but come with software for Windows that invisibly does the conversion the first time they are used. So these are really just Mac iPods. If you have access to a PC with MS Windows, you can use that to do the conversion to FAT32. (Thanks to Zach Hobbs for this information.)

A Linux system with a recent, FireWire-capable kernel (2.4.12 or later—now might be a good time to upgrade to RedHat 9.0 or similar)

Note that the version of RedHat Package Manager (RPM) that comes with RedHat 9.0 (Shrike) has an annoying bug: sometimes it will crash, and on subsequent executions, it will hang, waiting for a mutex (in the futex syscall, as can be observed using strace). If this happens, simply remove the */var/lib/rpm/__dbxxx* temporary files from the RPM database and try again.

A working FireWire interface

I use an Orange Micro PCMCIA card (*http://www.orangemicro.com/ firewire.html*; $59.00) for a laptop. It still seems that the kernel support for FireWire is a little flaky, so try to avoid issuing and/or interrupting commands unnecessarily, or removing the interface while the drivers are doing something.

The GtkPod package

GtkPod (*http://gtkpod.sourceforge.net*; free) is a graphical tool for transferring files to and from the iPod. It is the Linux equivalent of the iTunes software used for this purpose on the Mac.

I used the gtkpod 0.50 RPM, available free from *http://www.rpmfind.net*. This package requires the id3lib package.

You must use a tool such as GtkPod; you cannot simply copy files onto the iPod's hard disk, because the iPod's database must be updated for it to see the new tracks. Furthermore, the first time you use GtkPod, you must select File → Create Directories to set up the database on the iPod.

The grip package

Grip is a free, graphical tool for ripping CDs and encoding them as MP3s.

Note that when ripping CDs to files, the actual filenames are not important to the iPod. However, because its music database is populated from the ID3 tags embedded within the MP3 files, it *is* important that these are accurate.

This means that you should encode MP3 files from an album all together, or else you will lose the album track-numbering information. It also means that you can use convenient filenames (such as *track07.mp3*) instead of naming the files with the actual track names (e.g., *07. Voodoo Chile [Slight Return].mp3*); the shell metacharacters present in the latter make them a pain to work with.

Setting Up Your Linux Desktop

Assuming you're using a PCMCIA FireWire card, once the card is inserted, the cardmgr daemon should take care of loading the ieee1394 and ohci1394 modules. If you have a PCI card, these should be loaded by system startup (/etc/rc.local).

When you attach the iPod to the FireWire interface, the sbp2 module is loaded automatically. (If it's not, load it with modprobe.) You should see messages appear in dmesg indicating that the device is recognized. Additionally, /proc/bus/ieee1394/devices contains information on each device, including the string [Apple Computer, Inc.] for the iPod:

```
ieee1394: Host added: Node[00:1023]  GUID[00d0f5cd4008049d]  [Linux OHCI-
1394]
ieee1394: Device added: Node[00:1023]  GUID[000a2700020e545e]  [Apple
Computer, Inc.]
ieee1394: Node 00:1023 changed to 01:1023
SCSI subsystem driver Revision: 1.00
ieee1394: sbp2: Logged into SBP-2 device
ieee1394: sbp2: Node[00:1023]: Max speed [S400] - Max payload [2048]
scsi0 : IEEE-1394 SBP-2 protocol driver (host: ohci1394)
$Rev: 707 $ James Goodwin SBP-2 module load options:
- Max speed supported: S400
- Max sectors per I/O supported: 255
- Max outstanding commands supported: 64
- Max outstanding commands per lun supported: 1
- Serialized I/O (debug): no
- Exclusive login: yes
  Vendor: Apple      Model: iPod             Rev: 1.40
  Type:   Direct-Access                      ANSI SCSI revision: 02
Attached scsi removable disk sda at scsi0, channel 0, id 0, lun 0
SCSI device sda: 58595040 512-byte hdwr sectors (30001 MB)
sda: test WP failed, assume Write Enabled
  sda: sda1 sda2
```

The iPod appears as a fake SCSI device (typically /dev/sda if you have no other SCSI devices) and can be accessed using the regular Unix tools for block devices. However, if you are using a Mac iPod, fdisk will not recognize the partition map, and you will get a message resembling "Device contains neither a valid DOS partition table, nor Sun, SGI or OSF disklabel." In this case, it is time to follow the GNU instructions (for conversion).

At this point, the Linux IEEE1394 drivers (ieee1394, ohci1394) should have recognized the hardware:

```
% cat /proc/bus/ieee1394/devices
Node[00:1023]  GUID[001106000000649a]:
  Vendor ID: `Linux OHCI-1394' [0x004063]
  Capabilities: 0x0083c0
  Bus Options:
    IRMC(1) CMC(1) ISC(1) BMC(0) PMC(0) GEN(0)
    LSPD(2) MAX_REC(2048) CYC_CLK_ACC(0)
  Host Node Status:
    Host Driver     : ohci1394
    Nodes connected : 2
    Nodes active    : 2
    SelfIDs received: 2
    Irm ID          : [00:1023]
    BusMgr ID       : [00:1023]
    In Bus Reset    : no
    Root            : no
    Cycle Master    : no
    IRM             : yes
    Bus Manager     : yes
Node[01:1023]  GUID[000a2700020ec65a]:
  Vendor ID: `Apple Computer, Inc.' [0x000a27]
  Capabilities: 0x0083c0
  Bus Options:
    IRMC(0) CMC(0) ISC(0) BMC(0) PMC(0) GEN(0)
    LSPD(2) MAX_REC(2048) CYC_CLK_ACC(255)
  Unit Directory 0:
    Vendor/Model ID: Apple Computer, Inc. [000a27] / iPod [000000]
    Software Specifier ID: 00609e
    Software Version: 010483
    Driver: SBP2 Driver
    Length (in quads): 8

% cat /proc/scsi/scsi
Attached devices:
Host: scsi0 Channel: 00 Id: 00 Lun: 00
  Vendor: Apple     Model: iPod          Rev: 1.40
  Type:   Direct-Access               ANSI SCSI revision: 02
```

Performing the HFS-to-FAT32 conversion involves the following steps:

1. Save the first 32 MB of the second partition, which contains the iPod firmware image. Keep this file safe somewhere on your PC:

   ```
   % dd if=/dev/sda2 of=backup_firmware
   ```

2. Splat zeros all over the partition map so that all disk data is effectively erased. Unload and reload the sbp2 driver to update its world-view:

   ```
   % dd if=/dev/zero of=/dev/sda bs=1M count=10
   % rmmod sbp2 && insmod sbp2
   ```

3. Create two partitions. The first should be large enough to hold the 32-MB file you saved earlier; the second will hold the remaining 30 GB of the disk. Tag the two partitions as Empty and FAT32, respectively:

```
% fdisk /dev/sda
n    [make new partition]
p    [primary]
1    [first partition]
     [just press enter -- default first sector is 1]
5S   [5 sectors -- big enough to hold 32MB]

n    [make new partition]
p    [primary]
2    [second partition]
     [just press enter -- default first sector is 6]
     [just press enter -- default size uses all remaining space]

t    [modify type]
1    [first partition]
0    [first partition has no filesystem; ignore warning]

t    [modify type]
2    [second partition]
b    [second partition is FAT32]

p    [show partition map]

   Device Boot    Start      End    Blocks   Id  System
/dev/sda1             1        5     40131    0  Empty
/dev/sda2             6     3647  29254365    b  Win95 FAT32

w    [commit changes to disk]
```

4. Copy the firmware back to the first (small) partition:

```
dd if=backup_firmware of=/dev/sda1
```

5. Make a FAT32 filesystem on the second (large) partition:

```
mkfs.vfat -F 32 -n "My iPod" /dev/sda2
```

If all goes well, resetting the iPod (by holding down the Menu and Play buttons for 10 seconds) will cause it to reboot to the familiar menus. If not, go through the instructions again. Remember, the iPod is just a hard disk, so as long as you have the original firmware backed up correctly and safely on your PC, you can reformat it as many times as you like. (It worked for me the first time.) Be wary about installing different firmware from the one it came with, however.

At this point, you should be able to mount the disk in the usual way. Once this works, setup is complete and you are through to the normal usage instructions described in the following section.

Normal Usage

The Linux drivers for the iPod are still a little flakey; sometimes, the sbp2 driver gets stuck indefinitely in its initializing state and cannot be removed, and at other times the machine hangs.

To minimize the risk of such errors, I strongly advise you to follow a disciplined procedure for docking and undocking the iPod. Here's the order of events I usually employ:

1. Insert the IEEE1394 PCMCIA card into my laptop. Check that this succeeded by running lsmod and looking for ieee1394 and ohci1394.

2. Attach the iPod. This time the sbp2 driver should appear. If it does not, try detaching and reattaching it.

3. Mount the iPod as a disk, copy files across, and then unmount it again.

4. rmmod the sbp2 driver.

5. Detach the iPod.

6. Remove the IEEE1394 card.

Note that these steps are perfectly symmetrical. This seems to achieve greater reliability than performing them in an arbitrary order.

I use two scripts, *dock-ipod* and *undock-ipod*, whenever I attach or detach the iPod to or from the interface card. Here's *dock-ipod*:

```
#!/bin/sh

modprobe sbp2
mount /dev/sda2 /mnt/ipod/
```

And *undock-ipod*:

```
#!/bin/sh

umount /mnt/ipod
rmmod sbp2
```

They must both be run as root:

```
% su - root -c ./dock-ipod
```

or:

```
% sudo ./dock-ipod (if the user is a sudoer)
```

or:

```
% su - root
Password:
root$ ./dock-ipod
```

Downloaded MP3 Files and ID3 Tags

The iPod does not care about the filenames of MP3 files; all its database information is supplied by ID3 tags within the MP3 files. Therefore, these must be present for transferred files even to appear on the iPod.

You might want to add MP3 files that did not come from a CD (e.g., those downloaded from Napster, Kazaa, etc.) to your iPod. The ID3 tags in such files are often inappropriate; for example, because they feature the original artist/album name from the CD they came from, instead of the logical group to which they will belong on your iPod (e.g., *Misc/80s Synth Pop*). If you do nothing about this, you will find each song appearing in its own artist/album category, with no useful grouping. You'll also need to tag manually when CDDB lookup fails (e.g., for *non-industry* CDs) or for MP3 files that were hand-encoded from WAV.

To change the tags, you'll need a tool such as ID3ed (*http://www.dakotacom.net/~donut/programs/id3ed.html*; free). This tool is pretty straightforward, and it comes with a helpful man page. The synopsis says:

```
id3ed [-s songname] [-n artist] [-a album] [-y year]
[-c comment] [-k tracknum] [-g genre] [-q] [-SNAYCKG]
[-l] [-L] [-r] [-i] [-v] files...
```

Obviously, you don't need to include all of those options. Here's an example:

```
% id3ed -s "Red House" -n "Jimi Hendrix" \
-a "Are You Experienced?" -k 3 redhouse.mp3
```

Alternatively, you can use a graphical tool such as xid3 (*www.nebel.gmxhome.de/xid3/*; free), which has a Tcl/Tk-based front end for ID3-tag editing that makes it a lot easier to use for this information. The most important ID3 tags for the iPod are Artist, Album, Title, and Track Index (and Genre, if you actually bother to use that).

With minimal effort, your iPod will play nicely with Linux. No, you won't be able to buy songs from the iTunes Music Store, but you'll still have most of the functionality Macintosh and Windows users have.

—*Alan Donovan*

H A C K   Sync Your iRiver with Linux
#98   Use Linux to copy your songs and create the iRiver database.

Of the wide variety of "lifestyle" items that are competing for our disposable income, the personal music player is one of the most popular. Although many of us can remember the excitement of getting a personal cassette player when we were younger, the latest incarnation of music on the move is fully digital, and it can store your entire album collection.

A number of these personal music players are on the market, but one of the most intriguing is the iRiver series. Not only do these little boxes pack in upward of 40GB of storage, but they also support a variety of different codecs beyond plain MP3. Some of you might be aware that encoding MP3 is actually a legally foggy area, as the codec was created and licensed by Fraunhoffer, and many free encoders are not properly licensed. A free MP3 alternative called Ogg Vorbis exists that promises both higher quality and smaller file size. This format is gaining in popularity, and the iRiver, unlike the iPod, supports it out of the box.

To get songs on your iRiver, you need to rip your CDs to get the tracks onto the hard disk of your Linux machine, encode them as MP3 or Ogg Vorbis, and then upload them to the iRiver via USB. Optionally, you can then build the iRiver internal database for your MP3s (you cannot use the database for Ogg files). The iRiver IHP series of players use a special internal database that stores all the details of your song titles, albums, genres, and other information. One issue to bear in mind is that the iRiver lacks support of Ogg Vorbis tags. This means Ogg metadata will not be included in the database. If you want to use ID tags (these tags store information about the artist, album, track number, and so on), you need to rip your songs as MP3s.

This hack does not cover how to rip songs, but a number of great ripping tools are available, such as Grip, RipperX, KAudioCreator, and Jack. Most of these tools are simple and intuitive to use.

Transfer the Songs to the iRiver

You can transfer songs to the iRiver by plugging it into one of the USB ports on your computer. To transfer files, you need to ensure that you have USB support compiled into your kernel, and then you need to mount the device. These options are available in the kernel configuration tool [Hack #88] in the USB Support section. You should ensure that you have UHCU, UHCI Alternate Driver, or OHCI selected, depending on the type of USB support on your motherboard. You can find out which USB support you have from your motherboard's manual. With the USB support compiled in, you can mount the disk with the following command:

```
foo@bar:~$ mount -t vfat /dev/sda1 /mnt/iriver
```

You will probably need to change the mount directory */mnt/iriver* to something that is relevant to your system. Once it is mounted, if you look in */mnt/ iriver*, you will see either an empty directory if you have not uploaded any songs or a list of artist directories if songs are already on the iRiver. Now you can copy over files by using a file manager, such as Nautilus or Konqueror, or by using the following command if your Metallica songs are in */home/ joeblogs/Metallica*:

```
foo@bar:~$ cp -r /home/joeblogs/Metallica* /mnt/iriver
```

Rebuild the Database

The iRiver database is essential in terms of making the iRiver as usable as possible. This database contains a detailed list of artists, genres, albums, song lengths, track numbers, and more; many of the features in the iRiver are available only if you have created the database. You still can use the iRiver without the database, but you can choose your songs and albums only via the clunky file manager on the iRiver as opposed to its special menus. Unfortunately, the installation CD does not come with a tool to build the database for Linux, but a simple utility available on the Internet, called iRipDB, can do the job. You can download *iRipDB* from *http://www. fataltourist.com/iripdb/*.

Once you have downloaded the latest version of *iRipDB*, unzip it onto your hard disk with this command:

```
foo@bar:~$ tar xcvf iRipDB-x-x-x.tar.gz
```

Replace *x-x-x* with the actual version number of the *iRipDB* program. You need to ensure that you have the following libraries on your system before you compile the code:

libid3
    This library provides the use of ID3 tags in *songslibogg*.

libvorbis
    These libraries provide support for Ogg Vorbis files.

To compile the code, run the compilation script included with the code. Move into the directory where the code is stored, and run this:

```
foo@bar:~$ ./compile.sh
```

When the program is compiled, you will have an executable in the source directory called iripdb. Now you can run this to rebuild the database:

```
foo@bar:~$ ./iripdb /mnt/iriver
```

The preceding command runs the iripdb command on the directory where you mounted your iRiver. You can also use the -e switch to include files that have not had tags added to them:

```
foo@bar:~$ ./iripdb -e /mnt
```

To finish, you should unmount the device to ensure that all data has been copied over completely:

```
foo@bar:~$ umount /mnt
```

Now full support for your iRiver is available on your system. Although you will mostly listen to music on your iRiver, try copying some text files onto the device. On the IHP series, you will find that you can read them on the screen. This can be handy if you need to carry around some notes or other text with you.

HACK #99 Boost Hard-Drive Performance

Get the best possible performance from your IDE hardware.

To be on the safe side, your new Linux installation starts up with the least common denominator of disk drive performance capabilities—typically DMA-33—robbing you of 50–150% of your potential performance. Once Linux is installed, you are free and encouraged to start tweaking the configuration of your disk drive and its interface to squeeze the most of them.

Setting HDPARM parameters too aggressively—that is, in excess of the disk controller or drive capabilities—can lead to data loss.

It is best to test HDPARM settings on a fresh installation of the operating system before committing any applications or programs to the drive and prepare to back down on the settings and reinstall the OS if the drive is unstable or the HDPARM tests show erratic results or fail.

The tool needed, HDPARM, is included with the operating system (or available from your package manager). It can be adjusted manually and then put into a startup script to make your chosen settings effective every time the system starts up.

HDPARM is a command-line utility that provides powerful control over your hard drive parameters (HD PARaMeters). It can also tell you a lot about your disk drive. Everything you do with HDPARM, until you make a script for it, will be done at the command line.

You must be logged in as root to run HDPARM. You can also use the sudo command to run the command as root if you have sufficient privileges.

Assume /dev/hda is the designation for your hard drive. (This is the default for the first IDE drive; a SATA drive may appear as /dev/hde if your motherboard also has IDE interfaces.) Run the following command:

```
hdparm -i /dev/hda
```

You should get some info like the following:

```
/dev/hda:
Model=QUANTUM FIREBALLlct, FwRev=APL.1234, SerialNo=1234567
Config={ HardSect NotMFM HdSw>15uSec Fixed DTR>10Mbs }
RawCHS=16383/16/63, TrkSize=32256, SectSize=21298, ECCbytes=4
BuffType=DualPortCache, BuffSize=418kB, MaxMultSect=8, MultSect=off
CurCHS=16383/16/63, CurSects=-66060037, LBA=yes, LBAsects=39876478
IORDY=on/off, tPIO={min:120,w/IORDY:120}, tDMA={min:120,rec:120}
PIO modes: pio0 pio1 pio2 pio3 pio4
DMA modes: mdma0 mdma1 mdma2 udma0 udma1 udma2 udma3 udma4 *udma5
AdvancedPM=no
Drive Supports : ATA/ATAPI-5 T13 1321D revision 1 : ATA-1 ATA-2
ATA-3 ATA-4 ATA-5
```

This tremendous amount of data provided tells you:

MaxMultSect

> The maximum number of sectors your hard disk can read at a time.

MultSect

> The current number of sectors being read at a time.

PIO *modes and* DMA *modes*

> The modes supported by your hard drive. The one marked with an asterisk (*) is the one currently set.

AdvancedPM

> Indicates whether or not your hard drive supports Advanced Power Management.

Another command:

hdparm /dev/hda

reveals the following information:

```
/dev/hda:
multcount = 0 (on)
I/O support = 0 (16-bit)
unmaskirq = 0 (off)
using_dma = 0 (off)
keepsettings = 0 (off)
nowerr = 0 (off)
readonly = 0 (off)
readahead = 8 (on)
geometry = 2482/255/63, sectors = 39876480, start = 0
```

The items of interest are:

multcount

> The number of sectors being read at a time.

I/O support

> The operating mode of your hard disk (16/32/32sync).

using_dma

> Whether or not the drive is using the DMA feature. This may be on by default if your version of Linux properly detects and supports your chipset and drive's DMA capabilities.

keepsettings

> Whether the settings are kept after the drive resets (usually caused by errors).

readonly

> Whether the drive is read-only. Normally set to 1 only for CD-ROMs.

readahead

> How many sectors ahead will be read when you access the hard drive.

The HDPARM program provides two performance-testing features that are crucial to letting you know whether you're making improvements as you tweak along. The command:

hdparm -Tt /dev/hda1

will show results such as the following before enhancing the performance:

```
/dev/hda1:
Timing buffer-cache reads: 128 MB in 5.97 seconds = 21.43 MB/sec
Timing buffered disk reads: 64 MB in 17.97 seconds = 3.56 MB/sec
```

and then results like these after enhancing the performance:

```
Timing buffer-cache reads: 128 MB in 0.91 seconds =140.66 MB/sec
Timing buffered disk reads: 64 MB in 3.78 seconds = 16.93 MB/sec
```

The goal of this hack is to see the time in seconds decrease and the MB/sec to increase. You can do that by using a variety of parameters, invoked one at a time, then rerunning the performance tests to see if things are improving.

Mistakes during the setup process may damage your filesystem and all of its data, so it's best to do this after a fresh install of Linux or right after you've done a full backup.

Begin by setting the operating mode of the interface between the system and the disk drive using one of the following parameters:

```
hdparm -c0 /dev/hda  #sets operating mode to 16-bits
hdparm -c1 /dev/hda  #sets operating mode to 32-bits
hdparm -c3 /dev/hda  #sets operating mode to 32-bits synchronized
```

Mode 1 (-c1) is used most often for best performance. Mode 3 (-c3) only is needed for some chipsets.

Next set the data transfer parameters, which you can determine from the output of the "-I" command shown earlier (in that case 8 is the maximum supported):

```
hdparm -m8 /dev/hda
```

Next try activating DMA mode for your system interface:

```
hdparm -d1
```

Then set the drive mode (a value of X32 is most common; UDMA-5 is X69):

```
hdparm -X32 /dev/hda
```

or:

```
hdparm -X69 /dev/hda
```

Finally, try setting the read-ahead value, which is typically set to the same value as multcount from earlier, or 8:

```
hdparm -a8 /dev/hda
```

If any or all of these settings make incremental improvements in performance, remember them and create a script that sets them all sequentially or includes them all in one line. I prefer sequential lines to ensure the drive accepts each command separately and I do not lose a setting if another fails to take. From all of this, you might typically be using the following parameters:

```
hdparm -c1
hdparm -m8 /dev/hda
hdparm -d1
hdparm -X34 /dev/hda
hdparm -a8 /dev/hda
```

Another single-command example that may work best for your system is:

```
hdparm -X66 -d1 -u1 -m16 -c3 /dev/hda
```

Save to a file and make the file a script to place in the directory for the runlevel at which you normally use Linux. For example:

1. Using a text editor, create then save the script as */etc/init.d/hdparm.local*.

2. Configure it to start in runlevel 5 with the following command:

   ```
   ln -s /etc/init.d/hdparm.local /etc/rc5.d/S20hdparm.local
   ```

3. The rc5.d part of the parameter string indicates runlevel 5, which is the normal operating mode for most Linux systems. To find out your default runlevel, examine */etc/inittab* for the inittdefault entry, as in:

   ```
   id:5:initdefault:
   ```

The next step is to keep an eye on dmesg and/or */var/log/syslog*. In some cases, an error will cause the settings to be reset. So that's where the -k (keep) flag comes in. If you're 100% positive that these settings won't corrupt your data, you can add -k to the script.

—*Jim Aspinwall*

Accelerate Your Gaming

#100 Squeeze as much juice as possible out of your 3D graphics card with a commercial driver.

As Linux use grows, more device manufacturers are creating official Linux drivers; this is particularly true of video card manufacturers. The benefit of having official drivers is that the manufacturer, which has complete access to all the hardware specifications, is able to write a definitive driver that makes the device as usable in Linux as it is in other operating systems. The flip side to this benefit, however, is that some commercial drivers for graphics cards are written as closed source software, and sometimes they incorporate incomplete or unstable features. Some drivers have been particularly reliable, such as those from NVIDIA, but you should browse the Internet to see how reliable other official drivers are. Sometimes a driver's stability changes between versions, but not always for the better. So, your Internet searches might reveal that the best driver is not the most recent one.

This hack shows you how to install the binary drivers provided by the manufacturer for recent-model video cards from ATI and NVIDIA.

Preparing for the Installation

Many official drivers require that specific versions of software be used to build and run the driver. This required software usually includes the kernel, the kernel header files (used to compile the kernel itself), the C compiler (*gcc*), and X. You need to ensure that all of these requirements are present on your system; a process that can involve installing some of the missing pieces where needed. As many users have never compiled anything before, it is quite common to need to install a copy of *gcc*.

Before proceeding, you should ensure that your versions of the required programs are compatible with the software requirements for your driver. Virtually every program can report its version number. To find out the version of your kernel, you can run this:

```
foo@bar:~$ uname -a
```

To find out the version of your kernel headers, you need to ensure that you have the kernel headers package on your system. To check this on an RPM-based system, run this:

```
foo@bar:~$ rpm -qa | grep kernel-source
```

To check the version of the kernel headers on a Debian/APT-based system, run this:

```
foo@bar:~$ dpkg -l kernel-header*
```

To find out your version of *gcc*, run this:

```
foo@bar:~$ gcc -v
```

Finally, to find out your version of X, run this:

```
foo@bar:~$ X -version
```

Before you begin to install your driver, you should back up your X configuration file, as it might be overwritten when you configure the binary driver. This file is called *XF86Config* or *XF86Config-4* and is usually found in */etc/X11*. You should copy the file to a safe place as a backup:

```
root@bar:~# cp /etc/X11/XF86Config* /root/xconfigbackup/
```

Installing the NVIDIA Driver

One of the most popular closed source graphics drivers in use is the unified NVIDIA driver. Many people have chosen NVIDIA cards for their impressive performance and driver support, and because the full range of features on the cards are available in the Linux driver. You can download a single unified driver that supports all NVIDIA cards at *http://www.nvidia.com/linux*.

Once you have downloaded the driver package, you need to make it executable so that you can run it. Type the following commands as root:

```
foo@bar:~# chmod a+x NVIDIA-Linux-x86-x.x-xxxx-pkg1.run
```

> Before you run a graphics driver installer, you should ensure that you have exited X by logging out, and if you have a graphical login manager, you should shut this down, too. Using GDM as an example, you can do this in Debian with **/etc/init.d/gdm stop**. In Red Hat you can do the same with **service gdm stop**.

Then you can run the installer (make sure you are not in X):

```
foo@bar:~# ./NVIDIA-Linux-x86-x.x-xxxx-pkg1.run
```

The software compiles a driver on-the-fly and installs it to your system. The next step is to change your X configuration file to use the driver. For XFree86, you need to edit *XF86Config* or *XF86Config-4*, and for the Xorg version of X, you need to edit *xorg.conf*. Both configuration files are located in */etc* or */etc/X11*, and both use the same syntax.

Inside the file is a Device section, where you should change Driver "nv" to Driver "nvidia". In the Module section, you should add Load "glx" and comment the DRI and Glcore lines.

Now reboot or reload your modules and X to run the driver.

Installing the ATI Driver

ATI has made a number of drivers available for its Radeon range of cards. You install these closed source drivers in much the same way you install the NVIDIA drivers. You can download the drivers from *http://www.ati.com/support/driver.html*.

The drivers are available as RPM files, and you can install the RPM with this command:

```
foo@bar:~$ rpm -Uh --force driver.rpm
```

If you are on a system that does not use RPM as a package type, you can use Alien to convert the package to another type, such as a tarball or Debian package. Once you have opened the package, you can move to the directory that contains the driver and run the main tool that completes the installation for you:

```
foo@bar:~$ ./fglrxconfig
```

Within the program, you are asked numerous questions about how you want your video card configured (when in doubt, accept the default). Then you are asked if an *XF86Config-4* file should be generated. Select Y to accept this action and the installation is complete. If you are running the Xorg server, you will need to rename this generated file to *xorg.conf*, and put it in */etc* or */etc/X11* on your system. Then you can start X:

```
foo@bar:~$ startx
```

Now run the *fglrxinfo* utility; it should say this:

```
OpenGL vendor string: ATI Technologies Inc.
```

If this is the case, the driver installation process is complete.

Index

We'd like to hear your suggestions for improving our indexes. Send email to *index@oreilly.com*.

Mozilla, Wordview, 245
MTA (Mail Transfer Agent), procmail
    configuration, 185
multimedia keys on keyboard, 91
    LinEAK and, 96
multiple log-in screens
    command-line, 57
    GDM, 56
    KDM, 54
Mutt
    email text mode client, 29
    PDF documents, 172
    Word documents, 172

N

Nautilus
    file types, 156
    menu, scripts option, 155
    right-click actions, 154
    scripts, environment variables, 156
networks
    backups, 251
        rsync, 252
        single-shot, 252
    ifplugd utility, 240
    remote access, 105
    wireless
        Kismet and, 207
        scan for, 205
NTP (Network Time Protocol)
    clock synchronization, 220
    clocks and, 220
NVIDIA driver
    installation, 306
    mouse cursors and, 76
NX Client installation, 104
NX server
    commands, 105
    setup, 104
NXServer installation, 104

O

oooqs utility (KDE), OpenOffice.org
    and, 175
ooqstart-gnome, 176
OpenOffice.org
    oooqs utility, 175
    preloading items, 174
    quickstarts, 176
    respawn trick, 177

operating systems
    booting, 2
    non-Linux, booting and, 3
Orange, 293
Orange Micro PCMCIA card, iPod
    and, 293

P

pagers, colored files, 48
partition table, 5
partitions, cloning Linux and, 228
passwords
    KDE wallet system, 117
    Konqueror remote access, 117
    none, 238
    public key, 238
patches in experimental code, 134
PDF documents
    Mutt, 172
    terminal display, 170
performance
    hard-drive, 301
    prelinking and, 256
personal default cursor themes, 75
PGP (Pretty Good Privacy), 180
PIM (personal information
    manager), 90
plug-ins
    Java in Firefox, 196
    Macromedia Flash, 195
pointers, custom, 72
pop-ups as reminders, 84
port forwarding, 231
    firewalls, 249
PPTP Client, 211
    configuration, 211
prelinking, performance and, 256
printers
    ACPI (Advanced Configuration and
        Power Interface), 290
    redirected, 288
    unsupported, 286
printing overview, 287
private keys, generating, 238
procmail, 185
    configuration, MTA, 185
    recipes, 186
    usage, 186
prompt, command-line, space
    saving, 42

public keys
    generate, 238
    passwords and, 238

Q

Qingy
    configuration, 64
    installation, 62, 63
    login screens and, 60
    session choices, 66
    themes, 67
Quicktime media format, 214

R

RedDot directory, cursors and, 77
RedDotSource directory, mouse cursors
        and, 77
redirected printers, 288
refresh rate
    configuration, 286
    monitor, 284
reminder pop-ups, 84
reminders, script, 86
remote access, 105
    graphic file management, 239
    Konqueror and, 115
        one-click operation and, 120
        passwords and, 117
    passwords, none, 238
    XDMCP (X Display Manager Control
        Protocol), 108
remote systems, 103
resolution, configuration, 286
respawn, automation and, 226
respawn trick, OpenOffice.org, 177
restores, Debian and, 254
restricted media formats, 214
right-click menu actions
    GNOME, 154
    KDE, 130
rsync, 252
rxvt project, 167

S

screen
    LILO splash screens, 12–17
    mirroring and, 162

screen tool
    application sharing, 161
    disconnected, 161
    functions, 161
    monitor sharing, 161
    multiple users, 163
screenshots
    command-line and, 40
    command-line terminal, 41
    upload to Web automatically, 202
    X terminal, 40
script, 304
scripting
    cron, run automatically, 151
    DCOP, shell script writing, 129
    FetchYahoo, 178
    KDE, 127
    KDE actions, 132
    Nautilus, 155
        environment variables, 156
scrot screen-capture tool, 203
security
    firewalls, old computer as, 247–249
    viruses, 241
    X programs access, 106
SFTP, Konqueror and, 115
showkey command, 37
silent mode, booting, 20
Skype, 199
Smart Boot Manager, 4
SmoothWall, 247
source code
    CVS and, 258
    source control system, 258
splash screens
    boot splash utilities, 22
    LILO, 10
        color, 15
        custom, 12–17
SSH (Secure SHell)
    Konqueror, 118
    password, none, 238
    port forwarding, 231
    portforwarding and, 231
stalling browser, 192
starting applications, 124
    automation, 221–224
    kstart, 125
    shortcuts on desktop, 126
starting OpenOffice.org, preloading
        items, 174

VNC (Virtual Network Computer), 100
VPNs (Virtual Private Networks)
    Microsoft server, 211
    PPTP Client, 211

W

w3m packages, 169
wallpaper, GNOME, 149–151
Wavemon, 250
web browsers
    plug-ins
        Java in Firefox, 196
        Macromedia Flash, 195
    stalling, 192
web pages, screenshot upload, 202
webcams, GnomeMeeting, 200
window managers
    Fluxbox, 222
    minimalists, 163–165
    WindowMaker, 222
WindowMaker, 222
Windows
    access from Linux, 100
    convert to Linux
        cursor themes, 78
    documents, viruses and, 241–246
    emulators, viruses and, 241
    fonts, 80
        TrueType, 80
    machines as print server, 286
    VNC server, configuration, 102
windows
    drop shadows, 109
    KDE, 3D effects, 140
    translucent, 111
Windows Media (WMV) media
        format, 214

wireless networks
    Kismet and, 207
    scan for, 205
Word documents
    Mutt, 172
    terminals, 168
wvWare, 169

X

X programs, security, 106
X terminal, screenshots from, 40
X11
    black background, 71
    engine startup, Xservers and, 72
    introduction, 70
xcompmgr, 109
    automation, 225
    desktop startup, 110
    grep and, 227
    window manager startup, 110
XDMCP (X Display Manager Control
        Protocol), 108
XFce 4, automation and, 223
xid3, iPod and, 298
xinit command, 72
xinitrc startup script, automation
        and, 226
Xorg fork, 109
Xservers, X11 engine startup and, 72

Y

yaboot, 2, 3
Yahoo! mail, read from any client, 177

Colophon

Our look is the result of reader comments, our own experimentation, and feedback from distribution channels. Distinctive covers complement our distinctive approach to technical topics, breathing personality and life into potentially dry subjects.

The tool on the cover of *Linux Desktop Hacks* is a wood plane. For carpenters of the past, wood planes, which are used to smooth, shape, and straighten wood surfaces, were once indispensable tools. The typical carpenter lugged around an entire chest full of planes, each with a special function. This is not surprising considering a single piece of wood can potentially become bowed, twisted, cupped, sprung, and diamonded, all at the same time. Learning to use a wood plane is said to be a difficult and often frustrating task. If the proper techniques are not used, the plane will dig into the wood surface and ruin the board. Seasoned carpenters say that keeping a sharp blade and planing with the grain are the first steps in mastering this tool.

Bench planes, such as jointers and jacks, range in length from 9 to 22 inches or more. These are better than smaller planes for straightening edges, because their length enables them to bridge dips and rises in the wood's surface. Today, power tools, such as routers and power planers, have replaced bench planes for straightening boards, but hand or "block" planes are still the perfect tool for trimming swollen doorways and fitting shingles.

Sarah Sherman was the production editor and proofreader, and Audrey Doyle was the copyeditor for *Linux Desktop Hacks*. Lydia Onofrei, Claire Cloutier, and Colleen Gorman provided quality control. Johnna Van Hoose Dinse wrote the index.

Emma Colby designed the cover of this book, based on a series design by Edie Freedman. The cover image is an image source found at Photo.com. Emma Colby produced the cover layout with QuarkXPress 4.1 using Adobe's Helvetica Neue and ITC Garamond fonts.

David Futato designed the interior layout. This book was converted by Judy Hoer to FrameMaker 5.5.6 with a format conversion tool created by Erik Ray, Jason McIntosh, Neil Walls, and Mike Sierra that uses Perl and XML technologies. The text font is Linotype Birka; the heading font is Adobe Helvetica Neue Condensed; and the code font is LucasFont's TheSans Mono Condensed. The illustrations that appear in the book were produced by Robert Romano and Jessamyn Read using Macromedia FreeHand 9 and Adobe Photoshop 6. This colophon was written by Lydia Onofrei.

Keep in touch with O'Reilly

1. Download examples from our books

To find example files for a book, go to:
www.oreilly.com/catalog
select the book, and follow the "Examples" link.

2. Register your O'Reilly books

Register your book at *register.oreilly.com*

Why register your books? Once you've registered your O'Reilly books you can:

- Win O'Reilly books, T-shirts or discount coupons in our monthly drawing.
- Get special offers available only to registered O'Reilly customers.
- Get catalogs announcing new books (US and UK only).
- Get email notification of new editions of the O'Reilly books you own.

3. Join our email lists

Sign up to get topic-specific email announcements of new books and conferences, special offers, and O'Reilly Network technology newsletters at:

elists.oreilly.com

It's easy to customize your free elists subscription so you'll get exactly the O'Reilly news you want.

4. Get the latest news, tips, and tools

http://www.oreilly.com

- "Top 100 Sites on the Web"—PC Magazine
- CIO Magazine's Web Business 50 Awards

Our web site contains a library of comprehensive product information (including book excerpts and tables of contents), downloadable software, background articles, interviews with technology leaders, links to relevant sites, book cover art, and more.

5. Work for O'Reilly

Check out our web site for current employment opportunities:

jobs.oreilly.com

6. Contact us

O'Reilly & Associates
1005 Gravenstein Hwy North
Sebastopol, CA 95472 USA

TEL: 707-827-7000 or 800-998-9938
        (6am to 5pm PST)

FAX: 707-829-0104

order@oreilly.com
For answers to problems regarding your order or our products.
To place a book order online, visit:

www.oreilly.com/order_new

catalog@oreilly.com
To request a copy of our latest catalog.

booktech@oreilly.com
For book content technical questions or corrections.

corporate@oreilly.com
For educational, library, government, and corporate sales.

proposals@oreilly.com
To submit new book proposals to our editors and product managers.

international@oreilly.com
For information about our international distributors or translation queries. For a list of our distributors outside of North America check out:

international.oreilly.com/distributors.html

adoption@oreilly.com
For information about academic use of O'Reilly books, visit:

academic.oreilly.com

O'REILLY®

Our books are available at most retail and online bookstores.
To order direct: 1-800-998-9938 • *order@oreilly.com* • *www.oreilly.com*
Online editions of most O'Reilly titles are available by subscription at *safari.oreilly.com*

Related Titles Available from O'Reilly

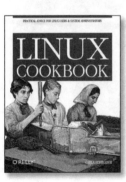

Linux

Building Embedded Linux Systems

Building Secure Servers with Linux

The Complete FreeBSD, *4th Edition*

Even Grues Get Full

Exploring the JDS Linux Desktop

Extreme Programming Pocket Guide

Knoppix Hacks

Learning Red Hat Enterprise Linux and Fedora, *4th Edition*

Linux Cookbook

Linux Device Drivers, *3rd Edition*

Linux in a Nutshell, *4th Edition*

Linux iptables Pocket Reference

Linux Network Administrator's Guide, *3rd Edition*

Linux Pocket Guide

Linux Security Cookbook

Linux Server Hacks

Linux Unwired

Linux Web Server CD Bookshelf, *Version 2.0*

LPI Linux Certification in a Nutshell, *2nd Edition*

Managing RAID on Linux

OpenOffice.org Writer

Programming with Qt, *2nd Edition*

Root of all Evil

Running Linux, *4th Edition*

Samba Pocket Reference, *2nd Edition*

Test Driving Linux

Understanding the Linux Kernel, *2nd Edition*

Understanding Open Source & Free Software Licensing

User Friendly

Using Samba, *3rd Edition*

O'REILLY®

Our books are available at most retail and online bookstores.
To order direct: 1-800-998-9938 • *order@oreilly.com* • *www.oreilly.com*
Online editions of most O'Reilly titles are available by subscription at *safari.oreilly.com*